Births From The Bristol Parish Register of Henrico, Prince George, and Dinwiddie Counties, Virginia, 1720-1798

Transcribed By

Churchill Gibson Chamberlayne

WITH A NEW INDEX

CLEARFIELD

Excerpted and Reprinted from
The Vestry Book and Register of Bristol Parish, Virginia, 1720-1789
Transcribed and Published by
Churchill Gibson Chamberlayne
Richmond, 1898

Reprinted with a New Index and Re-paged
Genealogical Publishing Co., Inc.
Baltimore, 1974, 1980

Reprinted for
Clearfield Company by
Genealogical Publishing Co.
Baltimore, Maryland
1990, 1996, 1998, 2004, 2007

Library of Congress Catalogue Card Number 74-8784
ISBN-13: 978-0-8063-0627-8
ISBN-10: 0-8063-0627-0

Made in the United States of America

Made in the United States of America

REGISTER.

A

Ephraim son of Wm. & Amy Andrews born 4th feb^{r} last bap^{t} sep^{tr} 1st 1721.

George son of Wm. & Anne Archer born 31st July last bap^{t} sep^{tr} 3d 1721.

Mary dau of Robt & Mary Abernathy born 16th Aprill last bap^{t} 9th Octob^{r} 1721.

Tho: son of Tho: & Ann Addison born 1st Aprill last bap^{t} 27th May 1722.

Isham son of Rich & Mary Andrews born 19th Aprill last bap^{t} July 7th 172–.

Tally son of Hen: & Mary Alley born 24th Augs^{t} 1721 bap^{t} March 27th 1722.

Ann dau of Abra & Mary Alley born 25th Instant bap^{t} 31st May 1722.

Fran: dau of Geo: & Mary Archer born 8th May last bap^{t} 19th August 1722.

Wm. son of Tho: & Mary Adaman born 2d July last bap^{t} 17th feb: 1722–3.

Geo: son of Wm. & Avis Andrews born 14th Jan^{r} last bap^{t} July 10th 1723.

Mary D. of Tho & Jane Andrews born 14th Aprill last bap^{t} July 10th 1723.

Judith D. of Geo & Mary Archer born 23d Aprill last bap^{t} 5th sep^{tr} 1724.

Winifred D of Wm. & Avis Andrews born 1st June last bap^{t} 16th sept^{r} 1724.

Drury son of Abra & Mary Allen born 1st X^{br} 1724.

Fran: son of Rich & Mary Andrews born 10th August last bap^{t} March 28th 1725.

Tho: Son of Tho: & Mary Adaman born 6th octob^{r} 1724 bap^{t} 12th Sep 1725.

John son of Rob[t] & Mary Abertnartha born 21th bap[t] 1723.

Mary Da[t] of Ann Andrews being Illigitimate born 18th octber last 1725.

Martha A negro of George Archer born Jan[r] 1725.

David Son of Rob[t] and Mary Abertnarthy born May 29th bap[t] June 6th 1726.

Wm Son of Elkana and Sarah Allen born 3d sep[r] 1726.

Sarah D of John and Catherine Adams born 30th Ap[r] 1726.

Winefritt D of Abraham and Mary Alle born 22d Aprill 1727.

Eliz D of Th[o] and Jane andrews born 11th Novem[r] 1726 bap[t] 15 1727.

Wm S of Rich[d] and Mary andrews born 13th May 1726 bap[t] 15 novem[r] 1727.

avice D of Wm and avice andrews Born 7th Dec[m] 1727 Bap.

Martha D of Wm. and ann Archer born 19th Bap[t] 19th Janr[y] 1727.

Mary D of George and Sarah Archer Born 25th June 1728.

Eliz[a] D of henry and Eliz[a] anderson Born 14th aprill 1729.

Ellinor female slave of Ditto Born 14th aprill 1729.

Sarah D of Elcanah and Sarah allin Born 28th Dec[r] Bap[t] 4th March 1728.

Henry Son of Richard & mary andrews Born 3d feb[r] 1729 Bap[t] 28th aprill 1730.

John Son of Wm and avis andrews Born 7th July 1729 Bap[t] 10th May 1730.

Mary D of abraham and Mary Alle Born 13th July 1730.

Thomas Son of Christophar and Mary Addison Born 12th Sept[r] 1730.

Eliz[a] D: of Robert and Mary Abernarthy Born 20th May 1730 Bap[t] 20th Sep[tr].

Frances D of William and Ann Archer Born 14th august 1730 Bap[t] oct[r] 12th.

Sarah D of George & Mary Archer Born 31th Dce[r] Bap[t] 21th feb[r] 1730.

anne of Thomas & ann addison Born 1th feb[r] 1730.

Martha Dat[r] of Tho[s] & Jean Andrews born 16th March 1731 bap[t] June 1st 1732.

Luciana dat[r] of W[m] & Avis Andrews born 9 Sep[r] 1731 bap[t] July 30th 1732.

Pheboe dater of Rich[d] & Mary Andrews born 26th March 1732 bap[t] July 30th 1732.

Jean Dat[r] of Geo & Mary Archer born 12th July 1732 bap[t] Sep[r] 3d 1732.

Clyborn of Henry & Elisabeth Born anderson 21th Dec[r] 1732 Bap[t] Jan' 14th 1732.

amy D of Robert & mary abernarthy Born 30th Jan[r] 1732 Bap[t] 26th March 1733.

Eleonore D of abraham & mary allen Born 11th ap[r] 1733 Bap[t] 27th may 1733.

Winifred D[r] of Christopher & mary addison Born 8th octb[r] 1732 Bap[t] 17th June 1733.

Phebe D: of Wm & ann archer Born 3d Sep[r] 1733 Bap[t] octb[r] 18th 1733.

Robert Son of John & martha alexander Born 2d Jan[r] 1733 Bap[t] 30 feb[r].

John Son of James & Elisabeth Anderson Born 4th May 1734 Bap[t] 4th august.

Field Son of field & Elisabeth archer Born 1th July 1734 Bap[t] 2d July.

George Son of Richard & Tabitha Archer Born 30 April 1734.

Ruth D. of Jane Anderson born July 12th 1733.

Amey D. of John & Elizabeth Anderson Born 18th June 1734.

Henry S of Henry & Elizabeth Anderson Born 4 Jan[ry] 1734.

Thomas S of Thomas & alice Archer Born Octob[r] 3d 1734 Baptiz'd the 25th.

Lucey D. of Abraham & Mary Allen Born Sep[t] 12th 1735.

Fredrick S of Thomas & Alce Archer Born November y[e] 13th 1740.

Mary D of Peter & Elisabeth Aldridg Born febuary y[e] 22nd 1739.

Miles S of Abraham & mary Allen Born may y[e] 18th 1741.

Lucy D. of David and Ann Abernothy B Feb[ry] 14th 1740.

John S of William & Agnis Abbet Feb[ry] 26th 1740.

William S. of Richard & Tabitha Archers born Sep[tr] 20th 1738 & Bap[t] Octob[r] 30th 1741.

Roger S. of Richard & Tabitha Archers Born May 10th 1741 & Bap[t] Octob[r] 30th 1741.

Mary D. of John & Elizabeth Atkinsons Born Sep[tr] 5th 1741 & Bap[t] Apr 11th 1742.

Robert S. of Robert & Sara Abernethys Born March 27th 1742 & Bap[t] June 13th 1742.

William S. of Charles & Ellis Abernethys Born Apr 4th 1742 & Bap[t] June 13th 1742.

Joanna D. of William & Ellis Aldrige Born Jan[y] 10th 1741–2 & Bap[t] May 11th 1742.

Elizabeth D. of Richard & Mary Aycock born Dec[r] 4th 1742 & Bap[t] Feb 20th 1742.

Martha D. of Elizabeth Allen born Octob[r] 28th 1742 and bapt[d] Aprile 10th 1743.

John S. of Peter & Elizabeth Aldrige born June 14th 1743 & bapt[d] May 9th 1743.

Sara D. of William & Mary Archers born Jan[r] 28th 1742–3 & bapt[d] June 12th 1743.

Mason D. of Abram & Mary Allens born Nov[r] 20th 1743 & bapt[d] Janry 1st 1743–4.

Mille D. of Peter & Elizabeth Aldridge born Janry 25th 1744–5 & bapt[d] Aprile 28th 1745.

Mary D. of William & Mary Archers born Septr 16th 1745 bapt[d] Octob —— 1745.

Frederick S. of John & Lucy Aberneathys was born Sep[t] 2d baptd Nov[r] 10th 1745.

Shade Son of Winifreid Alley born ——— —— Baptized May 12th 1751.

David Son of William & Jean Andersons born Novem[r] 29th 1750.

James Son of Ditto born January 21st 1753.

Sukey D of Drury and Abigail Alley born August 28th 1752.

Binns Son of Howell Adkins (of Sussex) & Susannah his Wife, born March 13th & bap. May 13th 1792.

Branchey a Negro Boy slave belonging to Roger Atkerson was Born April 23d 1761.

Samuel, Son, of Thomas Adams, & Mary his Wife, born August 11th & baptized September 22nd 1793.

William Archer (of Dinwiddie) was buried 23d June 1795.

B

Rob[t] son of Maj[r] Rob[t] & Anne Bolling born 30th octob[r] Last bap[t] 13th Nov: 1720.

Wm. son of Wm. & Mary Belsher born 4th June last bap' 24th octob' 1720.

Ruth dau: of Rich: & Agnis Barber born 14th octob[r] last bap' Jan[r] 1st 1720–1.

John son of Moses & Mary Beck born 4th Nov last bap[t] March 21th 1720–1.

Eliz: dau: of Andrew & Eliz: Beck born 26th octob[r] last bap' March 21th 1720–1.

Tho son of Tho: & Mary Burge born 31th may last bap[t] 17th sep[tr] 1721.

Rich: son of John & Eliz: Brown born 3d July instant bap' July 19th 1721.

Tho: son of Wm. & Mary Batt born 3d July last bap' Sept[r] 27th 1721.

Agnis dau of Edw: & Margret Birchet born 6th Jan[r] last bap' 27th August 1721.

Vide D: for Banks.[*]

Wm. son of Jo & Rebecca Bryerly born 9th sep[t] last bap' octob[r] 22th 1721.

James son of Rob' & Ann Bevell born 2d nov: Last bap' 25 decemb[r] 1721.

Jane dau of peter & Eliz Baugh born 15th Nov: last bap' March 5th 1721–2.

John son of Wm. & Anne Brown born 30th Augs: last bap' March 11th 1721–2.

Tho: son of Tho & Eliz Bott born 14th decem 1721 bap' Aprill 1722.

Cha: son of James & Mary Banks born sep' 18th Anno 1716.

Mary d: of ditto born Nov: 21th 1718.

Sarah d. of ditto born 10th Nov: 1721.

Tho son of Wm. & Mary Belcher born 28th June last bap' July 7th 1722.

Wm. son of Hugh & Mary Bragg born 20th March last bap' July 15th 1722.

John son of Rich: & Jane Burch born 7th March last bap' June 11th 1722.

*Three leaves, containing the first (and much the larger) part of the register of names in D, E and F, are missing.—C. G. C.

Annakin A Slave belonging unto Cap[t] Drury Bolling born in April 1720.

Sue A slave belonging unto ditto born in Nov: 1720.

Mingo A negro boy belonging unto ditto born in July 1722.

Benj[a] son of Benj[a] & Eliz Blick born 26th March 1721 bap[t] March 29th 172–.

John son of Rich & Agnis Barber born 21th Aprill last bap[t] 31th May 172–.

Cha son of Nico: & Ann Butterworth born 6th Jan: last bap[t] feb 14th 172–.

Agnis dau of Edw & Margaret Birchett 6th Jan: last bap[t] 27th August 1721.

Wm. son of Jn[o] & Anne Bradshaw born June 9th 1719.

John son of ditto 1st feb[r] 1721–2.

Wm. son of Edw & Mary Burchet born 30 xbr last bap[t] July 7th 1723.

Wm. son of Ja. & Eliz Baugh born 5th Aprill last bap[t] July 21th 1723.

Wm. son of John & Eliz Browder born 7th July last bap[t] 18th August 1723.

Tho. son of Geo. & Ann Brooks born 20th feb. last bap[t] Aug[t] 21th 1723.

prissilla dau of Jam. & Mary Panks born 31th Jan[r] last bap[t] Aug[t] 22th 1723.

Rob[t] son of Rob[t] & Ann Bevell born 10th oct[r] 1723.

Gabe A negro boy belonging to Cap[t] Drury Bolling born 10th of 9[br] 1723.

Bety A negro girl belonging to Mad. Anne Bolling born 28th Aprill 1723.

John son of Tho & Letitia Broadway born 10th May 1720 bap[t] Jan[r] 30th 1723–4.

Abigail D. of Rich: & Agnis Barber born 27th octob last bap[t] feb. 6th 1723–4.

Anne D. of Tho. & Eliz Bott born xb[r] ul[t] bap[t] feb 1st 1723–4.

prud. dau. of Jn[o] & Rebeca Broyely born 16th x[br] last bap[t] feb. 15th 1723–4.

Wm. son of Edm. & Mary Broadway born 4th June last bap[t] Aug 30th 1724.

Mason d of Maj^{r} Robt & Anne Bolling born 14th August last bap^{t} sep^{t} 22th 1724.

Andrew s of Andrew & Eliz Beck born 4th March last bap^{t} 18th Aprill 1725.

Randolph s. of Patrick & Rose Bardin born 12 March last bap^{t} May 2d 1725.

Tho. s. of Tho & Ester Backly Born 24th June last bap^{t} 7th March 1724-5.

Ann daughter of ditto born 28th May 1722.

Jam s. of Edw. & Margaret Burchet born 19th Nov. last bap^{t} June 13th 1725.

——— of John & Anne Bradshaw ———

Mary D. of Moses & Mary Beck born 27th May last bap^{t} 25th July 1725.

Luis s of Jno & Eliz. Baugh born 25th June last bap^{t} may 7th 1725.

John son of John burton and Catherine born 7th Sep^{tr} bap^{t} 12th oc^{tr} 1725.

Catherine burton Decs^{t} 10th Sep^{tr} 1725.

John Son of benj^{a} & Elis^{a} blick born 27th octb^{r} 1725.

Gower Son of Jno & Ann Bradshaw oct^{m} 24th 1724.

martha da^{t} of George and Ann brooks born 31th March 1725.

George son of henry and ann baly born 2d Day o June 1725.

Eliz^{a} Dat of Hugh and mary brag born 8th July 1725.

Mary Dat of George and Eliz^{a} Browder born 20th Augt 1725.

Eliz Dat of abraham and mary Burton born ap^{r} 1726.

Anne Da^{t} of simon and Martha Bursby born Jan^{r} 28th bap^{t} march 20th 1725.

Samuel burton son of Judith nunsry born august 8th 1725.

Wm son of James and Mary bankes born Ap^{r} ye 17th 1725.

Mol Slave of Capt Drury bolling Deceast. born 24th Sep^{t} 1726.

Mary D of Joseph and Margarit brewer born oct^{m} 7th 1725 bap^{t} 2d oct^{m} 1726.

Wm son of Robert and Ann Bevill born 2d oct^{m} bap^{t} 30th 1726.

Sarah D of Mary bly born 29th Aprill bap^{t} Dec^{m} 18th 1726.

Eliz^{a} D of Francis and Eliz bracy born 23d Dce^{r} 1724.

Handstess D of Edmond and martha browder born 30th Novr 1721.

James son of Ditto born 24th Augt 1725.

Edward son of Edward and Mary Brawdiway born 7th Decem[r] 1726.

Abram son of Lazarus and Winefred berten 17th Dce[m] 1726.

Mol female slave of Abr[a] burton born 4th Jan[r] 1722.

lego slave of Ditto born 14th february 1724.

peter slave of Ditto born 15th aprill 1726.

Robert son of Wm and Mary batte born 16th octem 1727.

Dorithy D of John and Rebekah Bryally born 30th feb[r] 1726.

Eliz D of John and ann Bradsho Born 20th July 1727 bap[t] 1. oct[m].

Eliz[a] Dater of Ishmail Bullock and Bersheba Chiswell Born 17th March 1721.

Frances D of Ditto born 2d March 1722 Bapt oct[m] 1th 1727.

Abraham son of Abr[a] and Mary Burton Born 28th Jan[r] 1727.

Rich[d] son of John and frances Byrge Born 29th March 1728.

Amie D. of Th[o] and Dorcorrs Booth Born 5th June 1728 Bap[t] 3d June.

John son of Henry and Avis Balie Born 23d oct[m] 1727 Bap[t] July 28th 1728.

Lucy D of John and Mary Beavil Born 19th Nov[m] 1727 Bap[t] July 4th.

Dol female slave of abraham Burton Born 18th July 1728.

Th[o] son of Wm and Mary Bryan Born 29th May 1728.

Mary D of John and Sarah Burton Born 15th June 1728.

Robert son of Wm. and Eliz[a] Bowman Born 14th March 1728.

Ann D of Rich[d] and agnis Barber Born 22d august 1728.

Edward son of Wm and Mary Belcher Born 10th March 1728.

Joel son of Hugh and Mary Bragg Born aprill 10th 1729.

William son of Edmond and martha Browder. Born 31th oct[m] Bap[t] 12th Jan[r] 1728.

Sarah D of Wm and Dorithy Browder Born 22d Dec[m] Bap[t] aprill 20th 1728.

amy D of andrew and Eliz[a] Beck Born 22d oct[m] Bap[t] feb[r] 16th 1728.

Peter male slav of John Burton Born 4th May 1729.

David son of Lasurous and Winfrit Benton Born 16th sep[r] 1729.

Sarah D of Mary Blaton 24th Jan[r] Decs[d] 1th feb[r] 1729.

Wm son of Jn[o] and Mary Blackston Born 9th May Bap[t] 27th June 1729.

John son of Th^{os} and ann Brooks Born 21th Dce^{m} Bap^{t} 15th Jan^{r} 1729.

John son of Wm and Mary Batte $Decs^{d}$ oct^{r} 8th 1729.

ann D of Ditto $Dces^{d}$ oct^{r} 6th 1729.

Ceasor male slave of Ditto $Dces^{d}$ oct^{r} 6th 1729.

Ditto Margery Sue. Jone Dinah Tom 11th 1729.

$Eliz^{a}$ D of John and frances Byrg Born 11th $Decm^{r}$ Bap^{t} 12th March 1729.

Jeane D of George and $Eliz^{a}$ Browder Born 29th Decr 1729 Bap^{t} 10th May 1730.

Martha Da^{t} of George and Ann Brooks born 31th March 1725.

George son of henry and amy baley born 2d June 1725.

$Eliz^{a}$ Da^{t} of hugh and mary brag born 8th July 1725.

Mary Da^{t} of George and $Eliz^{a}$ browder born 20th aug^{t} 1725.

Martha Da^{t} of Richard and Jane burch born 27th feb^{r} bap^{t} 29th May 1726 1725.

Tho. son of John and $Eliz^{a}$ Blanchet Born 22d feb^{r} 1729 Bap^{t} 10th May 1730.

John son of John and ann Butler Born 15th aprill 1730 Bap^{t} 10th May.

Wm. son of William and amy Bowen Born 2d $Dcem^{r}$ 1729 Bap^{t} 10th May 1730.

Phebe D of John and ann Bradsho Born 21th Decr 1729 Bap^{t} 10th March 1730.

$Eliz^{a}$ D of Simon and Martha Bursby 7th Jan^{r} 1729 Bap^{t} 2d March.

——— Dater of John and Mary Bentley Born 19th May 1730.

Phebe Dater of Abraham and Mary Burton Born 11th Sepr 1730 Bap^{t} 7th Dce^{r}.

Henry son of John and Johannah Burrough Born 26th $octb^{r}$ 1730 Bap^{t} 15th Nov^{m}.

Amy D of Richard and agnis Barber Born 30th august 1730.

Luciė D of Robert and avis Bowen Born 23th august 1730.

Abraham son of Edward and Margret Burchet Born 15th June 1730.

David son of David and Mary Barret Born 23d $octob^{r}$ 1730 Bap^{t} 12th Jan^{r}.

Joseph son of Robt & ann Beavil Born 11th Dce^{r} 1730 Bap^{t} 14th feb^{r}.

John son of Eliz[a] Butler Born 10th feb[r] 1725 Bap[t] 19th Sep[r] 1731.

Sarah D of William and Eliz[a] Butler Born 8th Dec[m] 1714 Bap[t] 11th Sep[r] 1731.

Eliz[a] D of Sam & Catharine Bartlet Born 25th Janr[y] 1730 Bap[t] 12th Sep[r] 1731.

Mary D of francis & Eliz[a] Bressie Born 3d 1731 Bap[t] 15th august 1731.

Sarah D of Mary Bly Born 29th ap[r] 1726.

Thomas son of Thomas & anne Brooks Born 10th June Bap[t] 11th octb[r] 1731.

Miles son Liewes & Eliz[a] Bobbitt 22d Janu[r] 1731 Bap[t] ap[r] 23[d] 1732.

Jo. male slave of abr[a] Burton Born Nov[r] 1730.

Jane female slave of Ditto Born Jan[r] 1730.

Benj[a] Son of Jn[o] & Ann Bradshaw born April 6th 1732.

Sam a Negro of James Boisseau born May 14th 1732.

Wm. son of William & Eliz[a] Bowman born Ap[l] 3d 1731 bap[t] May 21. 1732.

Sarah dat[r] of Jn[o] & Mary Bently bap[t] June 1. 1732.

Martha dat[r] of Jn[o] & Ann Butler born 23d Ap[l] 1732 bap[t] June 11. 1732.

George Son of Wm. & Mary Belcher born 18th July 1731. bap[t] 9th July 1732.

John son of Wm. & Mary Bugg born 1st Feb[y] 1731 bap[t] 16th July 1732.

Jn[o] son of Andrew & Eliz[a] Beck born 30th Ap[l] 1732 bap[t] 23d July 1732.

David of Wm. & Amy Bowen born 13th Nov[r] 1731 bap[t] 30th July 1732.

Ephraim Son of Rob[t] & Avis Bowen born 12th Feb[y] 1731 bap[t] 30th July 1732.

Fra[s] dat[r] of Rob[t] & Ann Burton born Oct[r] 11h 1732 bap[t] Sep[r] 20th 1732.

Martha dat[r] of Jn[o] & Sarah Burton born 25th May bap[t] Sep[r] 23d 1732.

Rice son of Jn[o] & Mary Blaxton born Sep[r] 16th 1732 bap[t] Nov[r] 5 1732.

Drury & Miles Sons of Simon & Martha Busby born 11th Dec[r] bap[t] y[e] 23 Dec[r] 1732.

Frances datr of Robt & Ann Bevell born ye 12th of Decr bapt Decr 24th 1732.

William Slave of Robt	Bolling born	18th Decr 1730.	bapt
Bouzer Slave of	Do	24th Novr 1728.	Decr 26
Anthony Slave of	Do	12 Octr 1732.	1732.

Robert Son of Abra & Mary Burton born 24th Augt 1732 bapt 26 Decr 1732.

John son of John & Frances Burg Born 10th novr 1732 Bapt dcer 29th.

George son of John & Eliza Browder Born 5 dcer 1731 Bapt 30 Janr.

Richard son of Richard & agnis Barber Born 17th febr 1732 Bapt apr 9th 1733.

Peter Son of William & Elisabeth Butler Born 20th octbr 1732 Bapt 26th. 1733.

Martha D. of John & Wilmet Banister Born 21th Decemr 1732 Bapt febr 4th.

Thomas Son of Francis & Eliza Bracy Born 25th March 1733 Bapt 22d apr 1733.

Susanna Dr of John & mary Beavil Born 4th Janr 1732 Bapt 27th may 1733.

amy Dr of Thomas & anne Brooks Born 17th febr 1732 Bapt 7th apr 1733.

William son ot Henry & avice Baly Born 10th may 1733 Bapt 17th June.

David son of David & Frances Burn Born 25th March 1733 Bap 2d June.

Will male slave of John Burton Born 5th March 1732.

amy D of william & Dorothy Browder Born 11th July 1733 Bapt 9th sepr.

Robin male slave of abraham & ann Burton Born 3d august 1733.

Judy of Ditto Born 15 sepr 1733.

William Son of Samuel & Cattorn Barttlet Born 6th July 1733 Bapt 28th Sepr.

Mary D. of James & Catherine Burow Born 1th Novr 1733 Bapt Novr 4th.

Robert Son of George & Eliza Belcher Born 4th Novr 1733 Bapt Dcer 10th 1733.

Robert Son of William & lettis Barten Born Dcer 1th 1733 Bapt febr 3d.

Phebe D. of William & Elisabeth Baldin Born 16th dec^r^ 1733 Bap^t^ Jan^r^ 30th.

Sarah D. of Thos & ——— Brawdiway Born 28th Sepr 1733 Bap^t^ 10th feb^r^.

John Son of Daniel & amy Wall Born 10th dce^r^ 1733 Bap^t^ 27th Jan^r^.

James Son of peter & Letisia Brewer Born 1th Novr 1733 Bap^t^ Jan^r^ 27th.

Jemmy slave of abr^a^ & Sarah Burton Born 13th Dce^r^ 1733.

Maryellis D. of John & Mary Bently Born 12th Dce^r^ 1733 Bap^t^ 10th March.

William Son of John & Eliz^a^ Blanchet Born 25th feb^r^ 1733 Bap^t^ 10th March.

anne D. of John & Eliz^a^ Browder Born 13th feb^r^ 1733 Bap^t^ 24th March 1734.

Lucy D. of John & Suffiah Blackman Born 29th Decr 1733 Bap^t^ 28th ap^r^ 1734.

Francis Son of John & Elisabeth Baugh Born 3d ap^r^ 1734 Bap^t^ 30th July.

William Son of George & Elisabeth Belcher Born 12th March 1733 Bap^t^ 28th July 1734.

Miles Son of Thomas & Elisabeth Bott 21th feb^r^ 1733 Bap^t^ 28th July 1734.

Presilia D. of George and Eliz. Brouder Born ye 2d of June 1735. Bap^t^ 6th July.

James S of John and Ann Butler Born 14 March 1734 Bap^t^ 17 Ap^l^ 1735.

Martha D. of John and Mary Bevel Born 4 March 1734 Bap^t^ 17 Ap^l^ 1735.

George S. of Thomas and Ann Brooks Born 28 May 1734 Bap Ap^l^ 19. 1735.

Nonney Male Slave belong^g^ to Theodirick Bland born Ap^l^ 22d 1735.

Rachell D. of John and Sarah Burton born 13th Feb^ry^ 1734.

Anthony Male Slave belonging to Richard Booker Born 11th January 1734.

Henry Son of Charles & Lovedy Burton Born 17th January 1734 Baptiz^d^ 26 March 1735.

Peter S. of William & Elizabeth Bowman Born ye 30th Xb^r^ 1734.

Elizabeth D of William & Elizabeth Burrow Born 5th Febry 1734-5.

John Son of John & Willmuth Banister Born 26th December 1734.

Robert Male Slave belongs to Ditto Born 2d Octobr 1734.

Mary F. Slave belongs to Ditto Born 25 July 1733.

Lady F. Slave belongs to Ditto Born 28th Xbr 1734.

Francis F. Slave belongs to Ditto Born 28th Xbr 1734.

Mary D. of John & Mary Blackstone Born 8th Novr 1734.

Martha D. of Henry & Avis Baley Born March 30th 1735 Baptizd 4th May.

Jesse S. of Wm. & Amy Bowyon Born March 11th 1734.

Martha D of Benjamin & Elizabeth Blick Born 5th May 1734 Bap. Octo. 25.

William S. of James and Margrett Baugh Born Octobr 7th 1735.

Martha D. of William and Margrett Butler Born 24th Sept 1735.

James S of James & Martha Baugh Born December ye 2nd 1740.

Nehemiah S of Henry & Ann Beckwith Born November ye 6 1740.

Abraham S of John & Sephirah Blackmun Born may ye 14 1741.

John Son of Thomas & Martha Butler B. June 25th 1740.

Woody Son of George & Lucy Belchair B Febry 22d 1740-1.

Debora D. of Richard & Joyce Burnet B Febry 17th 1740-1.

Sarah D of Wm. & Margaret Butler B June 30th 1740.

Eliz Daughter of James & Mary Boisseau B Septr 20th 1733.

James Son of the above Jams & Mary B May 22d 1736.

Sarah Daughter of the above James & Mary B March 3d 1738.

Nan Slave of the above Jas & Mary B July 3d 1740.

Fanny Slave of Ditto B Augst 16th 1740.

Patt Slave of John Bullington B July 14th 1740.

Samel S of Francis & Elisabeth Brasey B Febry 12th 1740.

Susanna D. of Capt James & Mary Boisseaus Born Octr 17th 1741 & Bapt Octobr 30th 1741.

Philip S. of Philip & Martha Burrows Born July 20th 1741 & Bapt Novr 1st 1741.

Frederick S. of Thomas & Mary Burges was Born Novr 5th 1741 & Bapt Janry 3d 1741-2.

Anne D. of Richard & Elizabeth Biggins Born June 24th 1741 & Bapt Janry 3d 1741-2.

Francis D. of John & Francis Burges Born July 7th 1741 & Bap^{t} Jan^{ry} 3d 1741-2.

Burwell S. of William & Elizabeth Browns Born Decr 13th 1741 & Bap^{t} Jan^{ry} 17th 1741-2.

Joseph S. of Senr John & Elizabeth Browders Born Feb^{ry} 2d 1741-2 & Bap^{t} Feby 28th 1741-1.

Winnie D. of George & Elizabeth Browders Born Jan^{ry} 7th 1741-2 & Bap^{t} Feb^{ry} 28th 1741-2.

Jane D. of George & Jane Bollings Born Decr 31st 1740 & Bap^{t} March 21st 1741-2.

Theoderick S. of Capt Theodorick & Francis Blands Born March 21st 1740 & Bap^{t} Ap^{r} 26 1742.[*]

Anne D. of James & Catharine Burrows Born March 28th 1742 & Bap^{t} May 2d 1742.

James S. of William & Mary Baxters Born Feb^{ry} 17th 1741-2 & Bap^{t} May 11th 1742.

Mary D. of George & Lucy Belchers Born May 9th 1742 & Bap^{t} June 13th 1742.

Isham S. of Thomas & Susanna Bonners Born Feby 7th 1741-2 & Bap^{t} June 13th 1742.

Edward S. of Robert & Jane Birchets Born March 17th 1741-2 & Bap^{t} May 30th 1742.

Patt A Negro Girll belonging to Robt Birchet Born March 15th 1741-2 & Bap^{t} May 30th 1742.

Phœbe D. of Joseph & Mary Becks Born Ap^{r} 16th 1742 & Bap^{t} June 27th 1742.

Thomas S. of Thomas & Francis Browns Born Aug. 12th 1741 & Bap^{t} July 25th 1742.

Mason D. of John & Mary Browders Born June 30th 1742 & Bap^{t} July 4th 1742.

Jesse S. of William & Margret Butlers Born Aug 2d 1742 & bap^{t} Octob 17th 1742.

Elizabeth D. of William & Margret Butlers born Septr 4th 1737.

Anne D. of Joseph & Mary Burreys born Aprile 1st 1742 & bapt^{d} Novr 14th 1742.

Thomas S. of Henry & Anne Bickwiths born Aug 17th 1742 & bapt^{d} Octob 31st 1742.

* Erased in original.—C. G. C.

Margret D. of William & Margret Browders born Nov[r] 16th 1742 & bapt[d] Dec[r] 19th 1742.

John S. of Mary Brandom was born Octob 22d 1740 & bap[t] June 12th 1743.

Charles S. of Mary Brandom born March 1st 1742 & bapt[d] June 12th 1743.

Joseph S. of William & Elizabeth Butlers born Jan[ry] 5th 1719-20 & bapt[d] Sept[r] 8th 1743.

Anne D. of John & Anne Butlers born Sep[tr] 25th 1743 & bapt[d] Octob 9th 1743.

Mary D. of John & Anne Baughs born Nov[r] 22d 1743 & bapt[d] Jan[ry] 6th 1743-4.

Lucretia D. of Richard & Elizabeth Biggins born Nov[r] 7th 1743 & bapt[d] Dec[r] 25th 1743.

Mary D. of Richard & Constance Bundy born Dec[r] 25th 1743 & bapt[d] Feb. 19th 1743-4.

Adam S. of James & Martha Baughs born Feb 1st 1743-4 & bapt[d] March 18th 1743-4.

Betty D. of Henry & Anne Berrys born Aug. 16th 1743 and bapt[d] March 18th 1743-4.

Charles S. of Joseph & Mary Becks born Jan[ry] 29th 1743-4 & bapt[d] Aprile 8th 1744.

Mary D. of Wm. & Agnes Batts born Ap[r] 16th 1744.

Charles S. of Charles & Elizabeth Butterworths born Apr. 18th & bapt[d] May 13th 1744.

Dinah a female slave belonging to Edward Burchet born Feb. 27th 1743-4.

Frederick S of Thomas & Mary Burge born Nov 21st 1741.[*]

Woodie S. of Thomas & Mary Burges born March 22d 1743-4 & bapt[d] March 25th 1744.

Mary D. of Thomas & Martha Baughs born March 20th 1743-4.

William S. of William & Frances Birchets born Dec[r] 20th 1744 & bapt[d] Jan[ry] 27th 1744-5.

Charles S. of Henry & Anne Beckwith born Octob[r] 28th 1744 baptized Feb[r] 3d 1744-5.

Robert S. of Robert & Jane Birchets born Apr 8th 1744.

---

* Erased in original.—C. G. C.

Noah S. of Noah & Elizabeth Browns born Jan^{ry} 26th 1744–5 baptized Aprile 7th 1745.

Wood S. of John & Sophia Blackmans was born March 22d 1744–5 & bapt^{d} May 19th 1745.

Frederick S. of John & Mary Browders was born Feb 22d 1744–5 & bapt^{d} June 23d 1745.

Susanna D. of William & Marg^{t} Browders was born June 18th 1745 & bapt^{d} July 3d 1745.

Nannie A Negro Child belonging to Mr. William Brodnax was born Octob^{r} 1st 1745.

Agnes D. of Henry & Mary Wilkisons born Septr 8th & bapt^{d} Octob^{r} 1745.[*]

William S of Mr. William Brodnax & Ann his wife born Novr 26th & bapt^{d} Decr 27th 1745.

Patty D. of Nathanael & Mary Burrows born Sep^{t} 22d & bapt^{d} Novr 3d 1745.

John S of Peter & Susanna Boilsys was born Octob^{r} 5th & baptd Novr 12th 1745.

Arthur S. of Richard & Elizabeth Biggins was born Octob^{r} 26th baptd Decr 8th 1745.

Hannah D of James & Margaret Bruce was born March 22d 1745–6.

Mary D. of Charles & Elizabeth Butterworths was born Jan^{ry} 16th 1745–6 bapt^{d} March 16th.

Phebe D. of Thomas & Martha Baughs was born Octob 13th 1745 bapt^{d} Feb 16th 1745–6.

Henry S. of William & Agnes Batts was born Feb 17th 1745–6 bapt^{d} Ap. 6th 1746.

Agnes } Negroes belonging to Mr James Boisseau
Billie }

born } Aug 15th 1745 } baptd May 1746.
} March 31st 1746 }

William son of Richard & Constant Burge born March 23d 1746.

Alexander S. of Thomas & Mary Burge was born June 6th 176.

Betty D of Sarah Brown Mulatto born March 28th 1745.

Ruth Female Slave of Noah & Eliz^{a} Browns born Feb^{ry} 14th 1747–8.

*Erased in original.—C. G. C.

James Son of Wm & Ann Baughs, Born July the 3d, Bap[t] October 5th 1749.

Elizabeth D of Theod[k] & Frances Bland born 4th Jan[ry] 1739.

Mary D of Ditto born 22d of August 1745.

Ann D of Ditto born 5th Septem[r] 1747.

Jane D of Ditto born 30th Septem[r] 1749.

Drury Son of John and Frances Birchet born 2d July bap[t] Novem[r] 2d 1749.

Lucy Female Slave belonging to Edward Birchet Sen[r] born Ap[r] 13th 1749.

Anthony Male Slave belonging to Ditto born 27th Septem[r] 1749.

John Son of Rob[t] & Jane Birchetts Born 17th October 1749.

Robert Son of Alexander & Susannah Bollings born —— March bapt[d] 28th Ap[r] 1751.

David Son of Edward Birchett Jun[r] & Sarah his wife born April 15th 1749.

Peter Son of Ditto born May the 6th 1750.

John Son of James & Mary Boisseau born Feb[ry] 12th 1747–8.

Dinah Female Slave belonging to ditto born June 1st 1746.

Tom Male Slave of ditto born 18th August 1747.

Millee Female Slave of Ditto born October 24th 1749.

Kate Female Slave of ditto born August 6th 1751.

Clitty Female Slave of Ditto born February 14th 1752.

Theoderick Son of Theod[k] & Frances Blands born 21st March 1741–2.

Rebeckah Daughter of Noah & Elizabeth Brown born 19th Novem[r] 1738.

Betty Daughter of Ditto born 27th Septem[r] 1740.

William Son of Ditto born 16th October 1742.

Noah Son of ditto born 26th January 1744.

Jesse Son of Ditto born 6th May 1747.

Burwell Son of Ditto born 11th Septem[r] 1749.

Boswell Son of Ditto born 1st May 1752.

Amy a Negro belonging to Ditto born 7th October 1738.

Roger male Slave belonging to D[o] born 29 March 1741.

Nanny Female Slave to ditto born 18th April 1743.

Titus Male do to d[o] born 5th Novem[r] 1745.

Ruth Female do to d[o] born 14th Febru[ry] 1747.

Bobb Male d[o] to d[o] born 27th Septem[r] 1750.

Martha D of Rob[r] and Jane Birchetts born October 14th 1752.

1752 Jane Daughter of Benjamin & ——— Blicks born ——— Bap[t] 12 Xber 1752.

Benj[a] Son of James & Mary Boisseau born 28 February 1753.

York Male Slave of Ditto 11th July 1752.

Joan Female Slave of d[o] 18 April 1753.

Quako Male Slave of d[o] 2d October 1753.

Frances Daughter of Theo[d] Bland born 24th Sep[t] 1752.

James Son of Robert and Jane Burchetts born 6th August 1755.

Molley holt Boisseau Daughter of James & Mary Boisseau Born Sep[r] 25 1756.

Charles a Negro Slave belonging Ditto son of Patt Born March 28 1755.

Nancy Ditto Daughter of Bess Born June 12th 1755.

Peter Ditto son of Chloe Born July 31 1756.

Silva a Negro Slave belonging to James Boisseau Born feb[r] 12 1757.

Hannaball Ditto son of Bess Born Jan[r] 29 1758.

Anthony Ditto son of Patt Born October 26 1758.

William son of Drury and Eliz[th] Birchett Born may the 12th 1756.

Eliz[th] Daughter of Drury & Eliz[th] Birchett Born January the 4th 1760.

Eliz[th] Daughter of John and Sarah Butler was born Jan[r] 23 1753.

Mary Daughter of John & Sarah Butler was Born Nov[r] 28 1755.

William son of John and Sarah Butler was Born Nov[r] 11 1758.

John son of Sarah and John Butler was Born July 6 1762.

Daniel Son of James & Anner Boiseau was born march y[e] 4th 1760.

James son of James & Anner Boiseau was born Nov[r] y[e] 13 1761.

A negro Girl slave belonging to Ditt[o] Namd Hannah born June 28 1760.

One Ditt[o] named Phillis belonging to Ditt[o] was born Jan[r] y[e] 1 1762.

Agness Birchett Daughter of Edward & Sara Birchett was Born April y[e] 6 1753.

d[o] Edward their son was Born June y[e] 6 1755.

d[o] Ephraim their son was born March the 5th 1758.

d[o] Henry their son was Born August the 5th 1761.

Drurey son of Drurey & Eliz[th] Birchett was Born July 23 1762.

William Son of William & Sarah Batte was Born November 19th 1763 About one in the Morning Baptiz[d] Jan[r] 12th 1764.

Daniel Birchett son of Edward & Sarah Birchett was Born ———— may the 12th 1764.

Ann daughter of Joseph & Fanny Butler born dc[r] 8 1766.

Eliz[th] Brandon Daughter of Mary Brandon was born April: 11th 1758.

John son of Mary Brandon was born Octob[r] the 4th 1760.

Aaron son of Mary Brandon was Born august the 1st 1762.

Judith Daughter of Mary Brandon was born July the 16th 1764.

Peter son of Mary Brandon was born Jan[r] y[e] 16th 1766.

Gabril son of Mary Brandon was born Octo[r] y[e] 2d 1767.

Rob[t] Bird son of Martha Bird was born July the 24th 1756.

Theoderick son of Edward & Sarah Birchet was born Jan[r] 23d 1769.

Nancy Brice Daughter of Wm & Margarett Brice was born Dec. 2d. 1766.

Molley their other Daughter was born Dec. 22. 1768.

Richard Bird Son of Elizabeth Bird was born July 7th 1767.

Susanna Burchet Daughter of Drury Burchet Baptised July 7. 1771.

Charlotte, Dau of Letty, a Negro Woman belonging to Sarah Brown, born December 29th 1791, & baptized Feb[y] 27th 1792.

James, Son of John Baxter & Patsey his Wife, born Nov[r] 4th 1791, & baptized March 11th 1792.

William, Son of Jeany, a Slave belonging to David Buchanan, born in December 1791 & baptized March 25th 1792.

John Bate, Son of John Baird & Polly his Wife, born February 8th & baptized March 31st 1792.

Mary D[r] of Richard Booker & Margaret his Wife, born March 19th & baptized June 3d 1792.

Aggy, D[r] of Aggy, a Negro Slave, belonging to the same, born Sep[r] 12th 1790, & bap. June 3d 1792.

Rebeccah D[r] of James Barnes & Elizabeth his Wife, born March 17th & bap: June 17th 1792.

Silias Dunlop Buchanan, the Child of David Buchanan, died the 15th & was buried the 16th of August 1792.

John. S. of William Bingham & Mary his Wife born March 27th, and baptized Sept[r] 19th 1792.

Mary Anne Jones, Dau[r] of Thomas Batte & Frances his Wife, born March 10th, and baptized October 2nd 1792. Chesterfield.

Robert Birchett, of Prince George County, was buried October 7th 1792.

Thomas, S. of Suck, a Negro Slave belonging to the Estate of Robert Birchett was born July 10th 1789. & baptized October 7th 1792.

Lid, Dau[r] of Sukey, belonging to the same, was born August 31st 1789, & baptized as above.

Milly, Dau[r] of Bet, belonging to the same, was born Nov[r] 20th 1789, & bap: as above.

Anna Buck. D[r] of John Bland & Mary his Wife, born March 12th & bap: June 25th 1792.

Robert Stith, Son of Robert Bolling was buried October 18th 1792.

Rebecah, Dau[r] of Tho[s] T. Bolling & Seigniora his Wife, was born March 18th & baptized October 20th 1792.

Mary Chambless Dau[r] of Nathaniel Barker, & Sally his Wife, born January 9th & baptized Nov[r] 15th 1792.

Patrick, S, of John Blick jun[r], & Sarah his Wife, born October 10th, & baptized Nov[r] 25th 92.

Sterling, S, of Sion Butler, & Dionicia his Wife, born Sept[r] 11th & baptized Dec[r] 23rd 1792.

Rebecca, Dau[r] of Robert Bolling & Catharine, his Wife, was born February 23rd & baptized May 12th 1793.

Anne, Dau[r] of John Blackwell & Martha his Wife, was born February 15th & baptized May 19th 1793.

Mary-Anne, Dau[r] of Joseph Benwood and Amy his Wife, born February 3rd & baptized June 9th 1793.

Mary Brooks Dau[r] of Richard Booker of Chesterfield County died July 24th & was buried August 7th 1793.

Richard Booker of Chesterfield County died August 27th & was buried Sept[r] 17th. 1793.

Betsey, Dau[r] of Thomas Brockwell & Jemimah his Wife, born Sept[r] 10. 1793.

Mary Johnson, Dau[r] of Robert Baugh. & Martha his Wife, born Sept[r] 30 & baptized Dec[r] 8th 1793.

Lucy Ann dau[r] of Rob[t] Bolling & Catharine his wife born 3d May and baptized 12th June 1795.

——— Broadie of the Town of Petersburg died Dec[r] 22d & D[o] 23d 1794.

Betsey Butler (of Petersburg) died Sept[r] 16th & buried 18th D[o] 1794.

John Bland (of P. George) died —— Dec[r] & buried 11th D[o] 1794.

Mrs Bonar Spouse of Jesse Bonar died ——— and buried May 1st 1795.

Robert Baugh was buried 26th April 1795.

Yelverton de Mallet Bolling Son of Thomas Bolling & Seigniora his wife born 10th Dec[r] 1795 & bapt[d] 29th Oct[r] 1796.

C.

Luis [ ] son of Barsheba Cristwell born 18th August 1718 bap[t] 26th feb: [ ].

Margaret dau of ditto born 16th Aug: 1720 bap[t] 26th Feb 1[ ].

peter son of Wm & Faith Coleman born 25th June last bap: feb: 9th 17[ ].

John son of Fran: & Mary Coleman born 11th June last bap: May 14th 17[ ].

Rich: son of Rich: & Mary Carlile born 2d May 1719.

Anne dau of Rob[t] & Mary Chappell born 8th feb[r] bap[t] may 21th 172[ ].

peter-hannor son of Rich: & Eliz: Cook born feb[r] 28th last bap[t] July 16th 17[ ].

Nutty a negro girl belonging unto Jn[o] Cureton born 25th of August 17[ ].

Bartho: son of Barth[o] & Eliz: Crowder born 3d June last bap[t] July 9th 17[ ].

Anne dau of Edw: & Tabitha Colvill born 10th August last bap[t] 17th sept[r] 1721.

Geo: son of Cha: & Margery Cousens born 9th sept[r] last bap[t] nov 2d 1721.

Nath: son of Rich & Mary Carlile born 2d Jan[r] Last bap[t] feb[r] 1st 1721-2.

Nutty a negro Girl belonging to Jno Cureton departed this life March 172[ ].

Cooke A negro slave belonging to John & Eliz: Edwards born Jan: 22th 1721-2.

Eliz dau of Jno & Mary Caudle born 17th Janr last bapt May 20th 1722.

John son of Cha: & Fran: Chapman born 26th Aug: last bapt June 16th 1722.

Hannah Wife of Titus Crecher bapt 30 octobr last 172[ ].

Mourning dau of Titus & hannah Crecher born 5th xbr 1716 bapt 30th octobr 17[ ].

Millesin dau: of ditto born 25th Janr 1719 bapt 30th octobr 172[ ].

Agnis dau: of ditto born 24 of Aug: last bapt 3th octobr 172[ ].

peter son of Wm & Faith Coleman born & bapt in August 17[ ].

Kasiah dau of Rich & Mary Carlile born August 24th 1715.

Eliz dau of ditto born Sept 4th 1717.

Amy dau of Tho: & ——— Clay born 9th March last bapt May 5th 172[ ].

Ruth dau of Rich: & Eliz: Cook born 1st Aprill last bapt Aug: 22th 17[ ].

Amy Dau of Fran: & Mary Coleman born 23d of May last bapt septr 29th 17[ ].

Wm son of Barth & Eliz: Crowder born 23th Augst last bapt Nov 7th 172[ ].

Tho: son of John & Mary Caudle born 5th Janr Inst bapt Janr 30th 172[ ].

Susanna d of Jno & Fra: Cureton born 19th Jan. last bapt March 7th 17[ ].

Moses s: of Robt & Katharine Cannell born 8 febr last bapt 10th Aprill 17[ ].

Robin a negro belonging to John & Fran Cureton born 19th July 1724.

Rich son of Hen: & Mary Crowder born 26th March last bapt Aug 30th 172[ ].

Sarah d of Cha & Fran: Chapman born 18 feb last bap 6th Novr 172[ ].

Frances D of Abra: & Fran: Crowder born 14th xb^{r} last bap^{t} feb: 7th 172[ ].

Benj^{a} s: of Dan: & Eliz: Coleman born 14th decem: last bap May 10th 172[ ].

Nutty A negro beling to Jno Cureton Died.

Wm son of patrick & Jane Doram.

Mary Dat^{r} of Jno & Mary Cawdle born [ ] 8th last bap^{t} Jul 22^{d} 172[ ].

Sarah Dat of Rich^{d} & Eliz^{a} Cook born 18th Dec^{m} 172[ ].

Jno Son of Robt and winiford Cook born 29th sep^{tr} 1724.

David Son of Samuel and hannah Crew born 28th Janr^{y} 1725.

Betty Slave of John and frances Cureton born march 16th 1725.

Amy D of batholomiew and Eliz^{a} Crowder born 20th Sep^{tr} 1725.

Jack m Slave of Jno and Mary Coalman born 6th febr 1726.

Martha D of Daniel and Eliz^{a} Coalman born 20th nov^{m} 1726.

John Son of John and Elliner Curtis born 22d feb^{r} 1726.

Febe D of Abraham and frances Crowder born 3d Jan^{r} 1726.

Lucretia D of John and Mary Cordle born 7 May 1727.

Eliz^{a} D of John and frances Curiton born 20th Jan^{r} 1726.

Jo male Slave of henry Cox born 10th oc^{tm} 1727.

William Son of Cornelias Cargell and Eliz^{a} Daniell born 15th June 1727.

Matthew Son of Th^{o} and Eliz^{a} Couch born 24th July 1725.

Peter M. S of Walter Childs born 14th January 1727.

[ ] of Wm and Mary C [ ] on Born 12 August 1727.

[ ] D of Wm and Sarah Coalman born 18th August Bap^{t} Sep^{t} 20th 17[ ]8.

[ ] D of Samuell and Ann Crews Born 19th Dec^{m} 1727 Bap^{t} 2d June.

[ ] female Slave of Henry Cox Born 2d sept^{m} 1729.

[Ge]orge & Richard sons of Bath^{o} and Eliz^{a} Crowder Born 13th oct^{r} 1727.

[Hen]ry son of Henry and amy Crowder Born 15th June Bap^{t} 24th Jan^{r} 1729.

[Ric]hard son of Jno and Dinah Cook Born 27th July Bap^{t} 24th Jan^{r} 1729.

[A]braham son of Robt and Eliz^{a} Chappell Born 6th May Bap^{t} 15 June 1729.

George son of Daniel and sandilla Carnill Born 31th March Bap^{t} 27th June 1729.

[J]one female slave of henry Cox Born 22d Nov^{m} 1729.

David son of Jno and Mary Cawdle Born 27th feb^{r} Bap^{t} 19th March 1729.

Alexander son of alexander and Mary Chisnall Born 25th Dcem: 1729.

Jamme male slave of Jno and francis Curiton Born 18th July 1730.

agnis female slave of Ditto Born 17th July 1728.

Thomas Son of John and Mary Crowder Born 19th July 1730 Bapt: 6th Sep^{tr}.

Abraham Son of abraham and frances Crowder Born 30th august 1730.

Abraham Son of abraham and Mary Cock Born 30th Sepr 1730 Bap^{t} 14th Dec^{r}.

Martha D of William and Sarah Coalman Born 10th Sepr 1730 Bap^{t} 8th octb^{r}.

Maryligon Coalman of John and Mary Coalman Born 18th July 1731 Bap^{t} august 10th.

anne D. of Charles & margry Cousins Born 8th Jan^{r} 1730 Bap^{t} ap^{r} 19th 1731.

Martha D of George & Eliz^{a} Crook Born 9th ap^{r} 1715.
Mary D. of Ditto Born 28th March 1717.
Tabitha D. of Ditto Born 8th feb^{r} 1719.
Joseph Son of Ditto Born 28th august 1722.
James Son of Ditto Born 27th Jan^{r} 1725.
Bap^{t} 11th Sepr 1731.

Nickols Son of Robt and Winnifred Cook Born 28th July 1731 Bap^{t} 12th Sep^{r}.

anne D. of Wm & Margaret Coalman Born 11th ap^{r} 1731 Bap^{t} 19th Sep^{r}.

Daniel Son of Daniel & Eliz^{a} Coalman Born 24th May 1731 Bap^{t} 14th Sep^{r}.

John Son of John and francis Curiton Born 27th Sepr 1731 Bap^{t} octb^{r} 20th.

Oather son of Robt Cobb born Jany 1st 1731.

Robt son of Robt & Eliz^{a} Chaple born 2d April 1732 bap^{t} May 7th 1732.

Drury Son of Edwd & Mary Burchett born Jany 1st 1731 bap^{t} May 29. 1732.

Wm Son of Wm & Sarah Coleman born 23d June 1732 bap[t] Aug[st] 13th 1732.

Jn[o] Son of Tho[s] & Mary Cheaves born 3d Aug[t] 1732 Bap[t] 14th Sep[r] 1732.

John son of Jn[o] & Mary Crouder born 11th Sep[r] 1731 Bap[t] May 22d 1732.

Frances d of Henry & Frances Chamlis born 7th Nov[r] 1732 Bap[t] 29th dce[r].

Mary d of ditto, born 26th May 1729 Bap[t] Dec[r] 29th 1732.

Isham son of John & Sarah Clayton Born 1th Nov[r] 1727 Bap[t] feb[r] 27th.

Sarah D: of John & Mary Cordle Born 19th octob[r] 1732 Bap[t] Jan[r] 14th.

Frances of Henry & amy Tucker Born 25th ap[r] 1733 Bap[t] 3d June 1733.

Isaac son of William & Eliz[a] Chandler Born 15th ap[r] 1732 Bap[t] 7th ap[r] 1733.

Susana D[r] of Robert & agnis Childers Born 28th august 1732 Bap[t] 7th ap[r] 1733.

Filis female Slave of William Crawley Born 15th July 1731.

Jenne female Slave of Ditto Born 29th March 1733.

Warner son of william & Eliz: Coalman Born 20th March 1732 Bap[t] 26th august 1733.

Jenne female slave of Walter Childs Born Dec[r] 1732.

Margery lucas D: of William & Margaret Coalman Born 24th Sep[r] 1733 Bap[t] 21th octb[r].

Rebeckah D: of Thomas & Martha Clemmonds Born 10th Nov[r] 1733 Bap[t] 5th Dce[r].

John son of Charles & Mary Clay Born 2d Jan[r] 1733 Bap[t] feb[r] 10th.

Sare female Slave of John Curiton Born 27th March 1734.

anne D: of Cornelias & Sarah Clensy Born 10th feb[r] 1733 Bap[t] 10th March.

Sarah D: of William & Sarah Coalman Born 20th March 1734 Bap[t] 28th ap[r].

Robin male Slave of Ditto Born 11th Dec[r] 1733.

Catharine D: of Thomas & Mary Covington Born 16th feb[r] 1733 Bap[t] 15th May 1734.

Tom male Slave of Sam[l] Cobbs Born 1th Sep[r] 1729.

Mol fe: slave of Ditto Born 7th Dce[r] 1732.

William Son of Francis & Mary Coalman Born 2d May 1733 Bap[t] July 2d.

David Son of abr[m] & frances Crowder Born 26th may 1733 Bap[t] July 2d.

Susanah daughter of Tho[s] & Mary Cheives Born Aug[t] 1st 1734.

William S of Joseph and Eliz Coleman Born 8th March 1734.

John S. of Robert and Agnis Childres Born 20 Ap[l] 1734 Bapt: Ap[l] 19th 1735.

Ben male Slave belong[g] to the Colledge of Wm & Mary Born March 1734.

Abraham Son of William & Elizabeth Chandler Born 26th Feb[ry] 1734.

Susanna Male Slave Belonging to Sam[l] Cobbs Born 11th June 1732 Bap[t] Octo[r] 6th 1734.

Fredirick S. of Robert & Winifrid Cook Born 15th Xb[r] 1734.

Dunnim S. of John and Elizabeth Coziear Born 28th July 1734 Baptiz'd 18th Octo.

William S of John and Mary Crowder Born y[e] 1st Octob[r] 1734.

Freeman S. of Thomas & Martha Clemmonds Born 26th June 1735.

Ann Ford D. of Martha Holy Cross being Illigitimate Born 24th Sep[t] 1735.

Sarah D of John and Lucretia Cox Born Nov[r] 2d 1735.

Martha D of Evin & affa Colbreth Born Febuary y[e] 8 1740.

William S of William & Mary Cheves Born December y[e] 22 1740.

Elisabeth D of John & Elisabeth Clark Born March y[e] 16 1740.

Daniel S of John & Margret Clark Born March y[e] 17 1740.

Joshua S of Henry & Francise Chambles Born May y[e] 15 1741.

Martha D of Solomon & Martha Crook B Feb[ry] 1st 1740–1.

George S. of George & Mary Cavanist B Jan[ry] 30th 1740.

Joseph S. of Abraham & Frances Crowder B Ap[l] 22d 1741.

Mary D. of William & Judith Caries Born Dec[r] 11th 1741 & Bap[t] Dec[r] 26 1741.

George S of John & Lucretia Cox Born Jan[ry] 12th 1741 & Bap[t] March 1st 1741–2.

Mary D. of James & Mary Christians Born May 31st 1741 & Bap[t] March 21st 1741–2.

William S. of Joseph & Elizabeth Clarkes Born Jan^{ry} 6th 1741-2 & Bap^{t} March 21st 1741-2.

Mary D. of Benjamin & Francis Coxs Born Apr 28th 1742 & Bap^{t} June 6th 1742.

John S. of John & Anne Chevers Born Jan^{ry} 18th 1741-2 & Bap July 25th 1742.

Thomas S. of Thomas & Martha Clemans born Decr 12th 1742 & bapt^{d} Feb. 6th 1742-3.

Silvia D. of Henry & Francis Chalmers born Decr 5th 1743 & bapt^{d} Jan^{ry} 22d 1743-4.

Elizabeth D. of Richard & Elizabeth Carliles born Aug 22d & baptized Septr 30th 1744.

James S. of John & Elizabeth Chamles born Octob 6th & baptized Novr 11th 1744.

Robert S of Thomas & Martha Clemmonds born Septr 13th & bapt^{d} Novr 11th 1744.

Martha D. of Mr. Burnell & Hannah Claibornes born Feb 19th and bapt^{d} March 20th 1744-5.

Sarah D. of Thomas & Mary Cheeves born Jan^{ry} 2d & bapt^{d} March 24th 1724-5.

Elizabeth D. of Benjamin & Frances Cooke was born March 15th 1745-6.

John Son of Richard & Elizabeth Carliles was born March 9th 1745-6 bapt^{d} Ap. 27th 1746.

William S. of Bolling & Phebe Clarke was born Jan^{ry} 26th 1745-6.

Lockie D. of Thomas & Martha Clemmonds was born Feb^{ry} 20th 1748.

Frances D. of John & Sarah Chambles was born Jan^{ry} 24th 1748-9.

Prissilla Daughter of John & Mary Clemonds born June 30th 1750.

Tabitha Daughter of Thos & Mary Cheeves born Septr 27th 1750 bap^{t} 3d March 1750-1.

Thomas Son of Thomas & Mary Cheves born 13th November 1738.

Elizabeth Daughter of Thomas & Mary Cheves born September 15th 1748.

Jemina D. of ditto born April 1st 1753.

Joshua Son of Tho[s] and Martha Clemonds born November 24th 1752.

Mary Daughter of John & Mary Clemonds born 16th May 1754.

John Cureton son of John & Winneford Cureton was born Nov[r] 13 1757.

Margret Daughter of John and Mary Clemons was born December th 3d 1757.

Louisey Cureton Daughter of John & Winneford Cureton born Jan[r] 28 1760.

Elizabeth Cox Daughter of Sam[l] & Ellinor Cox was born August 29th 1759 Baptiz[d] Octo[r] 21 1759.

Eliz[th] Daughter of John & Mary Clemons was born Decem[r] 25 1762.

Fran[s] Cureton daughter of John Cureton & Winifred his wife was born decem[r] 13th day 1762.

Charles Cureton Son of John & Winefred Cureton was born Sep[r] 20th 1765.

Henry, Son of Richard Cook, & Jean his Wife, born August 22d 1790, & baptized April 6th 1792. Sussex County.

Lucy Grice, Dau[r] of Richard Christian, (of Sussex County) & Anne his Wife, born March 10th 1791, & baptized April 6th 1792.

William son of William Cole & Anne his Wife, born Janu[y] 22d, & bap. June 19th 1792.

Jeany Dau[r] of Hannah a Negroe Slave belonging to William Call, born April 24th & baptized July 22nd 1792.

Walker, S of George Cheatham & Nelly his Wife, born April 2nd and baptized October 2nd 1792.

Maitland Mary Currie Maitland dau[r] of Mr. David Maitland of Blandford died 26th Jany and was buried 27th D[o] 1795.[*]

Elizabeth Corbin Daughter of William & Rosey Corbin was born April the 20th 1760.

William Son of John & Mary Clements was Born may the 28th 1760.

Rosey Daughter of William & Rosey Corbin was born feb[r] y[e] 27 1764.

* Erased in original.—C. G. C.

Joseph, S, of Ann Crews, was born Sept[r] 27th 1792 & bap: January 8th 1793.

Augustus Cæsar, S. of Susy a Negro Slave belonging to John Causy, was born November 25th 1792, & baptized March 31st 1793.

Thomas Son of the Revd John Cameron and Anne Owen his Wife, was born Jan[y] 16th and baptized April 1st 1793.

Richard Keith, Son of William Call jun[r] & Hellen his Wife, was born Oçtr 24th 1792 & baptized June 2nd 1793.

Clements, Son of James Clements, was buried 10th May 1795.

D.

Mary Davis Daughter of William & Maxey Davis, Born April 22d 1747.

Thomas Jones, son of William & Maxey Davis, was Born the 1st Novr 1752.

Samuel Davis the son of Ditto was born March ye 23d 1757.

Shepherd Davis their son was born June the 28 1759.

Mary Magdalene a Negro Girl slave belonging to Stephen Dewey Born March 1st 1761.

Maxey Daughter of Rob[t] & Sarah Smelt was born Decem[r] 30th 1763.

Eliz[th] Davis Daughter of Wm & Maxey Davis was born March 22 1744.

Lewis Burwell, Son of Thomas Dun & Lucy his Wife, born Oct 22d 1792, and baptized May 13th 1792.

Mary, Dau[r] of William Dun (of Sussex) & Jean his Wife, born July 4th & bap: May 13th 1792.

John Creagh, Son of John Denton & Margaret his Wife, born Dec[r] 12th 1789.

Rebeccah Hathorn D[r] of the same, born Sep[r] 9th 1791, & bap: June 24th 1792.

Polly Baugh Dau[r] of Shepherd Davis & Martha his Wife, born Dec[r] 17th 1792 and baptized July 7th 1792.

Samuel, S. of Samuel Davis & Sarah his Wife, born January 26th & bap: July 7th 1792.

Aggy Franklin, Dau[r] of William Dodson, and Mary his Wife, was born Jan[y] 11th and baptized March 21st 1793.

Mary Durand, was born June 1st 1776 & baptized July 1 1793.

Lucy Ann Kimbow Dau[r] of James Day & Levina his Wife, born April 20th & was baptized Oct[r] 13th 1793.

E

Lucretia, D[r] of John Eppes & Susanna his Wife, was born Feb[y] 7th 1791. & baptized March 11th 1792.

Richard Son of Buckner Ezell (of Sussex) & Elizabeth his Wife born Aug[t] 15th 1791. & bap. May 13th 1792.

Elizabeth Hall D[r] of Tinah, a Negro Slave belonging to Frank Eppes, was born January 27th & baptized May 27th 1792.

Richard Eppes (of City point) in Prince George County died the 8th and was buried the 23rd of July 1792.

Mary Danforth Dau[r] of Lewis Edwards & Mary his Wife, was born Jan[y] 4th & baptized April 1st 1793.

Mary Edwards, wife of Lewis Edwards, died Oct[r] 30th & was buried Nov[r] 1st 1792.

F

Thom[s] Francis, Son of Fran[s] & Sarah Finn was Born April 25 1753.

William Son of Ditto: was born January the 12th 1756.

John Son of Ditt[o] was Born the 18th May 1761.

Sarah Fernendo third Daughter of Benj[a] & Mary Feranondo was Born may the 16th 1764 about 4 oClock in the morning on a Wednsday.

Joel Son of Fra[s] & Sarah Fin was Born aug[st] 8th 1758.

Rosey Daughter of Ditt[o] was Born Octo[r] 13 1763.

David son of Fra[s] Lisenburg Finn and Sarah his wife was Born augs[t] 7th 1765.

Ann Fernando, y[e] 4th daughter of Benj[a] & Mary Fernando was born the 21st Day of September 1766. On a Sunday about 5 OClock in the Evening.

Ann Laughton, Dau[r] of Simon Fraser & Elizabeth his Wife, born January 18th, & baptizd April 7th 1792.

Arthur Son of Liza, a Negro Slave belonging to Simon Fraser, born March 8th, & baptized May 27th 1792.

Daniel, Son of John K. Fisher & Elizabeth his Wife, born the 2d & baptized the 7th June 1792.

Daniel Baugh, Son of Joel Fenn & Mary his Wife, born April 12th 1791, & baptized June 10th 1792.

Richard, S, of D^o & D^o born June 28th 1789.

Simon Fraser, of the Town of Petersburg, died October 28th, & was buried Novr 2nd 1792.

Clarissa Birchett, Dau^r of Betsey, a Mulatto Slave, belonging to the Estate of James Feild, born February 25th, & baptized Decr 9th 1792.

Lucy Dau^r of Edward Featherstone, & Sarah his Wife, born June 20th 1791 & baptized December 28th 1792.

Martha Edwards, Dau^r of D^o, born Septr 3rd & baptized as above.

Maria Deas, Dau^r of Thomas Fraser & Ann Loughton his Wife, was born July 3rd 92 & baptized January 16th 1793.

G

Peter son of Luis & Fran: Green born 16th Innstan. bap^t 20th octob^r 1720.

Nance son of Tho: & Eliz: Grigory born 10th Nov: last bap^t Jan 22th 1720–1.

Mary dau: of Hugh & Jane Golightly born 24th July last bap^t 7^{br} 18th 1720.

Margaret A Mollatto belonging unto Godfry & Eliz: Radgsdale born 7th Nov: last baptiz: May 28th 1721.

Tabitha dau of Tho: & Martha Goodwin born 25th Jan^r last bap^t July 18th 1721.

Nash son of Robt & Eliz Glidwell born 19th June last bap^t July 21st 1721.

Rebecca dau: of Harris & Frances Gillam born 18th July last bap^t Sep^t 30th 1721.

Anne dau: of John & Susanna Garret born 22th Sep^{tr} last bap^t Octob^r 2d 1721.

Anne dau of Wm & Mary Gent born 4th Aprill last bap^t 9th octob^r 1721.

Mary dau: of John & Mary Gibbs born 18th Sep^{tr} 1716.

Eliz dau: of ditto born 6th octob^r 1718.

John son of ditto born 30th Aprill 1719.

Wm son of Stephen & Martha Gill born 6th Inst bap^t Jan^r 20th 1721–2.

John son af Rob[t] & Rachel Glascock born 3d feb last bap 21th Aprill 1722.

Ann dau of John & Mary Gibbs born 23th decem last bap[t] 15th Aprill 1723.

Susan dau of Wm & Eliz: Grigg born 11th June 1720 bap[t] Aug 25th 1722.

Mary dau of John & Abigaell Green born 9th Aug: last bap[t] 4th Sep[t] 1722.

Abra son of Tho: & Mary Gent born 7th July last bap[t] 13th August 1722.

John son of Tho & Eliz: Grigory born 1st instant bap[t] Jan 30th 1722.

David son of Tho & Martha Goodwin born 27th Aug last bap Jan[r] 30th 1722.

John son of Tho: & Eliz Grigory born 1st Jan[r] bap[t] 31th instant 1723.

Ann dau of Joss: & Eliz: Gill born 30th May last bap[t] June 15th 1723.

Jn[o] son of Jn[o] & Ann Gillam born 2d May 1713.

Eliz: dau of Ditto born 16th Jan[r] 1716.

John son of Tho: & Martha Gunter born 19th octob[r] last bap[t] August 21th 1723.

Moses son of Wm & Mary Gent born 15th May last bap[t] August 22th 1723.

Susanna D: of John & Susanna Garret born 1st Sep[tr] & bap[t] 25th instant Sep[t] 1723.

Susanna D: of Luis & Susanna Green born 14th July last bap[t] octob[r] 21th 1723.

John S: of Hen: & Eliz: Green born 10th Jan[r] last bap[t] Sept[r] 22th 1724.

Mary D of Tho Gregory born 9th Sep[t] last bap[t] 1st Nov 1724.

Ralph S of Rich: & Mary Griffon born 16th feb[r] last bap[t] May 16th 1725.

Wm S of Harris & Fran: Gillom born 29th Jan[r] 1723 bap[t] 12th Aprill 1724.

Tho S of Hugh & Jane Golightly born 27th May lest bap[t] 3d June 1725.

Betty A Negro Girl belonging to ditto born 7th May 1725.

hugh lee golikely son of Jn[o] Golikely born 27th sep[tr] 1725.

Mary Dat of Thomas and Martha Gunter born 17th Dec^{m} 1724.

Wm Son of Wm and Ann Gower born 30th Aprill 1725.

Agnis D of Jno & Mary Gibs born Oct^{m} 6th 172[ ].

Jno son of Jno and Susannah Garrot born 10th July last 1726.

John Son of harris and francis Gilliam born 18th Ap^{r} 1726.

John Son of benj^{a} and Anne Grainger born 24th Dec^{m} 1726.

John Son of Joshua and Sarah Glass born 10th oct^{m} 1726.

Ann D of John and Abigall Green born 12th January 1725.

Dorcus D of henry and Eliz^{a} green born 27th Sepr 1726.

Wm Son of Wm and Mary Gamliin born 24th July 1727.

Mary D: of George and Rosamond Green born 24th ffeb^{r} 1721.

Eliz^{a} D of Wm and Ann Gower born 18th March 1726.

Eliz^{a} D of James and frances Grigg born 24th aprill 1726.

Phebe female Slave of John and ann gilliam born 29th June 1727.

Joseph Son of benj^{a} and Ann Grainger born 10th feb^{r} 1727.

Eliz^{a} Dater of Joshua and Sarah Glass born 15th aprill 1728.

John son of John and Ann Gilliam born 2d May 1712.

Eliz^{a} Dater of Ditt^{o} born 16th Jan^{r} 1714.

Edward Son of Wm and Susannah Gates Born 6th Novm^{r} 1727.

John Son of Richard and Mary Griffin Born 22d June 1727 Bap^{t} oct^{m} 1.

John Son of John and Eliz^{a} Gilliam Born 13th Dce^{m} 1725.

Lucy D of Ditto Born 17th Dce^{m} 1727.

Amie D of harris and frances Gilliam Born —— aprill 1728 Bapt 28th Sep^{t}.

Susan D of Robt & Eliz^{a} Glidewell Born 13th Novm^{r} 172[ ].

Margret D of John and Abigal Green Born 15th feb^{m} 1727 Bap^{t} 2d June.

Martha D of peter and Mary Green Born 27th May 1728 Bapt 2d June.

Susannah D of John and Mary Gibs Born 1th Dce^{r} 1728 Bap^{t} 20th aprill 1729.

Isack Son of John and Susan Garrot Born 9th Dce^{r} 1729.

James son of James and francis grigg Born 7th Jan^{r} Bap^{t} 24th 1729.

amy of stephen and Martha Gill Born 25th May Bap^{t} 30th august 1729.

Robt Son of Robt and Eliz^{a} Glidewell Born oct^{r} 23d 1722 Bap^{t} March 19th 1729.

Josiah son of Charles and frances Gilliam Born 30th March Bap[t] 30th 1730.

Sarah D of Joshua and Sarah Glas Born 24 Jan[r] Bap[t] 22d feb[r] 1729.

ann D of George & Rosomond Green Born 1th feb[r] 1729.

Harris Son of Harris and frances Gilliam Born 8th Sep[r] 1730.

Phebe D: of John and Mary Gibbs Born 1th Sep[r] 1730 Bap[t] 4th octb[r].

Thomas son of John & susannah Garrat Born 6th Dce[r] Bap[t] 4th Jan[r].

Benjamine son of Benjamine & ann Grainger Born 21th feb[r] 1730.

William Son of William & amy Hill Born 14th feb[r] 1731 Bap[t] ap[l] 23d 1732.

Winnifrid D of Henry & Eliz[a] Green Born 17th March 1731 Bap[t] 23 ap[r] 1732.

Abraham Son of John & Susan Garratt Born 3d July 1729.

Thomas son of Ditto Born 6th Dce[r] 1730.

Fanny female slave of Wm Green Born 4th Jan[r] 1731.

Tom a Male Slave of Jn[o] & Mary Gibbs Born 10th Feb[y] 1731.

Rich[d] Son of Corn[s] & Susanna Gibbs 22d June 1724 bapt May 29th 1732.

Susanna dat[r] of Ditto born 31 Jan[y] 1726 bap[t] Ditto.

Lucie dat[r] D[o] 15 Ap[l] 1728 Ditto.

Tho[s] Son D[o] 14 March 1730 Ditto.

Joshua Son of Joshua & Sarah Glass born 26th Ap[l] 1731.

Eliz[a] dat[r] of Charles and Francis Gilliam May 7th 1732.

Frances dat[r] of Benj[a] & Ann Granger born 2d Sep[r] 1731 bap[t] May 22d 1732.

Peter Son of James & Fra[s] Grigg born 6 March 1731 bap[t] Nov 5th 1732.

Mathew Son of Jn[o] & Mary Gibbs born 25th Sep[r] 1732 bap[t] Nov[r] 19th 1732.

Patty female slave of abraham Green Born 18th Dce[r] 1731.

Jemima d of John & abigal Green born 28th July 1731 Bap[t] 2d Jan[r].

Drury son of Thomas & Jane ———————

Mary D[r] of Joshua & Sarah Glass Born 17th feb[r] 1732 Bp[t] 8th ap[r] 1733.

James son of Harris & Frances Gilliam Born 13th May 1733 Bap[t] 24th June.

Johannah female Slave of abraham Green Born 25th May 1731.

Jonathan Son of John & Esther Green Born 29th Dce[r] 1732 Bap[t] 25th august 1733.

Mary D: of William & Susanna Gates Born 26th feb[r] 1732 Bap[t] 6th Sep[r] 1733.

Stephen Son of John & Susan Garret Born 9th ap[r] 1733 Bap[t] octb[r] 20th.

Mol fe slave of Wm Green Born 18th March 1733.

Tarance lamb son of Eliz[a] Glidewell Born 14th Jan[r] 1733 Bap[t] 24th March 1734.

ann son of Richard & Eliz[a] Green Born 25th feb[r] 1733 Bap[t] 26th May 1734.

Dol fe slave of Stephen Gill Born 5th feb[r] 1728.

Peg of Ditto Born 10th ap[r] 1733.

Joshua son of Charles & francis Gilliam Born 20th March 1733 Bap[t] 2d June.

Nan Slave of John & ann Gilliam Born 20th May 1734.

Martha D: of William & Amey Green Born 8th May 1734 Bap[t] 4th July.

Lucey daug[r] of Tho[s] and Jane Gregory Born 9 July 1734.

Lucey daughter of John & Mary Gibbs born 14 Novem[r] 1734 Bap[t] 9 Feb[ry] 1734-5.

Dick Male Slave belong[g] to Abraham Green Born February. 26. 1734.

Inde female Slave belong[g] to Ditto Born March y[e] 6th 1734.

Ann D. of Alex[r] and Mary Gray Born 20th May 1734 Baptiz'd Sep[t] 22d.

Edith D. of Benjamin & Ann Granger Born the 15th June 1734.

John S of John & Anne Fitz-Gareld Born July y[e] 25 1741.

John of Matthew and Ann Goodwyn B Ap[l] 20th 1740.

Susannah D. of Ditto B. December 17th 1736.

Toney Negro of The Same B: August 2d 1737.

Jimmey Slave of the Same B March 20th 1740-1.

Patty Slave of the Same B November 23d 1740.

Wm S of Richard & Mary Griffin B Nov[r] 21st 1740.

Burrell S. of Jessey & Amey Grigg B Aprill 28th 1741.

Wm of Abner And Mary Grig B March 6th 1740.

Lewis Burwell S of Burwell & Mary Greens Born Aug. 25th 1741 & Bap[t] Nov[r] 9th 1741.

Thomas S. of Thomas & Mary Ghents Born Dce[r] 8th 1741 & Bap[t] March 22d 1741-2.

Elizabeth D. of Richard & Hannah Garys Born Dce[r] 2d 1741 & Bap[t] Apr 4th 1742.

Peter S. of Nash & Martha Gloydwells Born Octob[r] 9th 1741 & Bap[t] June 13th 1742.

Katharine D. of Angus & Isabel Galbreaths born Octob 23d 1742 & bapt[d] Jan[ry] 15th 1742-3.

William Randolph S. of Burwell & Mary Greens born March 26th 1743 & bapt[d] May 24th 1743.

Daniel S. of Duncan & Barbara Galbreaths born May 31st 1743 & bapt[d] June 5th 1743.

Mary D. of William & Margret Galbreaths born Aug. 15th 1743 & bapt[d] Sept[r] 11th 1743.

John S of Richard & Hannah Gary born Dec[r] 4th 1743 & bapt[d] Janry 22d 1743-4.

Sarah D. of Charles & Mary Gees born Aug 22d 1743.

Peter S of Joseph & Elizabeth Grammers born Octob 11th & bapt[d] Nov[r] 11th 1744.

William S. of John & Elizabeth Gilliams born Nov[r] 29th 1744 & bapt[d] Jan[ry] 27th 1744-5.

John S of William & Martha Gibbs born Dec[r] 17th 1744.

John S of Charles & Mary Gees born Jan[ry] 18th & bapt[d] March 3d 1744-5.

Anne D. of Mr. John & Anne Geralds born June 17th & bapt[d] July 9th 1745.

James Williams son of Jane Gẹnt born Aug. 21st 1745.

Richard S. of Richard & Hannah Gary was born Sep[tr] 9th 1745.

Joseph S. of Joseph & Elizabeth Grammars was born March 14th 1745-6.

Pattie Daughter of Wm & Martha Gibbs born Nov[r] 12th 1750.

Sarah Rogers, Daughter of Archibald & Hester Gracie, was born December 14th 1791. & baptized February 12th 1792.

Mary Wright, Daughter of John & Priscilla Grammer, was born January 30th, & baptized February 26th 1792.

Wilson, Son of Richard Grigory & Elizabeth his Wife, born Sept[r] 28th 1791. & baptized March 18th 1792.

John, Son of John Gibbs & Martha his Wife, (of Chesterfield) born March 7th & baptized May 12th 1792.

Martha, Dau[r] of the same D[o] D[o].

Bristol, Son of Betty a Negro Slave belonging to John Gilliam, was born March 14th & baptized May 20th 1792.

Elizabeth Cain, D[r] of John Goodcy & Susannah his Wife, born Oct[r] 15th 1791, & baptized May 28th 1792.

Sarah D[r] of the same, was born July 18th 1790.

Betsy Philipps, Dau[r] of Peninah, a Negroe Slave belonging to William Gilliam, was born March 4th and baptized September 9th 1792.

Lucy Jones, Dau[r] of Erasmus Gill & Sarah his Wife, was born September 7th and bap: the 23rd 1792.

Lucy Jones, Dau[r] of D[o] buried September 23rd 1792.

Fanny, Dau[r] of little Aggy, belonging to Erasmus Gill, born the 2nd and baptized the 23rd of September 1792.

Erasmus, S. of Elsey, belonging to Erasmus Gill, born April 22nd & baptized Sept[r] 23rd 1792.

Hannah Scot, Dau[r] of Amy, a Negro Slave, belonging to John Grammar, born Sep[t] 27, & baptized Nov 4th 1792.

Elizabeth, Dau[r], of Josiah Gary & Sarah his Wife, was born Dec[r] 16th 1791 and baptized January 11th 1793.

Nancy Harrison Dau[r] of Richard Gary & Mary his Wife, was born May 10th 1792 & baptized January 11th 1793.

Delilah Peterson, Dau[r] of James Grantham, & Jean his Wife, born Dec[r] 17th 1792 & baptized January 27th 1793.

Harriott Dau[r] of Richard Gregory and Elizabeth his Wife, was born October 27th 1792 and baptized April 4th 1793.

Elizabeth, Daughter of William Gilliam & Christian his Wife was born Oct[r] 26th 1792, & baptized May 16th 1793.

Charles, Son, of Charles Gee & Susannah his Wife, was born April 9th 1792 & baptized June 2nd 1793.

Elizabeth Kid Dau[r] of James Geddy jun[r] & Euphan his Wife was born Feb[y] 14 & baptized July 7th 1793.

Thomas, Son of Charles Gee and Susanna his Wife, born 21st Nov[r] 1793 and baptized 20th Dec[r] 1794.

John Gilliam, Son of William Gilliam & Christian his wife born 15th April 1795 & bapt[d] 5th Feb[y] 1796.

William, Son of D[o] born ———— & bapt[d] 9th March 1798.

H

James son of Instant & Mary Hall born Jan^r^ 3d 1701-2.

Judith daughter of ditto born 17th June 1705.

Instant son of ditto born 28th october 1707.

John son of ditto born 18th Jan^r^ 1709-10.

Frances dau: of ditto born 20th July 1716.

George son of ditto born 20th Jan^r^ 1718-9.

James son of Tho: & Jane Hardaway born 10th July 1719.

Betty a negro girl belonging unto Allin Howard born 19th sep^t^ 1720.

Arthur son of Gab: & Grace Harrison born 15th Jan: bap^t^ 30th Jan 1720-1.

Mary dau: of Tho: & Mary Hobby born 29th Jan: last bap^t^ feb: 9th 1720-1.

Tim: son of Tim: & Anne Harris born 1st Aug: last bap^t^ 24th octob^r^ 1720.

Joseph son of John & Mary Hye born 28th March last bap^t^ July 18th 1721.

John & Rich: two sons born at one birth of Edw & Eliz Hall 1st of Octob^r^ last bap^t^ 18th July 1721.

Obedience dau of Rich: & Martha Hudson born 7th July 1720 bap^t^ 30th July 1721.

Anne dau: of Tho: & Jane Hood born July 26th last bap^t^ 19th August 1721.

Wm son of Inst: & Mary Hall born 22th Aprill 1721.

Robin a negro boy belongin unto ditto born 16th Aprill 1714.

Jeney a negro girl belonging to ditto born 18th Aprill 1717.

Micaell son of Micall & Eliz: Hill born 20th feb^r^ last bap^t^ Nov 2d 1721.

Jane Dau: of tho: & Jane Hardaway born 26th March last bap^t^ June 1st 1721.

A negro Man belonging to Bullard & Mary Herbert died April 7th 1722.

Wm son of James & phebe Hudson born 11th Jan: last bap^t^ June 17th 1722.

John son of Jeffry & Sarah Hauks born 10th feb: 1721 bap^t^ March 27th 1722.

John son of Christ & Marg^a^ Hinton born 29th July last bap^t^ 30th Aug: 1722.

Isaac son of Hall & Eliz: Hudson born 7th July last bap^{t} May 5th 1723.

Wm son of James & ——— House born 25th decem last bap^{t} June 16th 1723.

Grace dau of Wm & Joan Johnson born 31th octob^{r} 1721 bap August 21th 1723.[*]

Wm son of Tho: & Jane Hardaway born 12th June last bap^{t} 13th Octob^{r} 1723.

Geo: son of Timoth & Anne Harris born 27th feb^{r} last bap^{t} July 10th 1723.

Johanna D of Tho: & Jane Hood born 7th nov: last bap^{t} 30th Jan 1723-4.

Eliz: D: of Tho: & Johanna Hobby born 26th decem last bap^{t} 30th Jan^{r} 1723-4.

Tho: son of Chris: & Marg^{a} Hinton born 31th Jan^{r} last bap^{t} feb 6th 1723-4.

Wm s: of Tho: and Jane Hood born 14th of May 1711.

Sam son of James & Mary Huccaby born 19th May 1721.

Ann d of ditto born 9th of octob^{r} 1723.

John son of Bullard & Mary Herbert born 4th Aprill last bap^{t} 24th ditto 1724.

Eliz: d of John & Eliz: Hemans Born ————

Mary D: of ditto born 1st feb^{r} last bap^{t} Aprill 8th 1724.

Mary D: of Hall & Eliz: Hudson born 27th xb^{r} last bap^{t} sep^{tr} 12th 1724.

Heuen son of Tho & Eliz: Hudson born 4th Augs^{t} last bap^{t} 4th Novr 1724.

Mary d of Rich & Martha Hudson born Octob^{r} 9th bap^{t} 4th Nov 1724.

James son of James & Mary Hudson born 1[ ]th Augs^{t} last bap^{t} 6th Novr 1724.

John son of Christopher Hinton died Ult. October 1724.

Wm s: of Tho & Sarah Hackney born 28th Sep^{t} last bap^{t} 18th Aprill 1725.

Frances D: of Tho: & Jane Hardaway born 4th Aprill last bap^{t} 1725.

James S. of James & phebe Hudson born 10th July last bap^{t} June 13th 1725.

---

* Erased in original.—C. G. C.

Fran: D. of James & Ruth Hall. born 8th feb: last bap^{t} March 10th 1725.

Johannah D of thom and Johannah hobby born 14th march 1725.

Mary D of Samuel and Anne homes born 29th november bap^{t} 6th March 1725.

Lucainna Dat of Jno and Susan harwell born 18th oct^{m} 1725.

David son of Jno and mary high born 2d march 1725.

Patrick son of Edwd and Eliz^{a} hall. born 4th may 1724.

James son of John and Eliz^{a} hill born 17 July 1726.

Edward Son of timothy and Ann harris born 27th March 1726.

——— son of James and Ruth hall born 27th nov^{r} 1726.

John Son of Mical and Agnis hankings born 7th Jan^{r} 1721.

Jane Daughter of Ditto born 7th August 1723.

Joshua Son of Hall and Eliz^{a} Hudson born 9th June 1727.

John Son of Christopher ann Rowland born 20th May 1727.

Ann D: of buller and Mary herbert born 21th March 1726–7.

Blennum male slave of Ditto born 16th June 1727.

Moll female slave of Ditto born 10th Dce^{m} 1727.

David Son of Michael and agness hawkins born 3d June 1727.

James Son of Jo^{n} and Rebeckah Harwell born 9th June 1727.

Th^{o} Son of Th^{o} and Eliz^{a} hudson born 1th ffeb^{r} 1724.

Joshua Son of Micael and agnis haukins born 25th July 1725.

Susanah D of John and Mary high born 12th aprill 1727.

Sarah D of John and Eliz^{a} harwell born 22d aprill 1725.

Th^{o} Son of Ditto born 29th March 1727.

Theodrick Son of James and Ruth hall born 27th Nov^{m} 1726.

Tabitha D of Th^{o} and Eliz Hudson Born 29th march 1728 Bap^{t} July 28th.

John Son of Th^{o} and Jane Hood Born 1th octob^{r} 1728.

Mary D of Edward and frances Hill Born 15th Sep^{t} 1728 Bap^{t} No^{r} 12th.

Benj^{a} Son of Hall and Eliz^{a} Hudson Born 15th Jan^{r} Bap^{t} 3d March 1728.

Charles Son of Richard and Martha Hudson Born aprill 14th 1729.

Joseph Son of Th^{o} and Jane Hardiway Born 9th March 1728 Bap^{t} 7th aprill 1729.

frances D of Wm and amy Hill Born 2d Jan^{r} Bap^{t} 2d feb^{r} 1728.

Isack Son of sam^{l} and ann homes Born 16th Novm^{r} 1727.

Betty female slave of Mary herbert Born 12th oct^{m} 1729.
Liewes son of Jno and frances Hill Born 12 July Bap^{t} 12th august 1729.
Richard son of James and Phebe Hudson Born 18th July Bap^{t} 10th august 1729.
John son of James and Ruth Hall Born 2d march Bap^{t} 1728.
Wm Son of Jno & Rebeckah Harwell Born 20th august Bap^{t} Sep^{t} 6th 1729.
Eliz^{a} D of Jno and Mary High Born 17th June Bap^{t} 23d august 1729.
James Son of Christophar and Margret Hinton Born 25th Jan^{r} Bap^{t} 1729.
Frances D of Th^{o} and Sarah Hackney Born 20th Jan^{ry} 1729 Bap^{t} 30th May 1730.
William Son of William and Judith Jones Born 8th aprill 1730 Bap^{t} 10th may 1730.
Ann D of Wm Harris Born 7th March 1729 Bap^{t} 8th aprill 1730.
James markam son of Jno Frances Hardiway Born 21th Jan^{r} 1729 Bap^{t} 8th aprill 1730.
Frances D of Richard and Phebe Herbert Born 6th octb^{r} 1729 Bap^{t} 8th aprill 1730.
Catherine D of Robert and Jane Humphris was Born 20th July 1730.
Betty Slave of Saml Harwell Born 1th octb^{r} 1719.
John male Slave of Ditto Born 25th Novm^{r} 1724.
John Son of David and Eliz^{a} Hamleton Born 22d August 1728 Bap^{t} 13th Dec^{r}.
Ann D: of Ditto Born 5th may 1730.
Ruth D: of John & Eliz^{a} Hammond Born 8th feb: 1730 Bap^{t} 22d ap^{r} 1731.
Eliz^{a} D of Mical & agnis Hawkins Born 7th June 1731 Bap^{t} 12th august.
Samuel Son of Samuel & ann Homes Born 27th May 1731 Bap^{t} 7th Octb^{r}.
Thomas Son of John & mary High Born 22d Sepr Bap^{t} Novmb^{r} 7th 1731.
Jeane D: of John & Francis Hardiway Born 21th March Bap^{t} 14th November 1731.

William Son of william & amy Hill Born 14th feb[r] 1731 Bap[t] 23d ap[r] 1732.

Ludwell Son of Wm & Mary Jones Born 6th march 1731 Bap[t] 24th ap[r] 1732.

Frances D: of James & phebe Hudson Born 28th Jan[r] 1732 Bap[t] 24th ap[r] 1732.

Hanah Slave of Buller & Mary Herbert Born Novemb[r] 2d 1730.

Robert Slave of D[o] was Born Decem[r] 26th 1730 Baptized ——.

Martha dat[r] of Wm & Margery Hood born 8th May 1732 bap[t] June 1st 1732.

Tho[s] Boon Son of Edward & Eleanor Hawkins born May 3d 1720 bap[t] July 16th 1732.

Eliz[a] dat[r] of Tho[s] & Eliz[a] Hudson born March 9th 1731 bap[t] July 16th 1732.

Mary dat[r] of Wm & Fra[s] Harris born 11th July 1732 bap[t] 27th Aug[t] 1732.

Peter of Tho[s] & Phebœ Hamlin born 6th Aug[t] 1732 bap[t] Sep[r] 23d 1732.

John son of Jn[o] & Fra[s] Hardaway born 14th Sep[r] 1732 bap[t] Nov[r] 5th 1732.

Christopher Son of Christopher & Margrit Hinton Born 2d Dec[r] 1731 Bap[t] feb[r] 23d.

—— son of Wm & mary Hulem Born 29th Jan[r] 1732 Bap[t] March 10th.

Eliz[a] D: of william hudson and Charity smithis Born 18th octob[r] 1732 Bap[t] 14th Jan[r].

Drury Son of Thomas & Jane Hardiway Born 2d ap[r] 1733 Bap[t] ap[r] 7th 1733.

Mary D[r] of Isaac & anne Hudson Born 2d feb[r] 1732 Bap[t] 7th June 1733.

anne D[r] of John & Rebeckah Harwell Born 18th march 1732 Bap[t] 20th may 1733.

George Son of Joseph & Susanah Harper Born 24th Dce[r] 1732 Bap[t] 17th June 1733.

ann d: of John & ann Hill Born 19th Sep[r] 1732 Bap[t] 22d ap[r] 1733.

Drury Son of William & Martha Hawkins Born 25th may 1733 Bap[t] 29th July 1733.

John Son of William & margret Hatcher Born 13th July 1733 Bap[t] 25 august.
Anne D: of Thomas & Phebe Hamlin born 21th august 1733 Bap[t] 20th octb[r].
Sarah D: of Thomas & Jane Hood Born 21th feb[r] 1733 Bap[t] March 22th.
Joakim Son of Hall & Elisabeth Hudson Born 11th feb[r] 1733 Bap[t] 10th March.
William Son of William & Mary Hulone Born 13th ap[r] 1734 Bap[t] 5th May.
Hannah D: of Solomon & lucy Hawkins Born 15th Dce[r] 1733 Bap[t] 27th June 1734.
Robert Son of Christopher & Margrit Hinton Born 14th ap[r] 1734 Bap[t] 4th July.
anne D: of Thomas & Eliz[a] Hodges Born 19th June 1734 Bap[t] 28th July.
John Son of John & Eliz[a] Hammons Born 17th may 1733 Bap[t] July 15th.

Negro's belonging to Wm Hockins.

Amey female 12. August 1727.
Lewis male 1 May 1719.
Willo d[o] 26 Sep[t] 1719.
Scipio d[o] 4 March 1731.

Wm son of Will[m] & Martha Hawkins, Born 9 March 1734 Baptiz'd 4 May 1735.
Edward S: of Edward and Franis Hill Born 22d January 1734.
Thomas S: of John and Franis Hardaway Born the 20th Sep[t] 1734.
John S. of Thomas and Sarah Hackney Born March 9th 1734.
Phillis female Slave belong[g] to Thomas Hickman Born 4th day of June 1735.
Sawney Male Slave Belong[g] to Ditto. Born 22d day of June 1735.
Edmund S. of David and Mary Hattaway Born 31st January 1734.
Abraham S. of William and Magery Hood Born 11th December 1734.
Isham S of Edward & Jane Hawkins Born January y[e] 15 1740.
Harbud S of John & Ruth Hawkins Born December y[e] 22 1740.

Sibbinor female Slave belonging to Instance Hall Born may y 15 1741.

Susannah D of Thomas & Agnis Hardiway B Sepr 27th 1740.

Richard S of John & Rachell Hardey B. Augt 20th 1741.

James S of John & Katharine Hansell B Feb^ry 29th 1740–1.

Richard S of Richard & Elizabeth Harris B Feb^ry 18th 1740–1.

Hannah D. of Richard & Winnifred Heylins Born Ap^l 17th 1741 & Bap^t Novr 15th 1741.

John S. of Ussery & Mary Hitchcocks Born Decr 9th 1741 & Bap^t March 21st 1741–2.

Thomas S. of William & Elizabeth Harwells Born March 27th 1742 & Bap^t June 6th 1742.

Obedience D. of Robert & Sina Hudsons Born June 9th 1742 & Bap^t July 24th 1742.

Keren-happuch D. of John & Francis Hardaways Born Jan^ry 27th 1741 & Bap^t May 30th 1741.

Ainsworth S. of John & Francis Hardaways Born June 30th 1742 & Bap^t July 3d 1742.

William a Slave of William Hudson Born Sep^tr 11th 1741 & Bap^t July 25th 1742.

Winnifred a fem. Slave of William Hudson born Novr 25th 1739 & Bap^t July 25th 1742.

Lucy D. of Richard & Mary Hawkins Born May 14th 1742 & Bap^t Sep^tr 13th 1742.

John S. of Abram & Lucy Hawks born Decr 7th 1742 & bapt^d Jan^ry 9th 1742–3.

Edwards S. of William & Mary Hobbes born Decr 29th 1742 & bapt^d Feb^r 20th 1742–3.

John S. of John & Martha Halls was born Feb^r 3d 1742–3 & bapt^d March 27th 1743.

David S. of William & Elizabeth Harwoods born Jan^ry 28th 1742–3 & bapt^d May 29th 1743.

Elizabeth D. of Michael & Susanna Hills born July 18th 1743 & bapt^d Septr 4th 1743.

Lucy D. of Francis & Frances Haddons born July 15th 1743 & bapt^d Octob 16th 1743.

Mary D of Peter & Barbara Harwoods born Aug 5th 1743 bapt^d Apr 29th 1744.

Sarah D of Willm & Mary Hobbes born Ap^{r} 22d & bapt^{d} June 10th 1744.

William S. of Willm & Elizabeth Harvey born Apr 9th & bapt^{d} June 10th 1744.

Anne D. of Robert & Margret Hudsons born July 31st & bapt^{d} Sep^{tr} 17th 1744.

Edward S. of Francis & Frances Haddons was born Aprile 8th & bapt^{d} June 9th 1745.

Will a Negro Child belonging to Instance Hall born Sep^{tr} 23d 1745.

Anne D. of John & Martha Halls was born June 22d & bap^{td} Aug —— 1745.

Randolph S. of Peter & Barbara Harwells was born May 22d & bapt^{d} Septr 1st 1745.

Benjamin S. of Richard & Elizabeth Harrisons was born Jan^{ry} 25th 1745–6 bap^{td} Ap. 27th 1746.

Anne D. of Thomas & Anne Harmers was born March 2d 1745–6 baptd Ap. 27th 1746.

John S. of William & Elizabeth Harwells was born March 4th 1745–6 baptd Ap. 27th 1746.

Jesse Son of William & Mary Hobbs was born June 6th 1746.

Amie D. of Michal & Susanna Hills was born April 27th & bapt^{d} June 22d 1746.

Mary D. of Frances & Francis Haddons was born May 13th 1748.

Frederick son of John & Christian Hawks born 22d January 1750–1 bap^{t} 3d March.

Nann Female Slave of Instance and Mary Hall born September 30th 1749.

John Male Slave of Ditto born June 5th 1750.

George Male Slave of Ditto born February 7th 1752.

Frank Female Slave of Ditto born April 30th 1752.

Lucey Daughter of Joseph & Ann Hardaway was Born May the 25th 1755.

Drurey Hardway son of Ditto was Born August 13th 1756.

Mason Hardiway Daughter of Ditto Born February 6 1758.

Ann Hardaway Daughter of Ditto Born Septem^{r} ye 24 1759.

Rossey Hunt, Daughter of Samuel Hunt & Ann Lamboth Davis was Born August the 7th 1760.

Daniel Hair son of Thomas and Ann Hair was born ye 18th Decemb^{r} 1760 and Baptiz'd at Blandford Church, Bristol Parish March ye 1st 1761.

Mary Herringham Daughter of William & Prudence Herringham was Born august ye 3d 1739.

William Herringham their son was Born May the 15th 1742.

Betty Their Daughter was Born October the 11th 1744.

James son of Thomas and Ann Hair was Born April ye 7th 1762 and Baptiz'd at Blandford Church by Mr. McRoberts may ye 16th 1762.

Mary their Daughter was Born november ye 14th 1763.

Joel Stirdevent Hall son of Mary Hall was Born July the 30th 1760.

Sarah, D^{r} of Benjamin Hobbs & Molly his Wife, born March 11th 1789, & baptized March 11th 1792.

Edward, Son of Michael Heathcote & Mary his Wife, born Decr 29th 1791; & bapatized March 19th 1792.

Dolly Agness, Dau^{r} of William Heth & Elizabeth his Wife, born March 19th 1789, died Octr 31st 1791, & was buried April 5th 1792.

Dolly Anne, Dau^{r} of the same, born November 28th 1791, & baptized April 5th 1792.

Williamson Bonner, Son of Jesse Heth & Agnes his Wife, born February 16th & bap: May 13th 1792.

John Holmes, Son of Holmes Jones (of Sussex) & Susannah his Wife, born March 20th 1791, & bap: May 13th 1792.

Peyton, Son of Henry Harrison (of Sussex) & Elizabeth his Wife, born March 3d & bap: May 13th 1792.

Salley, Dau. of William Hall, & Elizabeth his Wife, born February 14th & bap: May 13th 1792.

Benjamin Stith, S, of Drury Hardaway & Anne his Wife, born Decr 30th 1791. and baptized July 8th 1792.

Peggy Dau^{r} of Nancy a Negroe Slave belonging to Edmund Harrison born February 15th & baptized July 22d 1792.

Edward Heathcote, Son of Michael Heathcote, deceased, of the Town of Petersburg was buried October 30th 1792.

Thomas Hope, of Petersburg, died Novr 3d & was buried Novr 5th 1792.

Peterson, S, of Francis Haddon & Becky his Wife, born March 8th & baptized Novr 25th 1792.

Mary Herbert Stith, Dau^{r}, of Instance Hall & Eliza his Wife, born May 20th & baptized Decr 13th 1792.

Drury Heath, of Prince George County, died Decr 16th 1792 & was buried January 27th 1793.

William Rives, S, of Thomas Heath & Selah his Wife, born September 6th 1791 & baptized January 27th 1793.

Armistead, S, of Drury Heath, & Elle his Wife, born Decr 25th 1792 & baptized January 27th 1793.

Robert, Son, of William Hiland & Lucy his Wife, was born April 15th & baptized June 30th 1793.

Delilah Ann Southall Dau^{r} of Thomas Hatton & Ann his Wife, born March 29th & baptized August 4th 1793.

Marry Murray Dau^{r} of Edmund Harrison & Mary his Wife, was born ———— & baptized May 2d 1793.

Andrew Hamilton of the Town of Petersburg died 8th and was buried 11th March 1794.

Martha Ann, and Mary Murray, Daughters of Edmund Harrison & Mary his Wife, died ———— and were buried 17th April 1794.

I–J

Peter son of Rich: & sarah Jones born 17th Nov: last bap^{t} Jan^{r} 8th 1720–1.

Frederick son of peter & Mary Jones born 4th decem last bap^{t} Jan^{r} 8th 1720–1.

James a Moll: belonging unto Mr peter Jones born 23d June 1720.

Susanna a Moll belonging unto Capt peter Jones born 24th July 1720.

Samuell son of Tho: & Mary Jones born 12th August last bap^{t} Aprill 30th 1721.

Eliz dau: of Ledbetter & Martha Jones born 7th Jan^{r} last bap^{t} feb^{r} 25th 1721–2.

peter A Moll: belonging to Abraham & Sarah Jones born 10th of May last 1721 & bap^{t} x^{br} 21th 1721.

Abra son of Abra: & Sarah Jones born feb: 16th 1720 bap^{t} Aprill 30th 1721.

James A Moll: belonging to Cap[t] peter Jones born 10th of x[br] 1722.

Hen: A Moll belonging to ditto born in March 1722-3.

Mary A Moll: belonging to ditto died 12th of Aprill 1723.

Edw: Son of Rich & Sarah Jones born 18th Aprill last bap[t] July 28th 1722.

——— Son of John & Eliz: Johnstone born 21th Jan[r] 1722-3.

Lucy dau of Wm & Mary Jones born 9th octob[r] last bap[t] 14th feb 1722-3.

Isaac son of John & Eliz: Johnstone born 22th Jan[r] last bap[t] may 5th 1723.

Prissilla dau: of Tho: & ——— Jones Born ——— bap[t] June 2d hard word 1723.

Grace dau of Wm & Joan Johnson born 31th Octob: 1721 bap[t] August 21th 1723.

Dan: son of Rich & Sarah Jones born 30th Octob[r] last bap[t] feb[r] [ ]th 1723-4.

Ann D: of Abra: & Sarah Jones born 11th May 1724.

Wm son of John & Eliz: Johnson born 25 Octob[r] last bap feb[r] 28th 1724-5.

Eliz: D: of Rich: & Eliz: James born the 8th Inst. bap[t] feb 14th 1724-5.

Pru: D: of Rich & Sarah Jones born 19th feb: last bap: 19th Aug 1725.

Sara A negro Girl belonging to Sam Jurden born 17th June 1725.

Francis and Amy Daughters of Ledbetter and martha Jones born 19th July last 1725.

Jane Dat of Wm and Mary Jent born 26th July 1725.

Wm son of Peter and Mary Jones born 25th March 1725.

Tom Slave of Abr[a] and Sarah Jones born 10th feb[r] 1725.

Benj[a] son of Wm and mary Jones born 8th feb[r] 1725.

Lucrece D of philip and Amy Jones born 11th March 1726.

Eliz[a] D of John and Susan Jones born 27th Jan[r] 1726.

Rebeckah Daughter of Wm and frances Jones born 16th Jan[r] 1726.

John Son of John and Eliz[a] Johnston born 4th March 1726.

Benjamine Son of Wm and Mary Jones born 19th ffeb[r] 1726.

Betty female Slave of Samuel and Mary Jordain born 18th oct[m] Decs[d] 2d Jan[r] 1727.

henry Son of Abr^{a} and Sarah Jones born 9th Jan^{r} bap^{t} 18th feb^{r} 1727.

Martin Son of Wm and Johannah Johnson Born 13th Novr 1713.

Wm Son of Ditto Born 16th Decr 1717.

Ann Dater of Ditto Born 8th June 1710.

Grace Dater of Ditto Born Octo^{r} 1720.

Ridly D of peter and Dorithy Jones born 5th august 1728 Bap^{t} 25th august.

Cadwaller Son of peter and Mary Jones Born 19th June 1728 Bapt 25th august.

Wm Son of Phillip and amie Jones Born 23d Sep^{t} 1728.

Dick Male Slave of Saml Jordain Born 30th Novm^{r} 1728.

Phebe female Slave of Abr^{a} and Sarah Jones Born 8th Dce^{m} 1728 Bap^{t} 23d august.

Mary D of Richard & Mary James Born ye 2d Jan^{r} Bap^{t} 2d feb^{r} 1728–9.

ann D. of ledbetter and martha Jones Born 15 Jan^{r} 1727.

Eleonar Dat^{r} of John and Susaner Jones Born 20th august 1729.

Pelletiah of Wm and Mary Jones Born 27th July 1729.

Mary of Wm and frances Jones Born 25th May Bap^{t} 30th June 1729.

William Son of William and Judith Jones Born 8th aprill Bap^{t} 10th May 1730.

Joshua Son of Joshua Irby and Mary Blyth Born 1th aprill 1730.

William Irby Son of Wm Irby and Mary Green Born 30th Decmb^{r} 1730.

Batte Son of Richard and Margrat Jones Born 30th Dce^{mr} 1729 Bap^{t} 2d may 1730.

Ridlie Dater of Dorithy and Peter Jones Born 9th August 1730 Bap^{t} 19th Sep^{r}.

William Son of abr^{a} and Sarah Jones Born feb^{r} 19th 1730 Bap^{t} 23^{d} May 1731.

Peter male Slave of Samuel and Mary Jordain Born 30th June 1731.

ann D of Thomas & Eliz^{a} Ivy Born 28th Jan^{r} 1730 Bap^{t} 21th feb^{r}.

Neptune Son of Thomas & Judith Jackson Born 30th Novm^{r} 1730 at sea Bap: 25th ap^{r} 1731.

Mary D: of James & Mary Jones Born 5th July 1731 Bap^{t} august 29th 1731.

peter Son of Peter & Mary Jones Born 28th March 1731 bap^{t} 14th Sep^{r}.

Sarah mulatto Slave of peter and mary Jones Born 11th March 1730 Bap^{t} 14th Sep^{r}.

Nathaniel Son of Tho^{m} & amy Jones Born 17th ap^{r} 1731 Bap^{t} 14th Sep^{r}.

Elisabeth D of Daniel & ——— Jackson Born 2d June 1731 Bap^{t} 1th august.

Peter Son of William & francis Jones Born 11th feb^{r} 1731 Bap^{t} 23d ap^{r} 1732.

Ludwell Son of Wm & Mary Jones Born 6th March 1731 Bap^{t} 24th ap^{r} 1732.

Eliz^{a} dat^{r} of Peter & Dorothy Jones Born 19th March 1731 Bap^{t} 30th May 1732.

Emanuel Slave of Ditto 30th Sepr 1731 Do.

Gideon Slave to Martha Jones Born 14th Augt 1731 Do.

Wilmoth dat^{r} of Joshua & ——— Irby born ——— Bap^{t} 4th 1732.

Richarda dat^{r} of Wm & Mary Jones born 18th Novr 1731 Bap^{t} Decr 26th 1732.

Rebecca of Rich^{d} & Margett Jones born & bap^{t} 28th Decr 1731.

Will a Melatto of Abra & Sarah Jones born 3d July 1730 bap^{t} 14th Sepr 1731.

Ja^{s} son of Wm & Judith Jones born 3d June 1732 bap^{t} July 16th 1732.

Dianah dat^{r} of Jno & Eliz^{a} Johnson born 16th May 1732 bap^{t} Sepr 29th 1732.

Thomas son of Thomas & Tabitha Jacob Born 14th Nov: 1731 Bap^{t} 30th dce^{r}.

Richard Son of William & Mary Jones Born 12th Novr 1732 Bap^{t} 28th Dce^{r}.

Jenne female Slave of Samuel Jordain Born 25th ap^{r} 1733.

Rachel D^{r} of Thomas & amy Jones Born 12th feb^{r} 1732 Bap^{t} 7th ap^{r} 1733.

Charles male Slave of Saml Jordain Born 26th May 1733.

Ursula D: of James & Mary Jones Born 28th July 1733 Bap^{t} 14th august.

Margrett D: of peter & Dorithy Jones Born 14th august 1733 Bap^{t} 28th Sep^{r}.

Phillip Son of Daniel & mary Jones Born 6th July 1733 Bap^{t} 28th Sep^{r}.

Isabell fe^{m} Slave of Thos & amy Jones Born 14th Sepr 1731.

Elisabeth D: of Thomas & Elisabeth Ivy Born 25th nov^{r} 1732 Bap^{t} 21th octb^{r} 1733.

Peter Son of abr^{a} & Sarah Jones Born 2d nov^{r} 1733 Bap^{t} 1th Dec^{r}.

George a mulatto Slave of Ditto Born 2d august 1732 Bap^{t} Dce^{r} 1th 1733.

Ned a mulatto of ditto Born 21th Dce^{r} 1732 Bap^{t} Dce^{r} 1th 1733.

William Son of William & Mary Jones Born 21th Jan^{r} 1733 Bap^{t} March 15th.

William Son of William & Mary Jones Born 21th Jan^{r} 1733 Bap^{t} 14th ap^{r} 1734.

Joseph Son of Daniel & Eliz^{a} Jackson Born 5th feb^{r} 1733 Bap^{t} 10th March.

John Son of Thomas & Tabitha Jacobs Born 26th ap^{r} 1734 Bapt 27th June.

Berriman Son of William & Mary Jones Born 18th March 1733 Bap^{t} 4th august 1734.

Moses Son of Joshua & Eliz^{a} Jane Born 1th July 1734 Bap^{t} 1th Sep^{r}.

David Son of Phillip and Amy Jones Born 4 March 1734 Bap^{t} ye 4 May 1735.

Amey D of Thomas and Easter Jones. Born 30 Novemb. 1734 Bap^{t} 4 May 1735.

Judith female Slave of Saml Jordan Born 27 March 1735.

Jenny female Slave belong^{g} to D^{o} Born 11 Ap^{l} 1735.

Aggey female Slave belong^{g} to D^{o} Born 18 October 1735.

Jane Female Slave belong^{g} to Daniel Jones Born 1st Novr 1734.

Elisabeth Slave Belonging to Abraham Jones Born May ye 8th 1741.

Toby male Slave of Samuel Jurdens Sr Born April ye 14 1741.

Thomas Son of Thomas & Tabitha Jones B July 21st 1740.

Mordica Son of Daniel & Mary Jones B July 22d 1741.

Anne D. of Mr. John & Elizabeth Jones Born May 29th 1742 & Bap^{t} aug 1st 1742.

John A Slave of Cap[t] Richard Jones born Nov[r] 15th 1741 & Bap[t] July 4th 1742.

Francis & Sara Negro Children belonging to Mrs Tabitha Jones Born July 4th 1741 & Bap[t] May 2d 1742.

Judith D. of William & Judith Jones born July 22d 1742 & bapt[d] Octob[r] 17th 1742.

John S of Abram & Sarah Jones born Dec[r] 14th 1742 & bapt[d] Jan[ry] 25th 1742–3.

Edward S. of Samuel & Milson Jordans born Feb 2d 1742–3 & bapt[d] March 27th 1743.

Anthony A Male Slave belonging to Mr. Abram Jones born Jan[r] 22[d] 1743–4.

Betty D. of Mr. John & Elizabeth Jones born Nov[r] 18th & bapt[d] Dec[r] 24th 1744.

Dorothy D. of Major Peter & Dorothy Jones born Jan[ry] 29th 1744–5 & bapt[d] May 5th 1745.

Mary D. of Samuel & Milson Jordans was born Aprile 30th & bapt[d] June 2d 1745.

Ann Daughter of Tho[s] & Lucy Jones born ——— bap[t] 3d March 1750–1.

Frederick Son of William Jones Jun[r] born ——— baptized 9th April 1751.

John Hall Jinkins son of William & Mary Jinkins was Born May the 13th 1768.

Sarah Johnson Daughter of Hubbard Johnson was Born Nov[r] 18th 1766.

Elizabeth D. of Tabitha Johnson, a free Mulatto, born May 4th 1791, & baptized March 4th 1792.

Anne Jeffries died Oct ——- 1792 & was buried July 4th 1793.

K

Olive dau: of Charles & Anne King born 30th decem: last bap[t] July 18th 1721.

Mary dau of Hen: & Mary King born 12th July 1720 bap[t] July 18th 1721.

Eliz: dau: of Rich & Agnis Kennon Born 12 day decem 1720.

Harry a negro boy belonging to ditto born Jan[r] 1720.

Tho Kent born about 50 years past baptized March 14th 1721–2.

John son of Robt & Cath: Kennell born in xb^{r} 1722 bap^{t} 3d feb 1722-3.
Ann dau of Capt Rich: & Agnis Kennon born 30th Nov: last bap^{t} 30th xbr 1722.
Rich son of Wm & Anne Kennon born 15th Aprill 1712.
Wm son of ditto born 9th feb 1713.
Fran: son of ditto born 3d sep^{tr} 1715.
Hen: Isham son of ditto born 22th Aprill 1718.
John son of ditto born 20th decem: 1721.

Negroes Belonging to Maj^{r} Wm Kennon.

Nutty born 3d octob^{r} 1711.
Pegg born March 18th 1716.
Lewis born 20th Aprill 1719.
Annake born 14th feb^{r} 1720.
Hannibal born 17th decem 1722.
Kate born 3d June 1723.

Sarah dau: of Hen: & Mary King born 31th Jan^{r} last bap^{t} Aug 21th 1723.
John son of Cha & Anne King born 4th Jan: last bap^{t} 10th Aprill 1724.
John son of Cornelias and Eliz^{a} Keeth born 24th Dec^{m} 1724.
Rebeckah Dat of henry and mary King born 1th July 1725.
John Son of Jno and Hannah King born 22d au^{g} 1724.
Sa^{m} Son of Cornelias and Eliz^{a} Keeth born 13th Dec^{m} 1725.
Sarah Da^{t} of Jo^{s} and Sarah Kimbal born 20th feb^{r} 1725.
Mary D of Wm and Mary Kally born 22d Septr 1725.
Ann D of Charles and Ann King born 3d oct^{m} 1726.
Robert Son of Richard and Agnis Kennon born 14th Aprill 1727.
John Son of John and Ann Kemp born 9th aprill 1710.
Jane Dater of Ditt^{o} born 11th May 1713.
Mary D: Wm and Sarah Kelly born 22d Sep^{t} 1725.
Nimrod Son of Robt and Jane Kileress born 28th July 1728.
Bille male Slave of Rich^{d} and agnis Kennon Born May 1723.
Mol female Slave Ditt^{o} Born august 1725.
Janne female slave of Ditto Born feb^{r} 1725.
Sue female Slave of Ditto Born Dcem^{r} 1727.
Dick male Slave of Ditto Born March 1727.
Mary D of Rich^{d} and agnis Kennon Born 29th Jan^{r} 1728.

Martha D of Charles and ann King Born 5th Dce[m] 1728 Bap[t] aprill 6th 1729.

Negros Belongine to Maj[r] Wm Kennon.

Hannah female Born 2d June 1723.
Harry male slave Born 1th March 1725.
Phillis female slave Born 1th March 1725.
Scippio male Slave Born 3d March 1727.
Lucy female Slave Born 10th July 1729.
Juno female Slave Born 5th July 1729.
Sampson Male Slave Born 1 decemb[r] 1729.
Phebe female Slave Born 2d Jan[r] 1730.
Sam Male Slave Born 4th January 1730.

Martha D: of Richard & agnis Kennon Born 30th august Bap[t] 17th octb[r] 1731.

Thomas Son of John & Mary Lenard Born 18th March 1733 Bap[t] ap[r] 7th 1734.

Thomas Son of Wm & Eliz[a] Loftus Born 27th august 1733 Bap[t] 7th ap[r] 1734.

Negro slaves belonging to William Kennon Gentleman.

Daniel male slave Born august 1732.
Cyrus male slave Born July 1733.
Molbrow male Slave Born June 1731.
Cato male Slave Born July 1733.
Prince male Slave Born Dce[r] 1733.
Adam male Slave Born Dce[r] 1733.
Jemmy male Slave Born March 1733.

Ann D. of William & Judith King Born 11th Nov[r] 1734.
Mary Slave of Mr James Keith B Dec[r] 20th 1740.
Molly D of John & Hannah Kinton B Jan[ry] 21st 1740.
James S. of Wm & Jane King B Dec[r] 18th 1740.
John S of John & Elizabeth Kirby. B April 18th 1741.
William S. of John & Hannah Kennons Born June 5th 1742 & Bap[t] July 4th 1742.
Williaw S. of Julian & Elizabeth Kings born Octob[r] 18th 1742 & bapt[d] Dec[r] 12th 1742.
Milly, Dau[r] of Eleanor Keown, born February 12th 1785 and baptized October 2nd 1792.

John Reading, Son of D° born June 25th 1790, and baptized October 2nd 1792.

Elizabeth Reading, Dau^r of D° born April 4 and baptized October 2nd 1792.

Betsy Collins, Dau^r of Stephen Knight, and Leah his Wife. Born December 9th 1791 and baptized October 2nd 1792.

Polly Cheatham, Dau^r of Josiah Knight & Milly his Wife, born Feby. 15: & bap: Novr 7. 1793.

Billy Stephens, Son of Stephen Knight & Leah his Wife born July 2 & baptized Nov. 7. 1793.

L

Mary dau: of Wm & Rebeca Ledbetter born 28th decem: last bap^t feb 26th 1720–1.

Fran: dau: of Sam: & Fran: Lee born 23th octob^r Last bap^t feb: 26th 1720–1.

Wm son of John & Fran: Ledbetter born 19th feb^r last bap^t July 23th 1721.

Tho son of Hugh & Mary Lee born 11th Nov: last bap^t March 4th 1721–2.

Mary dau of Jn° & Cath: Lee born 21th Jan^r Last bap^t Aprill 22th 1722.

Peter son of Tho: & Ann Leeth born 22th sep^{tr} last bap^t March 31th 1723.

Eliz: dau of peter & Abigaell Leeth born 19th octob^r last bap^t 16th xb^r 1722.

Jane dau: of Fran: & Jane Lajohn born 28th August bap^t 18th Nov: 1722.

John son of Wm & Elizth Laws born 29th March last bap^t Aug: 25th 1722.

Mary dau of ditto born 1th feb: 1719 bap^t Aug: 25th 1722.

Hannah dau of Tho & Eliz Lockett born 28th decem last bap^t March 10th 1722–3.

Peter son of Tho & Ann Leeth born 22th sep^t last bap^t 31th March 1723.

Wm son of Sam & Fran: Lee departed this life 29th Sep^{tr} 1723.

Eliz: dau of John & Mary Lewis born 21th Nov 1705.

Mary d: of ditto born 12th June 1707.

Ann: d of ditto born 16th Aprill 1710.

John son of ditto born 26th Sept[r] 1711.
Wm son of ditto born 22th Aprill 1713.
Fran: dau of ditto born 11th feb[r] 1715-16.
Susan: dau: of ditto born 11th Aprill 1718.
Tho: son of ditto born 29th Aprill 1720.
Frances dau: of Peter & Abigael Leeth bor 2d Nov[r] last bap[t] Jan[r] 19th 1723-4.
Sarah D of Matthew Lee & his Wife born 26th august 1721.
Amy D of ditto born 25 decem: 1722.
Eliz: dau: of Tho: & Mary Luis born July 27th 1722.
Susanna d: of Hugh & Mary Lee Jun[r] born 10th feb last bap[t] May 24th 1724.
Martha d of John & Anne Lile born 28th June last bap Nov. 2d 1724.
John Son of Joss & Mary Lantroop born 27th 8[br] last bap[t] 11th xb[r] 1724.
James S: of Wm & Elishaba Laws born —— March ——— bap[t] May 16th 1725.
Tho: S of Matt: & Eliz: Ligon born 7th feb: 1724-5.
Joss S of Wm & Elishaba Laws born 27th Jan[r] 1716.
Wm Son of ditto born 20th of feb[r] 1718.
John Son of ditto born 29th March last bap[t] August 25th 1722.
Mary D: of ditto born 1st feb[r] 1719 bap[t] August 25th 1722.
Mary D: of Matt: & Anne Lee born 30th May last bap[t] 4th Aug: 1725.
samuel son of Samuel and frances lee born 30th Aprill bap[t] 5th sep[tr] 1725.
Sarah Slave of bej[a] locket born 24th march 1725.
Charles Son of Th[o] & ann Leith born 23d Aug[t] 1725.
Robin Slave of Jn[o] Ledbetter Decst 30th march 1726.
tab Slave of Jn[o] & Mary Ledbetter born June 18th 1726.
Sarah D of Peter and Abigill Leath born 8th March 1727.
lucy female Slave of benj[a] and Winefrit locket born 12th May 1727.
Thomas Son of Thomas and Sarah lee born 12th Jan[r] 1726.
Joseph Son of Joseph and Mary lantrope born 16th Dce[m] 1726.
Eliz[a] D: of Wm and Elishabah Laws born 17th March 1725.
John Son of John and ann liles born 23d March 1726.

Eliz^{a} D of Matthew and Eliz^{a} Ligon born 9th Dece^{m} bap^{t} 9th feb^{r} 1727.

Thomas Son of John and anne Lanthrop born 30th Dce^{m} 1727 bap^{t} 14th aprill 1728.

Sam female Slave of matthew Elisabit Ligon born ye 12th may 1728.

ann D of Wm and Eliz Loftis Born 2d august 1728.

Edwd of Edward and Martha Liewes Born 3d octb^{r} 1728.

Mary D of Joseph and Mary lanthrope Born 24th Nov^{m} Bap^{t} 13th March 1728.

Winnifrit Wife of Benj^{a} locket Dces^{d} 25th Nov^{m} 1729.

Mary D of Peter and Abigal Leeth Born 5th aprill Bap^{t} 26th oct^{r} 1729.

Eliz^{a} D of John and Sarah Lovett Born 4th May 1730 Bap^{t} 10th May.

Margrat D of John and ann lantroup Born 21th May 1730 Bap^{t} 27 sb^{r}.

John Son of Thomas Liewes Born 3d august 1730.

William son of Joseph & mary Lantrop Born 13th Jan^{r} 1730 Bap^{t} ap^{r} 18th 1731.

Sarah D of Sam'l & Frances lee Born 20th March 1731 Bap^{t} august 30.

William Son of William & Eliz^{a} loftis Born 11th May 1731 Bap^{t} Sepr 6th.

Mary D of John & mary Leonard Born 20th august 1731 Bap^{t} Sep^{t} 6th.

Thomas son of Matthew & ann Lee Born 6th Dec^{m} 1731 Bap^{t} octbr 17th.

William son William & Jane Lovesy Born 14th March 1730 Bap^{t} 10th octbe^{r}.

John Son of Jno & Mary Lenoard Born 30th Jan^{r} 1731.

Martha D of peter & Tabitha Lee Born 16th octb^{r} 1731.

William son of Jno & Eliz^{a} Lile born July 3d 1732 bap^{t} 13th Augt 1732.

Joanah dat^{r} of Wm & Eliz^{a} Lewis born 7th July 1732 bap^{t} Octr 8th 1732.

Mary Wife of Joseph lantroup Decs^{d} 10th De^{r} 1732.

Elisabeth D: of Thomas & Elisabeth Lewis Born 16th Jan^{r} 1732 Bap^{t} 25th March 1733.

John Son of John & Sarah Loveit Born 14th Jan[r] 1732 Bap[t] feb[r] 25th.

Thomas Son of Samuell & Frances Lee Born 22d ap[r] 1733 Bap[t] 1th august 1733.

Henritta Dater of Williams & Frances Margret Lockley Born 9th ap[r] 1733 Bap[t] 1th august 1733.

Burrill Son of Thomas & Sarah Lee Born 30th august 1733 Bap[t] 11th Nov[r].

Littleberry Son of William & Elishaba Laws Born 23d June 1733 Bap[t] 14th July 1734.

Joshua Son of Catharine Lee Born 11th May 1734 Bapt 4th august.

William Son of Thomas & ann Lister Born July 7th 1734 Bap[t] 7th august.

Jesse Son of Thomas & anne Lewelin Born 11th March 1733 Bap[t] 28th July 1734.

Patrick Son of John & Mary Lenard Born 31st July 1734 Bap[t] y[e] Ap[l] 16. 1735.

Mary D. of John and Sarah Lovett Born 20. March 1734 Bap[t] 4 May 1735.

Mary Lee departed this Life the 8th day of January 1734-5 wife of Hugh Lee j[r].

Sarah D of John and Sarah Leveret. Born y[e] 2d November 1734.

Drury S of Richard & Johannah Ledbetter Born y[e] 24 Nov[r] 1734.

Elizabeth D. of Christopher & Mary Lane Born August 2d 1735.

Osbun s of Frances & ann Ledbetter Born Febuary y[e] 14 1740.

Elisabeth D of John & Rebacah Leeth Born January the 22 1749.

Frederick s of John & Mary Lenard Born March 22 1740.

Roland s of Daniel & Elisabeth Lee Born may y[e] 6th 1741.

Ann D of Richard and Mary Newman B March 30th 1741[*].

William S of Richard & Ha[ ] Ledbiter B March 22 1740.

Thomas S. of Thomas & Mourning Lenoye born Aug. 11th 1741 & Bap[t] Octob[r] 18th 1741.

Obedience D. of Joseph & Mary Lewis's Born Nov[r] 15th 1741 & Bap[t] Jan[ry] 17th 1741-2.

James S. of Thomas & Elizabeth Lewis's Born May 28th 1741 & Bap[t] Jan[ry] 17th 1741-2.

* Erased in original.—C. G. C.

Anne D. of William & Anne Lee Born Ap^{r} 22d 1742 & Bap^{t} Septr 19th 1742.

Mary D. of John & Elizabeth Lantrops born Octob^{r} 25th 1742 & bapt^{d} Feby 20th 1742.

Mary D. of Frances & Anne Leadbetters born Decr 5th 1742 & bapt^{d} Feb^{ry} 20th 1742.

Mary D. of Nathanael & Rebecca Lees born March 11th 1742–3 & bapt^{d} May 29th 1743.

Mary D. of George & Katharine Lewis born June 3d 1743 & bapt^{d} July 3d 1743.

Ephraim S of John & ——— Leadbetter born Decr 30th 1742.

Winifred D of John & Mary Lenard born May 31st 1743.

Anne Lee ———— Died Feb. 4th 1743–4.

Joseph S. of Willm & Mary Liffsay born March 20th 1743–4 & bapt^{d} May 27th 1744.

Drury S. of Daniel & Elizabeth Lees born Aug. 31st & bapt^{d} Octob. 28th 1744.

Frederick S. of Thomas & Mary Lees born Feb. 1st 1744–5 & bapt^{d} May 5th 1745.

Peter S. of John & Elizabeth Lantropes was born Aprile 2d & bapt^{d} May 19th 1745.

Woodie S. of Francis & Anne Leadbetters was born Aprile 5th & bapt^{d} June 9th 1745.

Mille D. of John & Keziah Loffsetts was born Novr 15th 1745 & bapt^{d} Jan^{ry} 5th 1745–6.

Frederick S. of William & Mary Loffsay was born Decr 19th 1745 & bapt^{d} March 16th 1745–6.

Shadrach Son of Thos and Hannah Lantrop Born 14th Decem^{r} 1749 bap^{t} 1st April 1750.

Winifred Daught^{r} of Amoss & Mary Love born 8ber 7th 1750.

Benjamin Son of Benjamin and ———— Lawsons born ——— bap. 3d March 1750–1.

Burwell Son of Thomas and Mary Lee born december 3d 1750 bap^{t} 17 March.

Elien Lang Daughter of James Lang & Elizth his wife was Born December the 20th 1766.

Elien Lang Departed this life the 4th of august 1767.

Elizth Lang Daughter of James & Elizth Lang was born July the 9th 1768.

Betsy, Daur of Euclid Landford (of Sussex County) & Elizabeth his Wife, born October 19th 1789, & baptized April 6th 1792.

Henry, Son of the same, born December 16th 1791, & baptized April 6th 1792.

Patsey, dau: of Robert Land (of Sussex County) & Martha his Wife, born October the 6th 1791, & baptized April 6th 1792.

Rebeccah Parham, Dr of John Lewis & Frances his Wife, born April 8th & bap: June 25th 1792.

Thomas S. of Samuel Leigh & Susannah his Wife, born Octr 21st 1791 & bap: July 6th 1792.

Francis Littlepage, S, of Winny Laurence, a free Mulatto, was born June 20th 1791, and was baptized August 26th 1792.

Mary Daur of John Taylor Leigh & Sarah his Wife born July 18th, and baptized September 30th 1792.

Becky, Daur of John Cotton, & Celah his Wife, born April 2nd and baptized September 30th 1792.

Rebecca Dressony, Daur of John Lanier & Catharine his Wife, was born June 5th 1791 & baptized Novr 2nd 1792.

Peter Singleton. S, of Francis Lard & Nancy his Wife, born Novr 2nd & bap: Decr 27th 1791.

Mrs Laniere (wife of ——— Laniere of the town of Petersburg) was buried 3d Novr 1794.

Samuel Son of Jesse Lee & Polly Marcum his wife born 1st May 1793 & baptized Jany 1st 1795.

Isham Randolph. Son of John Lanier & Anne his Wife born May 5th & baptized August 8th 1793.

M

Mary dau: of Sam & Mary Moor born 26th xbr 1719 bapt Aprill 10th 1720.

Mary dau: of Dan: & Mary Mellone born 20th March 1719–20 bapt ———.

John son of John & Cath: Moor born 8th decem 1720 bapt 19th March 1720–1.

John Bass son of Margaret Micabin born 26 July last bapt March 21th 1720–1.

Rosamund dau: of Fran: & Margaret Morrimont born 26th July 1719 bapt 22th June 1721.

Joshua son of Peter & Eliz: Mitchell born 26th feb: 1718 bap[t] July 18th 1721.

Tho: son of Tho: & Prissilla Man born 24th May last bap[t] July 6th 1721.

Marth: d of John & Julian Mays born 8th June Last bap[t] 18th ditto 1722.

Lucy dau: of Fran & Eliz: Man born 20th Aprill last bap[t] July 7th 1722.

Priscilla dau of James & Mary Moor born 1st June last bap[t] July 7th 1722.

Tho: son of Wm & Mary ——————————.

Dan: son of Peter & Eliz: Mitchell born 26th sep[t] last bap[t] June 11th 1722.

Ann dau of Rich: & ——— Massy born about Jan[r] or feb[r] last bap[t] June 14th 1722.

Eliz: dau of Sam & Mary Moor born 13th octob[r] last bap[t] 5th Aug: 1722.

Morgan son of Morgan & Sibilla Mackinney born 7th June last bap[t] 7th octob[r] 1722.

Fran: dau of James & ——— Matthews born 28th Aprill last bap[t] Sep[t] 30th 1722.

Joab son of Tho & Hannah Mitchell born 11th feb last bap[t] sep[t] 16th 1722.

John son of Ann Mackdaniell bass born 21th August 1721 bap[t] feb 3d 1722-3.

Eliz: dau: of John & Mary Maise born 30th sep[t] last bap[t] Jan 10th 1722.

John son of John & Cath: Moor born ——— bap March 19th 1720-1.

Sara dau of Ditto born 20th March last bap[t] 29th Aprill 1723.

John son of Tho & Ann Mitchell born 26th May 1704.

Tho: son of ditto born 19th Aprill 1705.

Fran: son of ditto born 18th June 1708.

Mary dau: of Tho: & Barbary Mitchell born 18th August 1713.

Barbary dau of ditto born 8th March 1715.

Nath: son of ditto born 4th decem: 1717.

Peter son of ditto born 3d Jan: 1719.

Sam son of ditto born 16th June 1722.

John son of Rob[t] & Anne Moody born 18th May 1723.

Mark son of Mark & Eliz: Moore borne 26th July last bap Nov 7th 1723.

John son of Morgan & Sibbilla Makinny born 12th febr last bapt 10th Aprill 1724.

Sarah d of Rich & Ann Massy born 27th Nov last bapt 10th Aprill 1724.

Rich son of Sam: & Mary Moor born 9th febr last bapt August 2d 1724.

Rich son of Hen: & Eliz: Mays born 1st of Aprill last bapt 6th Novr 1724.

Anne d of Fran & Marga Merimon born 26th June last bap Nov 6th 1724.

Mary d of John & Mary Mays born 2d last June bapt Octobr 11th 1724.

Seth Moor son of great John Moor born 9th Aprill 1692.

Rhuben son of phillip & Mary Morgan born 11th novbr bapt 20th febr 1725.

Anne Dat of Jno and Julia Mayes born 13th febr bapt 20th 1725.

John son of John & Julia Mayes born 29th febr 1719.

Martha Dat of John and Julia Mayes 8th June born 1722.

Thomas son of Thom and Jane Man born 4th June last bapt 30 July 1725.

Amey Dat of Joseph and Eleonore Mathes born 9th Decm 1724.

frances Dat of peter and Eliza Mitchel born 28th octm 1725.

martha Dat of henry and Martha Morris born 2 June 1725.

Priscilla Dat of Tho and Jane Man born 13th Decm 1725.

Winiford Dat of Wm and Eliza Mayes born 22d Augs 1725.

Jno and Richd sons of Ricd and Ann Massey born 14th febr 1725.

Jno Son of David and Eliz Murcollow born 14 Decm 1725.

Wm Son of Samuel and Mary More born 6th July bapt Octobr 9th 1726.

Wm Son of Jno and Mary Mayes born 11th June bapt octm 4th 1726.

Mark Son Mark and Eliza More born 10th June 1726.

James Son of Jno and Catherine More born 18th augst bapt 16th octm 1726.

Mary D: of Jno and dorithy Morland born 23d Sept bapt 30th octm 1726.

Mary gardiner D of Gardiner and Eliz^{a} Mayes born 13th Oct^{m} 1726.

Edward Son of Robert and Martha Munford born 1th No^{br} 1726.

James Son of Morgan and Sybellah Makinny born 7th feb^{r} 1725.

James Son of John and Mary May born 6th feb^{r} 1726.

Eliz^{a} D of henry and Susanah Morris born 6th Oct^{m} 1726.

Lucrecee D of Wm and Ann Mallone born 11th Jan^{r} 1726.

Robert Son of Jerimiah and Grace Mize born 10th May 1721.

Joshua son of Ditto born 10th March 1726.

Mary D of David and Eliz^{a} Murcollo born 7th June 1727.

Michaell son of Wm and Eliz^{a} Mixon born 15th aprill 1727.

Eliz^{a} D of henry and Susanah Morris born 6th oct^{m} 1726.

David son of David and Jane Miles born 17th aprill 1727.

Drury Son of Matthew and Eliz^{a} Mayes born 15th Jan^{r} bap^{t} feb^{r} 20th 1727.

Lucy Dat^{r} of Georg hunt and frances More born 22d Dce^{m} 1727.

James Son of John and Julia mayes born Monday ye 18th March 1727.

Agnis D of John and Mary Man Born 31t May 1728.

George Son of John and Mary Mayes Born 19th July 1728 Bap^{t} 6 ocb^{r}.

Jean D of John and Dorithy Moreland Born 21th Sep^{t} 1728 Bap^{t} 7th No^{r}.

Phebe Dat^{r} of John and Catherine More Born 22d oct^{m} 1728 Bapt 25th Dce^{m}.

henry Son of Henry and Susan Morris Born 22d octm^{r} Bap^{t} March 3d 1728.

Margret D of Th^{os} and Elionar More Born 13th aprill Bap^{t} 16th aprill 1729.

Dorithy D of John and Mary May Born 9th Dce^{mr} Bap^{t} 21 Dec^{m} 1728.

Martha D of James and Eliz^{a} munford Born 29th Sepr Bap^{t} 6th Jan^{r} 1728.

David Son of David and Eliz^{a} Murcollo Born 28th May Bap^{t} 3d august 1729.

Susannah D of Roger and Eliz^{a} More Born 27th aprill Bap^{t} 27 June 1729.

Lucia D of Jno and Mary More Born 24th May Bap^{t} 27th June 1729.

Frances D of David and Jane Miles Born 21 June Bap[t] 10th august 1729.

Zacariah son of John and Rachail Martin Born 22d Jan[r] 1729.

ann D of John and Mary Man Born 29th august Bap[t] 2d oct[r] 1729.

Lucy D of Th[os] & Jeane May Born 8th Jan[r] 1729 Bap[t] 28th aprill 1730.

Henry Male Slave of Wm and Mary Mayes Born 24th March 1725 Bap[t] 3d March 1729.

James Male Slave of Ditto Born 26th Jan[r] 1727 Bap[t] 3d March 1729.

Nancy female Slave of Ditto Born 27th Jan[r] Bap[t] 3d March 1729.

Phillip Son of Phillip and Mary Morgan Born 15th Dcem[r] Bap[t] 10th May 1730.

Joseph Son of Josep and Hellen Matthy Born 17th Janr: 1729 Bap[t] 10th May 1730.

Tabitha D of Richard and ann Massie Born 8th Jan[r] 1729 Bap[t] 30th May 1730.

Michal Son of Henry and Mary Matthews Born 27th Dce[m] 1729 Bap[t] 10th May 1730.

Eliz[a] D of George and frances More Born 1th Jan[r] Bap[t] 22d febr: 1729.

Robert Son of Wm and ann Marshall Born 23d Dcem[r] 1729 Bap[t] 3th March 1730.

Zachariah Son of Jn[o] and Rachald Martin Born 22d Jan[r] 1729 Bap[r] 1th March 1729.

Moses male Slave of Jn[o] and Julia Mayes Born 19th June 1730.

Sarah Dater of John and Julia Mayes Born 13th Decm[r] 1730.

Elisabeth Dater of John and Mary May Born 2d octber 1730.

Thomas Son of Roger and Eliz[a] more Born 20th Sep[r] 1730 Bap[t] 15th Nov[r].

Matthew Son of Marke & Mary fowler Born 4th Jan[r] 1730 Bap[t] augst 29th 1731.

Lucy D of John & mary mayes Born 26th Jan[r] 1730 Bap[t] 21th feb[r].

Sarah D: of michael & Eliz[a] Mackey Born 16th Dcm[r] 1730.

Betty rutherford Dater of John and Catharine more Born 25th June Bap[t] 2d octb[r] 1731.

mary D of Samuel & Mary More Born 29th ap^{r} Bap^{t} 7th Novmb^{r} 1731.

Elisabeth D: of Wm and ann marshal Born 13th July Bap^{t} 24th Sepr 1731.

Ja[ ] Son of David & Elisabeth Maccollo Born 29th Sepr 1731 Bap^{t} Decr 25th.

Laurana D: of Robert & ann Moody Born 29th Jany^{r} 1731 Bap^{t} ap^{r} 23: 1732.

Martha D: of Joseph & Eleanore Matthews Born 8th Jan^{r} 1731 Bap^{t} 23d ap^{r} 1732.

Frank male Slave of Jno & Julia mayes Born 28th Novr 1731.

John Son of Phillip & mary morgan Born 30th Novr 1731 Bap^{t} 23d ap^{r} 1732.

William Son of Rich^{d} & Eleanor McDearmon born May 18th 1732.

Jonathan son of Jonath^{a} & Sarah Mote born ——— bap^{t} Sepr 23d 1732.

Willm Son of Alex^{r} & Ruth Moor born 14th Sepr 1731 bap^{t} May 22d 1732.

Eliz^{a} Dat^{r} of Saml & Mary Morgan born Ap^{l} 20 1732 bap^{t} Decr 17th 1732.

James Son of James & Eliz^{a} Munford born Sepr 16th bap^{t} Decr 26th 1732.

Thomas Son of David & Jane Mils Born 29th dce^{r} 1731 Bap^{t} Jan^{r} 30th.

Johanna D: of Wm & Elisabeth Mayes Born 14 sep^{r} 1732 Bap^{t} Jan^{r} 19th.

William son of John & Mary May Born 28th Dce^{r} 1732 Bap^{t} 24th feb^{r}.

Dick male slave of Robt & martha munford Born 21th Decem^{r} 1732 Bap^{t} feb^{r} 4th.

Daniel son of James & leah more Born 11th feb^{r} 1732 Bap^{t} 2d ap^{r} 1733.

Roger son of Roge & Eliz^{a} more Born 8th Decr 1732 Bap^{t} 25th feb^{r}.

Robert Son of Francis & Eliz^{a} Man Born 7th feb^{r} 1732 Bap^{t} 8th ap^{r} 1733.

George Son of John & Mary More Born 23d Novr 1732 Bap^{t} 8th ap^{r} 1733.

Daniel Son of Nath^{a} & Mary Molone Born 15th Sepr 1732 Bap^{t} 17th June 1733.

avis D^{r} of Thomas & Eleonore More Born 27th March 1733 Bap^{t} 17th June.

Harry Male Slave of Jno & Julia Mayes Born 23d feb^{r} 1732.

Delilah D: of Matthew Mayes & Eliz: Born 20th July 1733 Bap^{t} 26th august.

frances D: of Robert & ann Moody Dcest novmber 1732.

David Son of Jonathan & Sarah Mote Born 13th ap^{r} 1733 Bap^{t} 20th octb^{r}.

Peter Son of John & Martha Manson Born 24th Dce^{r} 1733 Bap^{t} 30th Dce^{r}.

John Son of Samuel & Elizabeth Man Born 23d Dce^{r} 1733 Bap^{t} March 22d.

Matthew Son of John & Sarah Meuse Born 27th feb^{r} 1733 Bap^{t} 7th ap^{r} 1734.

Mary D: of John & Mary Man Born 28th feb^{r} 1733 Bap^{r} 10th March.

anne D: of william & anne Mershall Born 28th Jan^{r} 1733 Bap^{t} 10th March.

Joseph Son of George & ann marchbank Born 4th octb^{r} 1733 Bap^{t} 10th March 1733.

Susannah D: of James & Elisabeth Munford Born 29th March 1734 Bap^{t} 28th ap^{r}.

Richard son of william & Elisabeth Martin Born 27th august 1733 dces^{d} 22d November.

Micail son of Micail & Catharine Mikedermond Born 25th feb^{r} 1733 Bap^{t} 15th May 1734.

John Son of David & Jane Miles Born 27th ap^{r} 1734 Bap^{t} 26th May.

Benica female Slave of John & Julia Mayes Born 8th July 1734.

John Son of Saml & mary morgan Born 26th ap^{r} 1734 Bap^{t} 23d June.

Elizabeth, Daughter of Robt & Ann Munford born Sep^{t} 22d 1734 Bap^{t} 21st Octob^{r}.

John Son of John and Mary Moore Born ye 9th May 1735 Bap^{t} 6th July.

Vadrey S. of Wm and Susana Macbie Born 23 decem^{r} 1734 Bap^{t} Ap^{l} 19 1735.

Robert Son of Jam^{s} and Mary Moore Born ye 23d January 1734.
Daniel s. of Robert and Ann Moody. Born ye 2d Xb^{r} 1734.
John S. of John & Elizabeth Morris Born ye 24th Novr 1734.
William S of William Martin & Elizabeth his wife Born Novr 28th 1734.
Anne D. of David & Elizabeth M^{c}choller. Born 29th July 1735.
Jane D. of John and Ann Mooney Born Decr 13th 1735.
Henry Son of Henry & Sarah Mitchell Born 7th Augt 1735.
Betty D: of John & Agnes May was Born the 16th No^{vm} 1740.
William s of Daniel & Susanah Maccloud Born march ye 10 1740.
Martha D of John & Dorithea Moorland B Sepr 12th 1740.
Joel S. of Wm And Sarah Martin B March 18th 1740–1.
Wood S. of John & Mary Moor B March 27th 1741.
Elizabeth D. of David & Elizabeth Maccullochs Born July 23d 1741 & Bap^{t} Octob^{r} 30th 1741.
Anne D. of William & Isabel Martins Born Aug. 30th 1741 & Bap^{t} Octob^{r} 4th 1741.
Reuben S. of William & Anne Melones Born Sep^{tr} 26th 1741 & Bap^{t} Novr 15th 1741.
Lucy D. of Matthew & Elizabeth Martins Born Sep^{tr} 25th 1741 & Bap^{t} Decr 24th 1741.
Isham S. of Daniel & Jane Meadows Born Feb^{ry} 16th 1740–1 & Bap^{t} Jan^{ry} 3d 1741–2.
Hannah D. of Richard & Mary Meanlands Born Novr 13th 1741 & Bap^{t} Jan^{ry} 17th 1741–2.
Theodorick. S. of Capt Robert & Anne Munfords Born Feby 21st 1741–2 & Bap^{t} Feby 26th 1741–2.
Frederick. S. of John & Sara Mayes Born Feby 2d 1741–2 & Bap^{t} Apr 11th 1742.
Catharine D. of Malcom & Catharine MacNeils Born Feb 12th 1741–2 & Bap^{t} Apr. 26th 1742.
Jane. D of Humphry & Elizabeth Moodies Born March 30th 1742 & Bap^{t} June 13th 1742.
Susanna D. of John & Jane Meadlands Born Decr 13th 1741 & Bap^{t} July 25th 1742.
Mary D of Roger & Elizabeth Moors Born May 11th 1742 & Bap^{t} Aug. 15th 1742.
Richard S of John & Agnes May was Born December 20th 1742.

Benjamin S. of James & Elizabeth MacDowals Born Septr 27th 1742 & bapt^{d} Octob^{r} 3d 1742.

Addie D. of Henry & Sarah Mitchels born June 20th 1743 & bapt^{d} Jan^{ry} 6th 1743-4.

Anne D. of Mr Hugh & Jane Millers born March 13th 1742-3 & bapt^{d} Aprile 10th 1743.

Margret D. of Daniel & Susanna MacLauds born Jan^{ry} 8th 1742-3 & bapt^{d} May 22d 1743.

Elizabeth D. of John & Elizabeth Manns born Jan^{r} 28th 1743-4 bapt^{d} May 13th 1744.

Jane D. of John & Jane Meadlands born March 23d 1743-4 bapt^{d} Septr 22d 1744.

John S. of John & Agnes May born Decr 20th 1744 baptized Feb 24th 1744-5.

William S. of John & Elizabeth Man born Decr 11th 1744 bapt^{d} March 3d 1744-5.

Patrick Smith S of Margaret Malone born Feb. 27th 1744-5 baptized April 14th 1745.

Phyllis A female Slave belonging to Mr. Hugh Miller was born March 12th 1744-5.

Anne D of Mr. Hugh & Jane Milles was born March 13th 1742-3 & baptized Apr. 10th 1743.

Robert S. of Ditto was born March 28th 1746 & baptized ——.

Jane D. of Ditto was born Feb^{ry} 21st 1747-8 & baptized ——.

Betty born June 1740
Beck born —— 1742
Tony born Aprile 1746
Cutchnia born Sep^{t} 1746
Rose born Septr 1747
Isaac born March 1748
} Negroes belonging to Mr. Hugh Miller.

David Son of John May j^{r} and Agnes his wife Born —— 1749 Bap^{t} 5 Octo^{r}.

James Son of James and Anne Murray born July 10th 1743.

John Son of Ditto born September 13th 1744.

Anne Daughter of Ditto born October 30th 1746.

Margaret Daughter of ditto born February 8th 1748-9.

William Son of ditto born May 6th 1752.

Mary Daughter of Do born Feby 22 1754.

Thomas Son of Ditto Born Jany 13th Baptized ye 16th following 1757.

Negroes Belonging to James Murray Viz^t.

Moll a Mallatto Born Octo^r 1735. Patt a Negro B. Octo^r 1736.
Lucy a Negro. B. May 1739. Frank a Negro. B. Decr 1740.
Sarah a Mallato B. March 1742. Charles a Negro. Octo^r 1742.
Doll a Negro. B. April 1744. Billy a Negro. June 18. 1744.
Hannah a Negro. B. Octo^r 1744. Peg a Negro. July 1746.
Sue a Negro. Octo^r 1746. Tom a Mallato. Decr 1746.
Aggy. a Mallato. July 1748. Tom a Mallato Sep^t 1748.
Joe a Mallato. Augt 1749. Cate a Negro Octo^r 1748.
Will a Negro. Feby 1749–50. Kitt Novr 1751.
Nan, April 1753. Cate July 1753. Harry Octo^r 1753.
Jenny, January 1754. Cain March 1754. Poll. Jany 1755.
Latty, July 1755. Moll. Sep^t 1755. Jenny Novr 1755.
Betty, Decr 1757. Cyruss, March 1756. Patt. Decr 1756.
Easter, March 1757. Antony Sep^t 1757. Tabb. Octo^r 1757.
Matthew. Decemb^r 1757. Frank. March 1758.
Bobb, May 1758. Dick Sep^t 1758.

Joseph Moore son of John Moore & Mary his wife was Born Janury the 20th 1767 and Baptiz^d at the Brick Church of Bristol Parish March the 22d 1767.

Henry Son of George Wale Machen & Mary his Wife, Born March 7th 1780 Baptised May 11th 1780.

Elizabeth Daughter of William Edgar & Jane his Wife, Born Feby 6. 1780. Baptised May 11th 1780.

Jamy Cate, Son of Jeremiah Meacham & Milly his Wife, born October 26th 1791, & baptized March 21st 1792.

Louisa, Daughter of Aggy, a Slave belonging to John McLeod, born in March 1790, & baptized March 25th 1792.

Lucy Massenburg, Dau^r of John Mason (of Sussex County) & Lucy his Wife, born October 26th 1791, & baptized April 6th 1792.

John, Son of John McKenny (of Sussex County) & Rebeccah his Wife, born March 4th 1791, & baptized April 6th 1792.

David, Son of William McCarter & Susannah his Wife, born October 6th 1791, and baptized May 9th 1792.

Joshua Son of Fanny, a Slave belonging to David Maitland, born February 1st 1791, & baptized April 29th 1792.

Thomy Branch, son of Reaps Mitchell & Susanna his Wife, born Oct[r] 20th 1791 & bap. May 13th 1792.

John Malcolm died June 23d & was buried in St Pauls' Church-Yard, June 24th. 1792.

Elizabeth McMurdo, Wife of Charles J. McMurdo, died the 13th and was buried the 14th day of Sep:ember 1792.

Martha, Anne, Elizabeth, Dau[r] of Charles J. McMurdo, and Elizabeth his Wife, was born *(the 1st) of *(September) & baptized October 11th 1792.

Elizabeth McFarlane of Chesterfield County, was buried October 16th 1792.

Mary Wales, Dau[r] of Thomas Machen & Sally his wife, was born June 8th 1791 & baptized November 2d 1792.

Richard, S, of George May & Anna his Wife, born September 3rd & baptized December 29th 1792.

Lettice Hickman, Dau[r] of William Meredith & Anne his Wife, born Sept[r] 23rd & baptized Dec[r] 30th 1792.

Pleasant Meredith, a Child of John Meredith, died the 18th & was buried the 20th of January 1793.

John, S. of John McLeod, & Isabella his Wife was born Jan[y] 18 & baptized March 10th 1793.

James. Son of William McDowell & Susanna his Wife, was born January 20th & baptized May 5th 1793.

Elizabeth Agnes, Daughter of David Maitland & Susanna his Wife was born April 23rd & baptized June 20th 1793.

Lewis Lanier—Son of John Marks & Martha his Wife, born May 6th & baptized July 10th 1793.

Jemimah Wyat, Dau[r] of Jeremiah Meachen & Milly his Wife, born March 16th & baptized August 10th 1793.

Polly, Dau[r] of Edward Marks & Sally his Wife, born July 24th & bap: Sep[r] 11th 1793.

Johanna, Dau[r] William Marks & Eliza his Wife, born August 3rd & bap: Sep[r] 22 179[ ].

Ephraim May was buried 16th Octr 1794.

---

*These blanks filled up by her son C. J. Gibson Dec'r 12th 1848. The above note is in Dr. Gibson's handwriting.—C. G. C.

Mary Currie Maitland dau^{r} of David Maitland died 26th & buried 27th Jany. 1795.

Tazewell Son of Thos Mitchell and Rebecca his wife (of the County of Sussex) born 16th Augt 1794 and baptized 15th March 1795.

Alexander Campbell Maitland Son of William Maitland & Elizabeth his wife was born Augt 2d & baptized 9th D^{o} 1795. Died Octr 25th & buried Octr 26th 1796.

David Currie Maitland Son of Robert Maitland & Susan his wife, born 2d Nov^{r} & bapt^{d} 26th Decr 1796: died Octr 1797.

N

Mary dau: of Tho: & Margret Neel born 7th Nov: last bap^{t} March 31th 1721.

Phebe dau: of Dan & Eliz: Nance born in octob^{r} 1712.

Eliz: dau: of Ditto born 6th July 1719.

Elinor dau of John & Jane Nance born 25th May last bap^{t} July 19th 1721.

Fran: dau: of Raise & Ann Newhouse born 28th March 1720 bap^{t} July 1st 1721.

Tho: Son of ditto: born 1st sep^{t} 1712.

——— Son of Rich & Dina ————

James Son of Wm & Ann Norton born 2d of octob^{r} 1721 bap^{t} 30th octob^{r} 1722.

Elinor dau of Dan & Eliz: Nance born 9th sep^{t} last bap^{t} 28th Octob^{r} 1722.

——— D: of Tho & Margaret Neel born last summer bap^{t} Augs^{t} 6th 1723.

Tho: son of Jno & Jane Nance born 22th sep^{t} last bap^{t} Jan^{r} 19th 1723-4.

Peter son of Tho & Eliz: Nunnely born 3d Jan^{r} bap^{t} 2d feb^{r} 1723-4.

Tho son of Tho: & Marg^{a} Neel born 1 sep^{t} 1712.

John s: of Rich & Mary Nance bor 15 decem last bap^{t} 14th June 1724.

Mary d of Wm & Anne Norton born 9th Jan^{r} last bap^{t} Nov 1st 1724.

Frances Da^{t} of Thom and mary neel born: 7th may bap^{t} 25th July 1725.

Richard son of Jno and Jane Nance born 24th Jan^{r} bap^{t} 15th May 1726.

Eliz^{a} Da^{t} of Rich^{d} and mary nance born 7th Nov^{m} bap^{t} 15th May 1726.

Tho^{m} son of Thomas and Eliz^{a} nunnally born 27 sber: 1726.

Martha D: of John and Ann Nipper born 19th No^{m} 1726.

Mark Son of Robt and Eliz^{a} Nobles born 18th May 1727.

Sarhah female Slave of Th^{o} and Eliz^{a} Nunally born 11th May 1728.

Sarah D of Th^{o} and Margrat Neal Born 5th Jan^{r} 1727.

Eliz^{a} Dater of Daniel and Mary Nance Born 19th June 1728.

Wm Son of John and Jane Nance Born 12th July 1728 Bap^{t} July 29th.

Nan female Slave of Daniel nance Born Jan^{r} ye 5th 1727.

Sarah female Slave of Ditto Born aprill ye 10th 1728.

Obedience Dat^{r} of Rich^{d} and ——— Nunally Born 26th Novmber 1728.

John Son of Th^{o} and Eliz^{a} Nunally Born 4th Dce^{mr} Bap^{t} 12th Jan^{r} 1728.

Thomas Son of Thomas & Marget Neel Born 4th July 1730 Bap^{t} 9th august.

Leanord Son of Richard and Mary Nance Born 15th Decm^{r} 1730 Bap^{t} 4th Jan^{r}.

Lucy D of Daniel & Eliz^{a} nance Born 24th Dcember: 1730 Bap^{t} Jan^{r} 10th.

Daniel Son of Thomas & Eliz^{a} Nunally Born 28th march 1731 Bap^{t} august 15th.

Nathaniel son of Rich^{d} & Mary Nance born 9th Decr 1731 bap^{t} May 12th 1732.

Winny Slave of Danl Nance born Octr 1. 1732.

Mary D^{r} of Thomas & Eliz^{a} nunally Born 1th feb^{r} 1732 Bap^{t} 20th may 1733.

James son of John & margret nevil Born 1th July 1733 Bap^{t} 19th May 1734.

Zachariah Son of Thomas and Eliz. Nunnally Born 19th May 1735. Bap^{t} 6th July.

Jamey Male Slave Belonging to Danl Nance Sr Born Sep^{t} 1st 1735.

Giles S. of John and Martha Nance Born 4th May. 1735.

Thomas Son of William & Ann Nance Born 29th February 1735 Bap[t] 18th April 1736.

Ann D. of Richard & Mary Newman B March 30th 1741.

Anne D. of Richard & Mary Nances Born Jan[ry] 15th 1741-2 & Bap[t] June 13th 1742.

Sarah D. of William & Ann Nances born Jan[ry] 30th 1742-3 & bapt[d] Feb[ry] 27th 1742-3.

Will a male Slave belonging to Daniel Nance born Feb 6th 1744-5.

Ned a male Slave belonging to Ditto born Dec[r] 1743.

Sarah D. of Thomas & Priscilla Nantzs born Octob 19th 1745 & bapt[d] Jan[ry] 6th 1745-6.

Johney Nash son of John & Mary nash was Born Nov[r] 4th 1758.

Thomas, son of Thomas and Agness Norton was Born January the 23d 1755.

Sarah Norton their Daughter was Born October the 21st 1756.

Patty Norton their second Daughter was Born the 19th October 1758.

Frances Norton their third Daughter was Born June the 1st 1760.

William Norton their son was Born April 22d 1762.

Cressy, Dau[r] of Beck a negro slave, belonging to Mrs Lucy Newsum, was born March 15th and baptized September 23rd 1792.

O

James son of Nico: & Jane Overby born 5th sep[t] last bap[t] 4th octob[r] 1720.

Fran: dau: of Wm & Marg[a] Overby born 20th feb: last bap[t] 20th July 1721.

Rob[t] son of Rich: & Dina Overby born 18th Aprill last bap[t] 18th June 1722.

Adams son of Nico: & Jane Overby born 28th July last bap[t] Nov: 7th 1722.

Nico: son of peter & Ann Overby born 1st sep[t] last bap[t] Nov: 7th 1722.

Eliz: Dau of Drury & Anne Oliver born 8th June 1718.

John son of Ditto born 11th July 1720.

Wm Son of ditto born 26th July 1722.

Martha d of Rich: & Dinah Overbury born 8th decem last bap[t] feb: 6th 1723-4.

Martha D. of Drury & Amy Oliver born Nov: 25th last bap^t Jan^r 31th 1724-5.

Abraham son of James and Ann Overberry born 26th august last bap^t 17th sep^r 1725.

Mary D of nicholas and Jane Overberry born 9th August bap^t 17th Sep^t 1725.

Martha D of Drury and Amy Oliveer Deceast Sp^r ye 27th 1726.

Eliz^a D of howard and Margarat Owen born 24th July bap^t 2d oct^m 1726.

Drury Oliver Son of Wm and Eliz^a Olivier born 12th Aprill 1685.

Martha D of Drury and Amy olivier born 27th May 1727.

Jaminah D^t of Rich^d and Dinah overberry born 26th Jan^r 1727.

Peter Son of Peter and ann overberry Born 30th July 1727.

John Son of Th^o and anne oliver born 18th aprill 1728.

John Son of Howard and Margret owen Born 1th august 1728.

Mary D of Drury and amy oliveer Born 8th march Bap^t 20th aprill 1728.

Thomas Son of Howard and margret owen Born 2d July 1730 Bap^t 25th octb^r.

Rubin Son of Richard & Dinah overberry Born 12th august 1731.

Lucy D: of James & Eliz: overbury Born 29th July 1733 Bap^t 26th august.

Thomas Son of Richard & Dinah Overbury Born July 1st 1734.

William Son of Lanceford and Elizabeth Owen Born 23d December^r 1734.

Thamar D. of Richard & Dinah Overby Born 1st July 1734.

Ann D. of Drury & Elizabeth Oliver Born Sep^t 4th 1734 Baptiz'd Octob^r 27th.

Elizbth D of Edward & Joyce Owan Feb^{ry} ye 26th 1740.

Catharine D. of Nicolas & Elizabeth Ogilbys Born March 22d 1741-2 & Bap^t May 9th 1742.

Mildred D. of Isaac & Elizabeth Olivers born Octob 15th & bapt^d Octob^r 17th 1742.

Thomas S. of Isaac & Elizabeth Olivers born Octob 19th & bapt^d Decr 25th 1743.

Mary D. of James & Anne Olivers was born Septr 6th & bapt^d Decr 8th 1745.

William S. of Isaac & Elizabeth Olivers was born July 7th & bapt^{d} Aug 17th 1746.

Jean, Daughter of David Organ & Elizabeth his Wife, was born April 2nd & baptized June 30th 1793.

John Oliphant died the first day of Nov^{r} & was buried the 3d of Nov. 1793.

John Harrison Son of John Osborne & Jane his wife, born 19th July 1794 and baptized 4th Decr 1794.

P

Wm son of John & Judith Puckett born 15th sep^{t} last bap^{t} 17th decem: 1720

Smith son of John & Jane Pattison born 28th Aug: last bap^{t} Nov: 27th 1720.

Edith dau: of Wm & Mary Parsons born 7th Aug: 1719 bap: Nov: 27th 1720.

Nathaniell son of John & Fran: peterson born 12th Nov: last bap^{t} Jan^{r} 19th 1720–1.

Phebe dau: of John & Judith puckett born 11th Jan^{r} bap^{t} March 5th 1720–1.

Rich son of Rich: & Martha puckett born 7th March 1718–19.

Ephraim son of Womack & Mable Pucket born 24th Jan^{r} last bap^{t} Aprill 10th 1721.

Martha dau: of Wm & Rebecca Pearcy born 9th Jan^{r} last bap^{t} 4th June 1721.

Fran: son of John & Eliz: Perkinson born 5th August last bap^{t} Octob^{r} 8th 1721.

Wm son of John & Susanna Pride born xb^{r} 19th 1721 bap^{t} Jan^{r} 31th 1721–2.

Jeremiah son of Sara Patrum born 1st Jan^{r} bap^{t} March 21th 1722.

Eliz: dau: of Seth & Martha Pettypool born 8th May 1721 bap^{t} Octob^{r} 7th 1722.

Jamime dau: of Wm & Mary Parsons born 20th octob^{r} last bap^{t} 16 sep^{t} 1722.

Eliz: dau of John & Mary price born 7th June last bap^{t} 16th sep^{t} 1722.

Lewis son of Wm & Mary Puckett born 9th Jan^{r} 1722–3 bap^{t} May 5th 1723.

John son of Joss: & Mary Pritchett born 1st May 1716 bap[t] Aug: 25th 1722.

Wm son of ditto born 14th octo[br] 1719 bap[t] Aug 25th 1722.

Fran dau of John & Jane Paterson bor 28th May last bap[t] Aug: 13th 1722.

stephen son of Wm & ffrances pettypool jun[r] born 30th octob[r] 1721 bap[t] 14th feb 1722–3.

Wm son of John & Fran: peterson born 25 Octob[r] last bap[t] xb[r] 7th 1723.

Sarah D: of Seth & Martha Pool born 7th Nov: last bap[t] Jan[r] 30th 1723–4.

Joel son of John & Judith Pucket born 11th Nov: last bap[t] 7th March 1723–4.

Joseph son of Wm & Mary Persons born ——— bap[t] Aprill 12th 1724.

Isham son of Womack & Mable Puckett born 14th octob[r] last bap[t] Aprill 23th 1724.

——— A negro belonging to Mr Wm Poythers born 1st of August 1724.

Luis S: of Luis & Sarah Patrick born 17th Aug: last bap[t] Aprill 18th 1725.

Wm pool jun[r] had a Child born feb: 15th 1724–5.

Tho: s of Nath & Penellope Parratt born 30th xb[r] last bap[t] March 28th 1725.

Lucy D: of Seth & Mary perkinson born 6th instant bap[t] March 27th 1725.

Anne D: of Olive poxon died 30th July 1725.

Eady Dat of Jn[o] and Jane paterson born 28th July 1724.

phebe Dat of phebe parham born 9th oc[tm] 1725.

James Son of James and Mary pittillo born 23d Dec[m] 1725.

Ann Dat of James and mary plat born 13th Oc[tm] 1725.

Sheppyallin Son of Jn[o] and Judith pucket born 8th Nov[m] 1725.

Nathaniel Son of Nathaniel and penilopy parot born feb[r] 12th bap[t] 29 may 1726: 1725.

Anne Isham Dat of Wm and Sarah Poythris born 9th Ap[r] bap[t] 5th June 1726.

Jn[o] Son of Thomas and Isabell phillips born may 8th bap[t] June 7th 1726.

tabitha Dat of wm and Frances pool born oct[m] 13th bap[t] June 6th 1726.

Eliz[a] D of Wm and Mary pucket born 19th feb 1725.

Wm Son of Wm and Mary parsons born 24th may 1726.

John Son of John and & Mary powel born 16th march 1725 Bap[t] Aug[t] 22d 1726.

John Son of Seth and Martha pettypool born 6th Jan[r] 1725.

Sarah D of peter and frances plantine born 27th June 1726.

Joseph Son of John and Ann phillips born 6th Nom[r] 1726.

Th[o] Son of Edward and Eliz[a] Powell born 14th July 1727.

Ann D of Hezekiah and Batiah Powel born 16th June 1726.

Wm Son of Wm and Sarah poythres born 14th March 1727 bap[t] 26th may 1728.

Anna Dater of John and Mary Powell born 3d May 1728.

peter Son of Seth and Marth Pittypool Born 17th May 1727.

ann D of James and Mary pittillo Born 15th July 1728 Bap[t] 29th July.

Littleberry Son of liewes and Sarah Partrick Born 18th May 1728.

Batty Son of Wm and mary parsons Born 22d August 1728.

Stephen Son of John and Judith Pucket Born 17th octb[r] 1728 Bap[t] No[v] 10.

Mary D of Nath[a] and Penilopy Parrot Born 21th Novmber 1728.

Mason of Th[o] and Isabell phillips Born 23d July Bap[t] 16th Sep[r] 1728.

Phebe D of John and Judith Pucket Born 2d Jan[r] 1728.

Liewes son of John and Mary Patterson Born 28th august Bap[t] 2d feb[r] 1728.

Ephraim son of Wm and frances Pucket Born 2d March Bap[t] 30th June 1729.

William Son of Tho[s] & Mary Parram Born 22d Sep[r] 1729.

Alice D of Seth & Mary Perkinson Born 15th June 1729 Bap[t] 27th June.

Martha D of Joshua & Martha pritchett d[o] 15th April 1729.

William Son of William ——— ———.

William Son of Zedekiah and Bathua Powel Born 26th aprill 1729 Bap[t] may 31th 1730.

William Son of peter and frances plentine Born 5th Sep[r] 1729 Bap[t] 31th mam 1730.

Pucket Son of John and Susana Pride Born 2d Sep[r] Bap[t] 1th march 1729.

Eliz[a] D of francis and hannah Poythris Born 1th feb[r] 1729 Bap[t] 8th aprill 1730.

John Son of peter and Rebeckah pott Born 6th Sep[r] 1729.

Richard price servant of Drury oliver Des[t] 29th June 1730.

sarah Dater of Edward & Mary Parham Born 16th Dce[r] 1730 Bap[t] 24th Jan[r].

Mary D of Thomas & Isabel phillips Born 9th march 1730 Bap[t] 19th ap[r] 1731.

Isham of Seth pirkinson Born 8th may 1731 Bap[t] June 22d 1731.

James Son of Nathaniel & penellope Parrott Born 12th febr: 1730.

Phillip Son of Wm & Frances pool Born 13th march 1730 Bap[t] 12th Sep[r] 1731.

Sarah D: of William and Sarah poythris Born 7th august 1731 Bap[t] 7th octb[r].

John Son of John & mary Parham Born 26th Sep[r] Bap[t] 6th Novmb[r] 1731.

Mary D: John & anne phillips Born 11th ap[r] Bap[t] Nom[r] 14th 1731.

Nathaniel Son of John & martha Peterson Born 25th ap[r] 1732.

Rebeccah dat[r] of Hezekiah & Bathia Powell born 26th ffeb[y] 1730 Bap[t] June 18th 1732.

Frances dat[r] of Sam[l] & Amy Pitchford born 5th Jan[y] 1731 bap[t] July 9th 1732.

Jane Dat[r] of Peter & Rebecca Pott born 10th ffeb[y] 1731 bap[t] Aug[t] 13th 1732.

Joshua of Josh[a] & Catherine Pritchett born 9th May 1732 bap[t] Aug[t] 13 1732.

Rob[t] Son of Wm & Mary Perkinson born 13th Sep[r] & bap[t] y[e] 28th 1732.

Obedience Dat[r] of Jn[o] & Pricilla Pickins born 26th Oct[r] 1732 bap[t] Dec[r] 26th 1732.

Elisabeth D of Gower & archer parham Born 20th octb[r] 1732 Bap[t] 24th feb[r].

Penellope D[r] of nathaniel & Penellope Parrott Born 8th may 1733 Bap[t] 20th may 1733.

anne D^{r} of Edward & mary Parham Born 14th march 1732 Bap^{t} 8th ap^{r} 1733.

Eliz^{a} D^{r} of George & Jane penticost Born 3d feb^{r} 1732 Bap 20th may 1733.

Eddith D: of Seth & Elisabeth pirkenson Born 20th July 1733 Bap^{t} 28th august.

Mary D: of Edward & Elizabeth powell Born 12th august 1733 Bap^{t} nov^{r} 4th.

Charles Son of Charles & Sarah Pistole Born 15th Sepr 1733 Bap^{t} 11th Nov^{r}.

Frances D: of william & Frances Pettipool Born 18th apr^{l} 1733 Bap^{t} Dce^{r} 10th.

anne D: of Seth & martha Pettipool Born 25th Sepr 1733 Bap^{t} dce^{r} 10th.

Henry Son of James & mary Pittillo Born 31th octb^{r} 1730 Bap^{t} feb^{r} 9th.

Lucy D: of Ditto Born 11th Novr 1733 Bap^{t} Jan^{r} 20th 1733.

anne D: of Seth & martha pettipool Born 25th Sepr 1733 Bap^{t} dce^{r} 6th.

Robert Son of John & Mary powell 17th Novm^{r} 1733 Bap^{t} feb^{r} 10th.

Isham Son of Thomas & Mary Parham Born 17th Sepr 1732 Bap^{t} feb^{r} 12th.

John Son of Thos & Mary Pott Born 12th octb^{r} 1732 Bap^{t} 12th feb^{r} 1733.

Drury Son of John & Judith Pucket Born 25th Jan^{r} 1733 Bap^{t} 12th feb^{r}.

Rebeckah d of Hezekiah & Bathia Powell decest 26th march 1734.

martha D: of Charles & mary Parrish Born 10th May 1734 Bap^{t} 4th august.

Rachel D: of Philip & Rachel Prescot Born 3d March 1733.

Thomas Son of Charles & Sarah Pistol Born 2d May 1735 Bap^{t} 6th July.

Thomas S of Thomas and Mary Parham Born Septem^{r} 22. 1734 Bap. 4 May 1735.

Jane female Slave belonging to Wm Parsons Born May 1st 1729.

Betty female Slave belonging to D^{o} Born June 15th 1733.

Dick male Slave belonging to D^{o} Born June 19th 1731.

Dick male Slave belonging to D^o Died Augt 22 1731.

Batty Son of William and Mary Parsons departed this life Octo^r 11th 1734.

James Markham Son of William and Mary Parsons Born the 31 March 1731.

James Markham Son of William and Mary Parsons departed this life Octo^r 26th 1734.

William S. of Gower & Archer Parham Born the 2d July 1735.

William S. of George and Jane Penticost Born 2d August 1734.

Sarah D. of William & Juliana Peirce Born 17th Aug^{ts} 1734.

James S. of Thomas & Izabella Phillips Born Sep^t 12th 1734.

Lucy D. of George & Jane Pentycost Born January ye 25 1740.

John S. of John & Elisabeth Porter Born ye 20 of febuary 1740.

John s of John & Anne Phillips Born August ye 20 1740.

John Son of Wm. And Juliana Peircy Sepr 30th 1740.

Susannah of Kaleb & Frances Pritchet B Aug 24th 1740.

Patty D of Thomas & Mary Presise B Decr 10th 1740.

Magdaline D of Israell & Elizabeth Peterson Born Novr 21st 1740.

Wm. S. of Charles & Sarah Pistol B Decr 19th 1740.

Ann D of Morgan & Ann Purreah B August 1st 1741.

John S of Aron & Ann Pricheat B Feb^{ry} 26 ye 1740.

Thomas S of Thomas & Mary Presise Born Decr 27 1735.

Mary Daughter of D^o Born March ye 29th 1738.

Elizabeth. D. of Major Willm & Sara Poythress's Born Sep^{tr} 21st 1741 & Bap^t Novr 22d 1741.

Henry. S. of William Petty & Francis Pools Born Jan^{ry} 27th 1740–1 & Bap^t Novr 29th 1741.

Sara. D. of Daniel & Francis Pegrams Born Decr 29th 1741 & Bap^t Feb^{ry} 28th 1741–2.

Mary. D. of Gower & Archer Parhams Born Decr 23d 1741 & Bap^t March 14th 1741–2.

William. S. of Thomas & Mary Perrys Born Ap^r 19th 1742 & Bap^t May 9th 1742.

William. S. of Edward & Mary Pegrams Born June 18th 1742 & Bap^t July 4th 1742.

Mary D. of Edward & Amy Paynes Born Oct. 16th 1741 & Bap^t July 24th 1742.

Anne D. of Joshua & Lucy Porters born Octob 7th 1742 & bapt^{d} Decr 12th 1742.

George S. of John & Anne Phillips born Feb^{ry} 15th 1742–3 & bapt^{d} May 29th 1743.

Anne D. of George & Jane Pentecost born Sep^{tr} 8th 1743 & bapt^{d} Octob^{r} 9th 1743.

Reuben S. of Abram & Esaia Peebles was born Aprile 11th & bapt^{d} June 9th 1745.

Frances D of Mr John & Martha Petersons was born Septr 3d & bapt^{d} Octob. 27th 1745.

Elizabeth D. of John & Anne Phillips was born Feb. 5th 1745–6.

Luke S. of Edward & Elizabeth Powels was born May 8th & bapt^{d} Aug. 3d 1746.

William Son of Joseph & Frances Parsons born May 9th bapt^{d} 29th May 1750.

Edith Daughter of Wm. & Mary Parsons jun^{r} Born 22nd May bap^{t} Sep^{t} 16th 1750.

Two Twins, Mary & Elizabeth Brown Daughters of William Brown & Servant Probey was Born July 20th 1761.

William Son of Lewis & Sarah Parham was Born april the 22d 1761.

William Paterson son of James Paterson & mary was born Sepr 12th 1768.

David Parrish Son of James Parrish Baptised July 4. 1771.

Henry, Son of Lewis Parham (of Sussex County) & Rebeccah his Wife, born January 28 & baptized April 6th 1792.

Lotty Williams, S. of Page a Negroe Slave belonging to Thos G. Peachy, born July 1st and baptized August 19th 1792.

William Parsons, and his Wife (of Prince George) were buried September 3rd 1792.

Jean Peachy Dau^{r} of Samuel Peachy, was buried October 11th 1792.

David, S, of William Perkins & Margaret his Wife, born October 11th & baptized December 23rd 1792.

Ann, Dau^{r} of Wm Parry & Phœbe his Wife, born September 7th 1789 & bap: Decr 28th —9[ ].

Peggie, Dau^{r} of James Peebles & Betsy his Wife, born Sept 19th & bap: January 27th 1793.

William Poythress died 15th and was buried 18th Octr 1794.

Hannah Dau of Baldwin Pearce & Rebeccah his Wife, was born February 23rd and baptized April 2nd 1793.

Sarah H. Pope. Dau^{r} of Ralph Pope, died June 19th & was buried June 20th 1793.

James Son of William Prentis & Mary his Wife, born August 3. & baptized Septr 23rd 1793.

Mary, Dau^{r} of William Poythress & Mary his Wife, born Septr 24 & bap: Nov. 7. 1793.

R

Mary dau: of Christ^{o} & Sarah Robinson born 3d June last bap^{t} 17th decem: 1720.

Wm A Moll belonging unto Hen: & Eliz: Royall born 7th Aug: 1720 bap^{t} Jan^{r} 30th 1720–1.

Martha dau of Hen: & Martha Rottenbery born 1st sep^{t} last bap^{t} 12th octob^{r} 1720.

Matthew son of Israel & Sarah Robinson born 22th Nov: last bap^{t} Aprill 30th 1721.

Margaret A Mollatto belonging to Godfry & Eliz: Ragsdale born 7th Novr last bap May 28th 1721.

Daniel son of Wm & Fran: Rowlet born 10th June last bap^{t} July 30th 1721.

John of John & Mary Rackly born 14th day of June 1720 bap^{t} 18th July 1721.

Fran: Son of Hen: & Eliz: Royall born 10th Jan^{r} last bap^{t} July 4th 1721.

Mary dau of Wm & Mary Russell born 2d decem 1719 bap^{t} octob^{r} 9th 1721.

Martha dau of Wm & Eliz Russell born 14th decem^{br} Last bap^{t} Aprill 8th 1722.

Tab: dau of Godfry & Eliz Radgsdale born 13th March last bap^{t} May 20th 1722.

Jack a negro boy belonging to Dan: Radgsdale born Octob^{r} 8th 1722.

Ann dau of Hen: & Eliz: Robinson born Jan: 6th 1719 bap^{t} August 25th 1722.

Faith dau of peter & Alice Radgsdale born 24th octob^{r} last bap^{t} 27th decem 1722.

peter son of Hen: & Eliz: Robinson born 27th ——— last bap^t Jan: 10th 1722.

Nath son of Christ & Sara Robinson born 21th octob^r last bap^t Jan 10th 1722–3.

Rich son of Jno & Rebecca Raburn Born 28th May last bap^t Aug: 21th 1723.

John son of Israel & Sarah Robinson born 8th May last bap^t Aug 21th 1723.

Nath: son of John & Mary Robinson born 21th June last bap^t Aug^s 21th 1723.

Edward son of Godfrey & Eliz: Radgsdale born 8th decemb^r last bap^t Jan 12th 1723–4.

Rich: son of Hen: & Marg^a Rottenberry born 30th June last bap^t 29th July 1724.

Dan: son of Benj^a & Martha Radgsdale born 7th May last bap^t sep^t 6th 1724.

Mary d of Ja & Eliz Rigsby born 10th octob^r last bap^t 11th x^{br} 1724.

Patt a negro girl belonging to Mr. Peter & Mary Rowlett born 15th feb: 1724–5.

Joseph son Peter & Alice Radgsdale born 17th Jan^r last may 23th 1725.

Israil Son of Israil and Sarah Robertson born 14th nov^m 1725.

Abr^{a}ham Son of Jno and Mary Robertson born 20th July 1725.

Daniel A negro slave of Ge^o and mary Rob'son born Decr 1723.

Matthew A negro of D^o born sep^r 1724.

Harry A negro of ditt^o born May 1726.

Cesar a negro of ditto born aprill 1726.

Daniel Son of Josep and Sarah Reeves born 31th august bap^t 11 sep^t 1726.

John Son of tho^m and Eliz^a Rhaynes born 5th July bap^t 2d oct^m 1726.

Mary D of thomas and Hannah Roberts born 17th August 1726.

Sarah slave of George and Mary Rob^{t}son born 17th July 1726.

Lot Slave of Ditto born 17th 1726.

Rachail D of benj^a and martha Ragsdail born 28th June 1726.

Martha D of Christopher and Sarah Robinson born 27th ffebuary 1724.

Liewes Son of henry and Eliz^a Robinson born 17th March 1723.

Thomas Son of John and Rebeckah Rayborn born 16th Sep[tr] 1726.

ann Daughter of James and Eliz[a] Rigsby born 19th Jan[r] 1726.

John Son of Christopher and ann Rowland born 20th May 1727.

ann D of peter and alce Ragsdail born 25th May 1727.

ffrances D. of John and Mary Robinson born 3d March 1726.

Jemiah D of Wm and Mary Reed born 9th Dce[m] 1724.

John Son of Benj[a] and Martha Ragsdail Born 23d June 1728.

Deborah Son of henry and Eliz[a] Robertson Born 14th March 1727 Bap[t] 2d June.

David Son of Israil and Sarah Robertson Born 19th august 1728.

Francis Son of Tho[s] & Mary Reese born 5th of Decem[r] 1727.

John Son of Henry & Eliz Royall born 23d October 1729.

Mark Son of Jn[o] & Mary Robertson born 23d June 1729.

John Son of Jn[o] and Rebeckah Rayborn Born 30th Novm[r] 1729.

Peter Son of Roger and Sarah Ranie Born 20th March 1729 Bap[t] May 29th 1730.

Prissilla D of Hug and Sarah Riss Born 21th feb[r] 1729 Bap[t] 10th May 1730.

agnis D of Christophar and ann Roland Born 7th Jan[r] Bap[t] 22d feb[r] 1729.

Tho: Son of Thomas and Mary Rees Born 2d novm[r] Bap[t] 22d feb[r] 1729.

Benj[a] Son of John and Eliz[a] Roland Born 6th feb[r] Bap[t] 2d march 1729.

James Son of Partrick & Isabellah Royall Born 20th June 1730.

Mary D of Joseph and Sarah Reeves Born 20th Sep[r] 1730.

Baxter Son of Godfrey and Eliz[a] Ragsdail Born 16th June 1730.

Nicholas Son of Thomas and ann Rollings Born 4th octb[r] 1730.

Negro Slaves of M[r] George Robertson Minister.

Daniel male Slave Born 5th Dce[r] 1723.

Matthew male Slave Born 25th sept[r] 1725.

Harry male Slave Born 26th March 1726.

Lott male Slave Born 10th May 1726.

Sarah female slave Born 16th July 1726.

Cesar male Slave Born 4th Dce[r] 1727.

Nanny female Slave Born 4th July 1728.

Tom male Slave Born 26th Dce[r] 1728.

amy female Slave Born 25th July 1730.
Liewess male Slave Born 3d august 1730.
George male Slave Born 2d Sep[r] 1730.
Betty female Slave Born 5th Sep[r] 1730.
Jo: male Slave Born 29th March 1731.
Ned male Slave Born 15th Sep[r] 1730.

William Son of Roger & Sara: Reiny Born 13th ap[r] 1731 Bap[t] 12th Sep[t]

——— Son of Shanes & mary Raines Born 12th Sep[r] 1731 Bap[t] 20th octb[r].

Nicholas Son of Israil & Sarah Robinson Born 12th sep[tr] Bap[t] novmbr 7th 1731.

Isham Son of John & anne Ratlif Born 10th octb[r] 1731.

Edward Son of John & Mary Robertson Born 22d Dce[r] 1731 Bap[t] 23d ap[r] 1732.

Winfred daughter of Benj[a] & Martha Ragsdale born ffeb[y] 17th 1731.

Martha dat[r] of Roger & Eliz[a] Reese born ffeb[y] 9th 1730 bap[t] May 21st 1732.

Jean Dat[r] Rich[d] & Jean Raybon born 28th Ap[l] 1732 bap[t] Aug[t] 13th 1732.

Martha dat[r] of Jn[o] & Sarah York born 3d June 1732 bap[t] 13 Aug[t] 1732.

Frederick son of Rich[d] & Jane Rains born 9th June 1732 bap[t] Sep[r] 14th 1732.

Alse dat[r] of Tho[s] and Eliz[a] Reams born 31st March 1732 bap[t] Sep[r] 24 1732.

Sarah dat[r] of Christ[o] & Ann Rolland born 26th Sep[r] 1732 bap[t] Dec[r] 17 1732.

Rachel D: of peter & alice Ragsdail Born 27th feb[r] 1732 Bap[t] march 15th.

William Son of James & Sarah Rutlidge Born 9th may 1732 Bap[t] ap[r] 7th 1733.

Isham Son of hugh & Sarah Reese Born 8th august 1732 Bap[t] 20th may 1733.

John Son of Thomas Reese Born 30th Sept[r] 1731 Bap[t] 20th may 1733.

Josept Son of Joseph & Sarah Reaves Born 5th Dec[r] 1732 Bap[t] 1th august 1733.

Francis son of Thos & Hanah Roberts Born 29th June 1733 Bapt 5th Augt

Charles Son of Israil & Sarah Robinson Born 24th July 1733 Bapt 28th Sepr.

——— of Roger & Sarah Rainy Born 12th octobr 1733 Bapt Dcer 10th.

Charles Son of Roger & Eliza Reese Born 3d apr 1733 Bapt 30th dcer.

Phill male Slave of Thomas Ravenscroft Born 8th June 1734.

Benjamine Son of Benjamine & Martha Ragsdail Born 28th March 1734 Bapt July 14th.

Michael Son of John & Judith Roberds Born 7th may 1734 Bapt 30th June.

Thomas Son ot Thomas & Elisabeth Reams Born 10th Janr 1733 Bapt 28th July 1734.

Robt S of John and Mary Robinson Born June 10th 1734.

Ann d of Henry & Ann Robinson Born May 8th 1734.

Mary D. of Thomas & Mary Reese Born 8th Octobr 1733.

Sarah D. of Hugh & Sarah Reese Born 10th Octobr 1735.

Isham s of Joseph & Sarah Reaves Born January ye 25 1740.

John s of Hugh & Elisabeth Ray Born June ye 14 1741.

Thomas S of Robert and Hannah Rivers B June 28th 1740.

Thomas S of John & Mary Reess B Febry 12th 1739.

George S of Martha & Sarah Robarson B Decr 6th 1740.

Mason D of Thomas & Mary Reess B July 10th 1740.

James S of Hugh & Sarah Reess Born August ye 29 1741.

Hannah female Slave of of Judath Roberts Born Decm ye 1st 1735.

Jack male Slave of Dito was Born January ye 29th 1737.

Sarah female Slave of Dito was Born July ye 15th 1741.

William S. of Samuel & Anne Rawthorns Born Novr 4th 1741 & Bapt May 2d 1742.

Peter S. of Henry & Susanna Robertsons Born Mar: 21st 1742 & Bapt July 25th 1742.

David & Lowerel twin Childn of Charles & Anne Roupers were Born June 29th 1742 & Bapt Aug. 15th 1742.

Elizabeth D. of Hugh & Elizabeth Raes born April 25th 1743 & baptd May 22d 1743.

Usiller D. of Timothy & Mary Reeves born July 7th 1743.

Sarah D. of Peter & Sarah Roshill born march 1st 1743–4 bapt[d] apr 29th 1744.

Judith D. of William & Priscilla Reeves born Aug. 10th & baptized Octob[r] 14th 1744.

John S. of Philip & Mary Rogers born Aprile 14th & bapt[d] July 21st 1745.

Elizabeth D. of Patrick & Sarah Roney was born March 5th 1745–6.

Neil S. of Hugh & Elizabeth Raes was born Feb. 19th 1745–6 bapt[d] Apr 2d 1746.

Sarah Slave to partrick & Sarah Roneys born Septem[r] 3d 1754.

William Reaves Son of John & France[s] Reves was Born July y[e] 13 1743.

Mary Reves Daughter of Ditto was Born July y[e] 17 1745.

John Reves Son of Ditto was Born Nov[r] the 15th 1747.

Richard Reves the Son of Ditto was Born Octo[r] the 5th 1750.

Thomas Reves their Son of Ditto was Born Sep[r] the 15 1753.

Thomas Roney son of Patrick and Sarah Roney was born Jan[r] 19 1756.

John Roney the son of Ditto Born October the 8th 1757.

Richard Russell Son of Wm and Rachel Russell was Born 1759 Sep[r] y[e] 10th.

Tim, Son of Nanny, a Slave belonging to William Robertson, born August 28th 1791, & baptized March 25th 1792.

Thomas, Son of Jeany, a Slave belonging to William Robertson, born January 4th & baptized March 25th 1792.

Susannah, Dau[r] of Joel Reading (of Sussex) & Martha his Wife, born Nov[r] 6th 1791, & bap. May 13th 1792.

Elizabeth Archer, D[r] of James Robertson, & Martha F, his Wife, born Nov[r] 27th 1791, & bap[d] May 30th 1792.

Robert, S, of Robert Russel and Jenny his Wife, born the 6th & baptized the 12th of August 1792.

Edmund Ryan of the Town of Petersburg died the 25th, and was buried the 26th of October 1792.

John Fetherstone, S, of Jacob Reese & Diancy, his Wife, born May 14th, & baptized December 15th 1792.

Littleberry S, of William Royal & Sarah his Wife, born Nov[r] 2nd & baptized Dec[r] 27th 1792.

Anne, Dau[r] of William Robertson & Elizabeth his Wife, was born Nov[r] 25th, 1792 & baptized January 6th 1793.

——— Reeves wife of James Reeves buried 20th Dec[r] 1794.

Col. John Reeves (of Sussex) buried March 15th 1795.

Patrick, Son of Robert Roe & Nancy his of Albemarle Parish—Sussex County—was born April 9th 1792. & baptized May 26th 1793.

John Alexander Son of James Robertson & Martha Feild his Wife born May 29th & baptized August 7th 1793.

S

Thompson son of Thompson & Ruth Staples born 12th instant bap[t] Nov: 27th 1720.

Jeny a negro girl belonging unto Ja: Sturdivant born 6th March 1720–1.

Rebecca dau of Wm & Rebecca Scoggin born 7th Jan[r] last bap[t] Aprill 30th 1721.

John son of Rich: & Mary Scoggin born 22th July last bap[t] 17th Sep[tr] 1721.

Griffin son of Drury & Eliz: Stith born 28th Nov: last bap[t] July 18th 1721.

John son of Wm & Mary Spain born 22th March last bap[t] octob[r] 23th 1721.

Catherine dau: of John & Mary Sturdivant 16th instant bap[t] 23th octobe[r] 1721.

Edw: son of Eliz: Stuard born 19th August last bap[t] octob[r] 29th 1721.

Eliz: dau: of James & Eliz Sandert born 23th May last bap[t] July 29th 1722.

Mary dau: of Tho: & Mary Stonebank born 10th Octob: last bap[t] 2d decem 1722.

Phebe bast dau of Ann Shipton born 9th July 1721 bap 22th July 1722.

Agnis dau of Rich & Agnis Smith born 9th Arill last bap[t] 25th July 1722.

Angelica dau of Geo & Ann Stell born 18th decem: 1718 bap[t] 25th August 1722.

James son of ditto born 17th Aprill 1720 bap[t] Aug: 25th 1722.

David son of Geo & Eliz: Smith bor 2d instant bap 13th Aug: 1722.

James son of John & Agnis Smith born 15th Nov last bap: 13th Aug: 1722.

Phebe dau of Wm & Mary Smith born 7th May last bap Aug: 13 1722.

Eliz dau of Ann Shipton born 26th Novem: Last bap[t] 27th decem 1722.

Wm son of Wm & Mary Spain born 9th of March last bap[t] May 5th 1723.

Rich son of Rich & Mary Scoggin born 15th fe[b] last bap[t] May 26th 1723.

Wm son of Wm & Rebecca scoggin born 18th march last bap[t] May 26th 1723.

Eliz: dau of Rob[t] & Eliz: Stoker born 14th octob[r] last bap[t] Nov: 7th 1723.

John son of Drury & Eliz Stith born 20th march last bap[t] Aprill 10th 1724.

Wm son of John & Eliz: Sturdivant born 12th Nov: 1723 bap[t] 2d feb. 1723-4.

——— a negro born belonging to ditto born 12th Sep[t] 1723.

Rinnian A negro boy belonging to Dan Sturdivant born 4th May 1724.

Phillis A negro Girl belonging to ditto born May 5th 1724.

Han: d of Wm & Marg[a] Stow born ——— bap[t] May 24th 1724.

Sarah d of Rich & Agnis Smith born 30th Aprill last bap[t] 2d July 1724.

fran d of Thompson & Ruth staples born 14th May Last bap[t] June 21th 1724.

Joss s: of Geo: & Eliz: Smith born July 2d last bap[t] 27th ditto 1724.

Fran: D. of Jmes & Mary Sturdivant born 25th August last bap[t] decem: 31th 1724.

Catherine D. of Wm & Mary Smith born 25th octob[r] last bap[t] Aug: 22th 1725.

Joshua son of Wm and Mary Spain born 10th July last 1725.

David son of wm and Rebeckah Scogin born 27th nov[m] 1725.

Sarah Dat of Jn[o] and agnis Smith born 15th ap[r] 1725.

Mary Dat of Rob[t] and frances Stanfield born 6th Jan[r] 1724.

francis son of Rich[d] and mary Scogin born 22d augst 1725.

Elizab Dat of Th[o] and mary Satterwhite born 22d Ap[r] bap[t] 8th may 1726.

matthew son of Jn[o] and mary Sturdivant born Ap[r] 29th bap[t] 8th may 1726.

Olive Da[t] of Jn[o] and Jane Stroud born 17th feb[r] bap[t] June 6th 1726.

Mary D of Thomas and Ann Stunks born 12th Aug[t] 1726.

Jane D of Wm and Mary Smith born 28th November 1726.

Abrattam Son of Wm and Marg[t] Stow born 6th oct[m] 1726.

Matthew Son of Eliz[a] Stuard born 6th Jan[r] 1726.

John Son of Wm and Margaret Stroud born 29th Nov[m] 1726.

Eliz[a] D of Th[o] and Mary Sturdifant born 18th Nov[m] bap[t] 18 feb 1727.

Eliz[a] D of Th[o] and Ann Stunks Born 25th aprill 1728.

Jane D of George and Eliz[a] Smith Born Jan[r] last 1727 Bap[t] 2d June.

Eliz[a] D of Rich[d] and ann Stanley Born 26th June 1727 Bap[t] 29th July.

Priscilla D of William and Eliz[a] Standley Born 10th august 1728.

Mary Dat[r] of John and mary Sturdifant Born 21th Novm[r] 1728 Bap[t] Dec[m] 25th.

Samson male Slave of Ditt[o] Born 20 aprill 1728.

Rob[t] Son of Rob[t] and Frances Stanfield Born March 11th 1729.

Jonathan son of samuel and Mayr Sental Born 26th May Bap[t] 6th June 1729.

Barthurst Son of Drury and Eliz[a] stith Born 19th sep[t] 1729.

Mary D of James and Mary Sturdivant Born 18th august 1729.

Tom Male Slave of Ditt[o] Born 31th august 1729.

Martha & Lutia D[rs] of Rich[d] & Mary Scoggan Born 11th of July 1729.

William Son of William and Eliz[a] Stanley Born 11th Jan[ry] Bap[t] 19th March 1729.

Matthew Son of Robert and Eliz[a] Stoker Born august 21th Bap[t] oct[r] 2d 1729.

Wm son of Joseph and Mary Stroud Born 22d feb[r] 1729 Bap[t] 10th may 1730.

Eliz[a] D of Lewellin and Mary Sturdvant Born 19th Nov[r] 1729 Bap[t] 31 may 1730.

frances D of Th° and Martha Spain Born 9th Dcem^r 1729 Bap^t 30th march 1730.

Mary D: of Jn° and Jean Stroud Born 29th aprill 1730 Bap^t 12th July.

Toby Male Slave of James Sturdivant Born 1th Sepr 1730.

Eliz^a D of Wm & Mary Spain Born May 30th 1731 Bap^t august 1th.

Mary D. of Jacob & Mary Summerell Born march 1th 1730 Bap^t august 1th 1731.

amy female Slave of William & mary Spain Born 7th march 1730 Bap^t 29th august 1731.

Prissilla D of Thomas & anne Stunks Born 25th august 1731 Bap^t 10th octbe^r.

Thomas william Shorie Son of William shorie Born 6th feb^r 1726.

Prisilla D: of Tho^m & martha Spain Born 7th Sepr Bap^t 24th Sepr 1731.

Thomas son Drury & Eliz^a Stith Born 29th Dce^r 1731 Bap^t 24th ap^r 1732.

Elisabeth female Slave of Drury & Eliz^a stith Born 12th June 1725.

Poll female Slave of Ditto Born 20th June 1725.

Liewess male Slave of Ditto Born 3 feb^r 1726.

Christian female Slave of Ditto Born 5th Novr 1727.

Martha female Slave of Ditto Born 4th Novr 1728.

Hannah female Slave of Ditto Born 30th april 1730.

Ned male Slave of Ditto Born 29th Jan^ry 1731.

Moses son of Jn° & Eliz^a Smith born Novr 28th 1731 Bap^t May 8th 1732.

Ann Dat^r of Robt & Eliz^a Stoaker born Jany 30th 1731 Bap^t June 10th 1732.

Joell Son of Jn° & Mary Sturdivant born May 18th 1732 Bap^t June 16 1732.

Fra^s a girl Slave of D° born Ap^l 15 1730 D°.

Roben a boy Slave of D° born June 11 1732.

Eliz^a Dat^r of Biggen & Sarah Sturdivant born Ap^l 28th 1732 Bap^t June 18th 1732.

David son of Joseph & Mary Stroud born 19th March 1731 Bap^t June 18th 1732.

Mary dat^{r} of Rich^{d} & Mary Scoggan born 1st July 1732 bap^{t} 20th Augt 1732.

Mary dat^{r} of Lewellen & Mary Sturdivant born 20th Novr 1731 bap^{t} Sepr 20th 1732.

Ann Dat^{r} of Thos & Mary Savage born Decr 28 bap^{t} Decr 31. 1732.

——— Son of Jacob & Mary Summerrell Born 25th June 1727 Bap^{t} octb^{r} 15th.

Thomas Son of Partrick & Eliz^{a} Smith Born 23d octb^{r} 1731 Bap^{t} Jan^{r} 30th.

Phillis fe^{m} slave of James & mary sturdivant Born No^{r} 1731.

Ceasor male slave of ditto Born 15th feb^{r} 1732.

Mary Mullatto girl of Elizabeth stuart Born 19th Sepr 1732 Bap^{t} feb^{r} 4th.

Thomas son of Thomas & sarah suttawhite Born 15th Febuary 1732 Bap^{t} 26 march 1733.

Rebeckah D^{r} of James & Mary Sturdivant Born 22d ap^{r} 1733 Bap^{t} may 8th.

Roger male Slave of william & mary Spain Born 29th 1732 Bap^{t} 8th ap^{r} 1733.

antony male Slave of Ditto Born 7th feb^{r} 1732 Bap^{t} 8th ap^{r} 1733.

David son of Thomas & Martha Spain Born 1th march 1732 Bap^{t} 8th ap^{r} 1733.

Batt peter son of william & mary Spain Born 9th Sepr 1733 Bap^{t} 21th octb^{r}.

Bolling Son of Wm & Mary Starkes Born 21th Sepr 1733 Bap^{t} 11th nov^{r}.

Jane D: of Samuell & Mary Sentall Born 5th March 1733 Bap^{t} 20th May 1734.

Thomas Savage Decs^{d} 7th June 1734.

anne D: of John & Mary Shern Born 3d march 1733 Bap^{t} 23d June 1734.

anne D: of Richard and Mary Scogin Born 25th May 1734 Bap^{t} 11th august.

William Son of Jacob & Mary Summerell Born 29th May 1733 Bap^{t} July 2d.

Henry Fitz Son of Ann Sental Born 18th July 1734 Bap^{t} 26 day Septemb^{r}.

Isaac S of Luellin & Mary Sturdivant Born June 8. 1734.

James Son of James and Mary Sturdivant Born March 28. 1735 Bap[t] 27 Ap[r].
John S. of John and Mary Stuart. Born 16 Octob[r] 1734 Bapt 19 Ap[l] 1735.
Margaret D of Robert and Elizabeth Stoaker Born Aug[t] 26. 1734 Baptiz[d] Sept 6th.
James S of William and Elizabeth Stanley Born Octob[r] 16th 1734.
James S. of Daniel and Sarah Sturdivant Born 18th June 1735.
Henry S of James & Elisabeth Smart Born December y[e] 15 1740.
Martha D of Daniel & Sarah Sturdefant Born March y[e] 22 1740.
Abby female Slave belonging to James Sturdivant Born March y[e] 15th 1740.
Dennice Male Slave of James Sturdivant Born August y[e] 5 1741.
Thomas s of Thomas and Mary Short was Born August y[e] 6 1741.
Wm son of George and mary Smith Born August y[e] 4th 1739.
Fanney D of Ann Steward B August 1st 1740.
James S of Wm and Elizabeth Stanley B. Novem[r] 11th 1740.
Elizabeth D of Thomas & Susannah Snipes B Nov[r] 28th 1740.
James S. of John & Mary Still B Feb[ry] 28th 1740–1.
Mary D. of Archiball & Mary Smith B May 11th 1741.
Susannah D of George and Mary Smith B Apr[l] 8th 1741.
Hardship D of Clemond and —— Stradford B Decem[r] 2d 1740.
Frederick S. of Matthew & Sarah Smart B Feb[ry] 8th 1740.
Wm S. of Richard Cross & Frances Still B April 13th 1740.
Benjamine Son of Richard & Agnis Smith Born June 22 1741.
Lidey female Slave of James Sturdavant B Febuary y[e] 25 1741.
Phebe female Slave of John Sturdavants B Febuary y[e] 20 1741.
Anne D of John & Mary Saunders Born Nov[r] 9th 1741 & Bap[t] Feb[ry] 28th 1741–2.
Patie Tadlock D. of Mary Stephens Born Aug. 25th 1741 & Bap[t] Feb[y] 14th 1741–2.
Matthew S. of John & Anne Scoggins Born Dec[r] 31st 1741 & Bap[t] Ap[r] 11th 1742.
John S. of Susanna Stewart Born Aug. 30th 1741 & Bap[t] July 4th 1742.

Martha D. of Elizabeth Stewart Born Octob 3d 1741 & Bapt July 4th 1742.

John a Slave of Coll John Stith Born July 16th 1741 & Bapt July 25th 1742.

William S. of William & Rebecca Saunders Born March 7th 1741-2 & Bapt July 4th 1742.

Susanna D. of Francis Sturdivant Born Mar. 13th 1741-2 & Bapt Aug. 7th 1742.

Drury S. of Patrick & Elizabeth Smiths Born Aug. 7th 1742 & Bapt Sept 19th 1742.

Agge Slave of James Sturdavant was Born February 23d 1742.

Answich Female Slave of Ditto was Born April 24th 1743.

Agge D. of Mary Sauntie born Decr 25th 1731 & baptd Novr 14th 1742.

Clement S. of David & Obedience Smiths born Novr 27th 1742 & baptd May 15th 1743.

David S. of John & Priscilla Smiths born Decr 18th 1742 & baptd June 12th 1743.

Sylvana D. of James & Elizabeth Smarts born April 16th & baptd June 12th 1743.

Joshua S. of George & Mary Smiths born Septr 9th & baptd Octob 16th 1743.

Mary D. of George & Goodith Stillmans born Octob 8th & baptd Novr 13th 1743.

Martha D. of Mr Thomas & Mary Shorts born Decr 26th 1743 & baptd Janry 22d 1743-4.

Joseph S. of Henry & Catharine Spires born Septr 5th 1743 baptd ap. 29th 1744.

Mally D of Daniel & Sarah Sturdivants born Aug 5th & bapd Sept 17th 1744.

Lucy D. of Patrick & Elizabeth Smiths born Octobr 12th & baptd Novr 25th 1744.

David & Elizabeth Children of David & Obedience Smiths born Decr 24th 1744 baptd Janr 7th 1744-5.

William S. of Mr John & Jemima Scotts born Septr —— 1740 baptized March 18th 1744-5.

Stephen S. of Mr John & Jemima Scotts born Aug. 31st 1742 baptized March 18th 1744-5.

Jumbo born Octob^{r} 6th 1738
Sarah born Aprile 1739
Lucy born Novr 15th 1741
Nann born May 3d 1744
Harry born Decr 22d 1744
Doctor born Sep^{tr} 14th 1745
Antony born Octob^{r} 27th 1745
} Slaves belonging to Capt Thomas Short baptized Jan^{ry} 5th 1745-6.

Millinton S. of George & Mary Smiths was born Decr 7th 1745.

George S. of George & Elizabeth Scoggins was born Jan^{ry} 28th 1745-6 & baptd Feb 19th 1745-6.

Daniel S of Daniel & Sarah Sturdivants was born March 29th & bapt^{d} June 1st 1746.

Cesar born March 29th 1748
Argan a female born 29th of Aprile 1748
} Slaves belonging to Mr William Skipwith

Charles Son of Matt Steward and Mary Toney born Decem^{r} 22d 1750.

Thompson son of John & Ann Sturdivant born Sepr 11th 1752.

Rachel a Negro Girl slave Belonging To Sr William Skipwith was Born May 13th 1761.

Mary Epes Stirdevent Daughter of John & Ann Stirdevent was Born Jan^{r} 18 1750.

Ann Isham Stirdevent Daughter of Ditto was Born Octo^{r} 10th 1754.

John Stirdevent son of Ditto was Born may 20th 1756.

Salley Stirdevent Daughter of Ditt^{o} was Born July 20th 1758.

Joel Stirdevent son of John & Ann Stirdevent was Born January ye 15th 1764.

Elizabeth, Daughter of William Stainback & Ann Lamboth his wife, was Born Novr ye 20th 1766.

John Sturdivant ye 3d Son of James & Mary Sturdivant was born the 22d day of September 1766. on a Monday between three & four OClk in the afternoon.

Ann Grant Spencer Daughter of Richd Spencer & Elizth his wife was Born February the 15th 1767.

Ann the daughter of William & Ann Stainback was born feb^{r} 20th 1769.

Rebecka Stainback Daughter of Wm and ——— Stainback Born Feby 4. 1770.

Sally Hall, Daughter of Charles & Ellen Stimpson, was born January 24th & baptized February 26th 1792.

Elizabeth Dr of Polly Spruce, a free Mulatto, born May 1st 1791, & baptized March 4th 1792.

Sarah Feild Dr of Alexander Glass Strachan & Sarah his Wife, born January 22d and baptized March 18th 1792.

William Allfriend Son of Nancy a Slave belonging to Alexr Glass Strachan, born January 13th & baptized March 18th 1792.

William, Son of William Smith (of Petersburg) died April 8th & was buried April 9th 1792.

James, Son of William Scoggin & Selah his Wife, born April 7th 1790, & bap: May 13th 1792.

Sally Daur of the same born Novr 17th 1791, & baptized May 13th 1792.

Sarah Feild Daur of Alexander G. Strachan died May 17th & was buried May 19th 1792.

John Taylor, Son of Judy, a Negroe Slave belonging to Anthony Sidner, was born December 18th 1791, & baptized May 27th 1792.

Letty Rays Dr of Sally Rays, a Mulatto Slave belonging to Thomas Shore, born Augt 9th 1791, & baptized June 17th 1792.

Mary Anne Thompson, Dr of Joel Sturdivant & Frances W. his Wife, born July 9th 1789.

Sally Servant, Dr of the same, born May 1st & baptized June 17th 1792.

Johnny S, of Jeanie, a Negroe Slave belonging to Zachariah Shackleford, born June 16th & baptized July 15th 1792.

John Benjamin, Son of Benjamin Smith, and Anne his Wife, was born September 23rd and baptized October 27th 1792.

Nathaniel Birchett, S. of James Sturdivant & Patsey his Wife, was born March 7th 1790, and baptized October 7th 1792.

Robert S. of Do, born January 9th & baptized October 7th 1792.

Margaret Lang, Daur of William Sharp, & Winnifred his Wife, born, June 5th & baptized Decr 25 1792.

Sarah Howlet, Daur of Launcelot Stone & Elizabeth his Wife, was born January 30th & baptized May 5th 1793.

Sarah Daughter of John Shore & Anne his wife, was born —— of ——— & baptized June 28th 1793.

John Sturdevant sen[r] died August 25th & was buried Sept[r] 5th 1793.

Thompson Sturdevant died August 25 & was buried Sept[r] 5. 1793.

——— Shore dau[r] of Dr. John Shore buried 29th Nov[r] 1794.

John Sturdevant died 18th & was buried 19th Feb[y] 1795.

——— Sturdivant Son of Daniel Sturdivant buried 20th May 1795.

Daniel Sturdivant was buried Jan[y] 21st 1798.

Helen Stott dau[r] of Ebenezer Stott & Elizabeth his wife, born 15th Aug[t] & bapt[d] 18th of Sept[r] 1796: died 5th Sept[r] 1797.

T

Drury son of John & Cath: Tucker born 24 sep[t] 1719 bap[t] octob[r] 24th 1720.

Anne dau: of Rob[t] & Martha Tucker born Aug: 29th last bap[t] octob[r] 9th 1720.

Geo: son of Hen: & Hannah Thweat born 7th March last bap[t] Aprill 18th 1720.

John son of John & Judith Thweat born 11th Jan[r] last bap[t] 17th Aprill 1720.

Tabitha dau of Geo: & Mary Tilman born 14th sep last bap xb[r] 17th 1720.

Rob[t] son of Joss: & Martha Tucker born 3d of Octob[r] Last bap[t] May 28th 1721.

Hen: son of Hen: & Mary Tatum born 28th May last bap[t] 11th June 1721.

Amy dau of Francis & Anne Tucker born 12th May last bap[t] July 9th 1721.

Abra: son of John & Anne Talley born 2d sep[tr] last bap[t] octob[r] 21th 1721.

John son of John & Judith Thweat born 21th March Last Bap[t] ————————.

Sara dau of John & Ann Tucker born 12th Jan[r] last bap[t] May 13th 1722.

Micael son of James & Mary Tucker born 11th July 1721 bap 7th Octob[r] 1722.

John son of Hen: & Hannah Thweat born 12 Aprill last bap^{t} 20th May 1722.

James son of John & Judith Thweat born 12 March last bap^{t} May 20th 1722.

John son of Rich & Eliz Tidmust born 28th decem 1721 bap^{t} 29th March 1722.

Joseph son of Robt & Martha Tucker born 22th June last bap^{t} 15th Aprill 1723.

Fran: son of Sam: & Mary Tatum born 17th of Aprill 1721.

susanna dau of Wm & Eliz: Tucker born 19th of Aprill 1721 bap 14th feb 1722–3.

John son of Sam: & Phebe Tatum born 7th June 1710.

Wm son of Sam: & Eliz: Tatum born 26th June 1717.

Eliz: dau of ditto born 29th of Nov: 1718.

John son of John Thweat died June 10th 1722.

Sam: son of Sam: & Eliz: Temple jun^{r} born 7th Jan^{r} 1720.

Mary dau: of ditto born 20th Sep^{t} 1722.

Wm son of Geo: & Mary Tilman born 21th May last bap^{t} Augt 22th 1723.

Nath: son of Nath: & Katheren Tucker born 20th feb^{r} last bap^{t} July 10th 1723.

Fran: son of Fran: & Anne Tucker born 1st Nov last bap^{t} 7th Nov 1723.

Lucy d: of Ja: & Mary Tenheart born 10th May last bap^{t} 15th sep^{r} 1723.

Tho Temple had A Child born June 4th And died 7th ditto 1724.

Frances D of Thompson & Ruth Staples born 14th May last bap^{t} June 21th 1724.[*]

Eliz d: of Jno & Judith Thweat born 11th March last bap^{t} May 24th 1724.

Mary d: of Ja: & Mary Thweat born 28th feb last bap^{t} May 24th 1724.

Susanna d: of Hugh & Mary Lee born 10th feb: last bap^{t} May 24th 1724.

Frances D of Hen: & Mary Tatun born June 6th bap^{t} 12th July 1724.

---

*Erased in original.—C. G. C.

Geo S: of Wm and Eliz: Tucker born 4th Sep^{tr} 1723 bap^{t} 11th octob^{r} 1724.

Ruth d of John & Anne Tally born 28 Jan^{r} last bap^{t} Novr 6th 1724.

John son of John & Anne Tucker born 9th Sep^{tr} last bap 6th Nov 1724.

Geo: Son of Wm & Eliz: Tucker born 4th sep^{t} 1723 bap^{t} 11th octob^{r} 1724.

Obedience D: of Hen: & Hannah Thweat born 15th sep^{t} last bap^{t} 1st Nov 1724.

Eliz: D: of Wm & Eliz Temple born 7th March last bap^{t} May 16th 1725.

Dan: of Robt & Martha Tucker born Jan^{r} lest bap^{t} May 10th 1725.

Geo S of Roger & Mary Tilman born 21th Jan^{r} last bap^{t} May 30th 1725.

phebe D of Edmond & Elisabeth Trayler born 2d Sepr bap^{t} 18th octob^{r} 1725.

Frances Da^{t} of Allen and mary Tye born 16th march last 1724.

Frances Da^{t} of James & Ann Thweat born Dce^{m} ye 25 bap^{t} ye 8th Aprill 1725.

Jno son of Jos and Eliz^{a} turner born 11th Dce^{m} 1725.

Jamey slave of Jo^{s} Turner born 19th Aprill 1726.

Dinah slave of D^{o} born 8th may 1726.

Wm son of Wm and Mary Totty born Dec^{m} 5th 1725 bap^{t} May 30 1726.

John son of Frances and Ann Tucker born 25th June bap^{t} 28th sep^{tr} 1726.

——— Da^{t} of Jno and Anne Tucker born ———.

Robert son of Nathaniel and Emelea Tatam born 30th Janr^{y} 1725.

John Son of Jno and Judith Thweat born 22d august 1726.

Daniel Son of William and Eliz^{a} Tucker born 29th Jan^{r} 1725.

Amy D of John and Mary tucker born 23d August 1726.

francis Son of John and Ann tucker born 3d Jan^{r} 1726.

Anne D of of James and Mary Thompson born 3 feb^{r} 1726 bap^{t} 25: 1727.

Eliz^{a} D of Roger and Mary tillman born 15th Nov^{m} 1726.

Martin Son of Rich^{d} and Mary tally born 15th July 1727.

Agnis D of henry and Mary Tatam born 14th Oct[m] bap[t] 26th November 1727.

Eliz[a] D of Roger and Mary Tillmon 15th Nov[m] 1726.

Martha D of Rob[t] and frances Tucker born 10th July 1727.

Eliz[a] D of Henry and Hanna Thweat born 20th august 1727 bap[t] 1t octb[r].

Judith D of John and Martha Traylor Born 6th March 1727.

Wm Son of Wm and Mary Totty Born 15th March 1727 Bap[t] 3d June.

Th[o] Son of Th[o] and Eliz[a] Tucker Born 30th March 1728 Bap[t] 28th July.

Holenberry Son of Joseph and Eliz[a] Turner Born 14th June 1728 Bap[t] July 28th.

archer of John and Mary Traylor Born aprill 20th 1729.

Roger Taylor Dces[d] 7th June 1729.

Wm Son of John and Judith Thweat Born 11th Sep[r] Bap[t] 4th March 1728.

ann Dau of James and Mary Thompson Born 3d feb[r] 1726.

Elizabeth D of Henry & ——— Tucker Born 2d Sep[r] 1729.

Lucretia D. of James & Mary Tucker. Born. 5th June 1729.

ann D of francis and ann Tucker Born 19th feb[r] Bap[t] 19th March 1729.

Matthew Son of Matthew and Mary Tolbert Born 27th Novm[r] 1729.

Christian D of James and ann Thweat Born 9th feb[r] 1729 Bap[t] 31th May 1730.

David Son of Joseph and Martha Tucker Born 24th Dcember 1729 Bap[t] 31th May 1730.

William Son of allen and Mary Tye Born 10th May 1730 Bap[t] July 12th 1730.

Thomas Son of Thomas and Eliz[a] Totty Born 5th aprill 1730 Bap[t] 12th July.

David Son of John and Mary Tucker Born 25th Sep[r] 1730.

William Son of Robert & Mary Taylor Born 22d august Bap[t] 20th Nov[r].

Nevil Son of Daniel & Eliz[a] Tucker Born 25th aprill 1730.

Kezia Dat[r] of Jn[o] and Judith Tally Born 23d Sep[r] 1730.

William Son of Jn[o] and Phelis Thacker Born 10th Nom[r] 1730.

Ann D: of Joseph & Eliz[a] Turner Born 8th Nom[r] 1730.

Hanna D: of George & frances Tucker Born 30th March 1731 Bap^{t} 29th august.

Frances D of Robert & Frances Tucker Born 11th March 1730.

——— D of Henry & ELisabeth Tucker Born 8th May 1731 Bap^{t} 29th august.

Amy D: of William & Eliz^{a} Temple Born 3d June 1731 Bap^{t} octb^{r} 17th.

Lucretia D of Joseph & Lucretia Tucker Born 15th august 1731 Bap^{t} 10th octbe^{r}.

Sarah D: of George & Mary Tillman Born 8th octb^{r} Bap^{t} novmb^{r} 6th 1731.

Martha D: of James & anne Thweatt Born 29th Sepr Bap^{t} 14th novmb^{r} 1731.

Littleberry Son of peter & mary Tatam Born 10th ap^{r} Bap^{t} 18th novm^{b} 1731.

Marth D: of John & Judith Thweat Born 21th octb^{r} 1732 Bap^{t} Dce^{r} 17th.

Littlepage of Hen^{y} & Judith Tally Born 13th Jany 1731 Bap^{t} May 7th 1732.

Warner son of James & Mary Tucker born 15th April 1732 bap^{t} 1st June 1732.

Jno son of Roger & Eliz^{a} Tayler born Novr 12th 1731 bap^{t} Decr 20th 1731.

Jane dat^{r} of Jno & Eliz^{a} Tomlinson born July 16th 1732 bap^{t} Sepr 20th 1732.

Burrell son of Miles & Sarah Thweat born 4th July 1732 bap^{t} Sepr 17th 1732.

Wilmut dat^{r} of Jno & Mary Trayler born 19th Augt 1731 bap^{t} May 22d 1732.

Rebeckah d of Thomas & Frances Temple Born 18th Novr 1732 Bap^{t} 29th Dce^{r}.

Blanch d of Edmond Eliz^{a} Traylor Born 17th Sepr 1732 Bap^{t} dce^{r} 31th.

Martha D^{r} of Francis & ann Tucker Born 21th feb^{r} 1732 Bap^{t} march 3d.

Isham Son of Jno & mary Tucker Born 1th feb^{r} 1732 Bap^{t} 3d march.

Joseph Son of John & mary Tucker Born 14th Novr 1732 Bap^{t} Jan^{r} 14th.

Joseph Son of Joseph & Eliz[a] Turner Born 2d ap[r] 1733 Bap[t] 20th may 1733.

William Son of Robert & Frances Tucker Born 15th ap[r] 1733 Bap[t] 3d June 1733.

Agnis D[r] of allen & mary Tye Born 9th March 1732 Bap[t] 3d June 1733.

James Son of Matthew & Mary Tolbot Born 7th Nov[r] 1732 Bap[t] 7th ap[r] 1733.

Frances of Henry & amy Tucker Born 25th ap[r] 1733 Bap[t] June 3d 1733.

Margret D: of William & Mary Totty Born 30th feb[r] 1732 Bap[t] octb[r] 20th 1733.

William Son of Edward & Mary Traylor Born 12th June 1733 Bap[t] 21th octb[r].

Robert Son of George & frances Tucker Born 3d dce[r] 1733.

Judith D: of George & Eliz[a] traylor Born 8th march 1733 Bap[t] 7th ap[r] 1734.

Martha D: of Henry & Judith Tally Born 31th Jan[r] 1733 Bap[t] 10th March.

John Son of John & Margret Tillman Born 20th ap[r] 1734 Bap[t] 26th May.

Lucia D: of William & Sarah Tate Born 19th feb[r] 1733 Bap[t] 20th May 1734.

William Son of Roger & Eliz[a] Taylor Born 16th May 1734.

Willmoth D: of Richard & Eliz[a] Thorn Born 10th June 1734 Bap[t] 4th august.

Elizabeth daugh[r] of James & Ann Thweatt Born Aug[t] 5 1734.

William Son of Miles & Sarah Thweatt Born 14th Sept[r] 1734 Bap[t] y[e] 9 Feb[ry] 1734-5.

Peter S. of Peter and Elizabeth Thomas Born 2d Xb[r] 1734.

Lucretia D. of John and Mary Traylor Born Aug[t] 16th 1734.

Ann D. of William & Sarah Trayler Born Aug[t] 23d 1734.

Solomon S. of Allen and Mary Tye Born 20th March 1734.

Abraham S. of John and ——— Tucker Born 22d Jan[ry] 1734 Bapt. 7th March.

Elizabeth D. of Joseph and Elizabeth Turner Born 6th Octob[r] 1735.

Nathan S of William & Sarah Tate Born the 23 april 1736.

William S of William & Sarah Tate Born august 26 1738.

John Son of Charles & Frances Thomson B Aug[t] 28th 1740.
Rebeckah D. of Thomas & Mary Twitty B Sep[r] 5th 1740.
Mary D of Richard & Mary Thomas B March 12th 1739-40.
David S of Peter and Elisabeth Thomas B Dc[r] 24th 1740.
Thomas. S. of Thomas & Anne Tunks Born Oct. 29th 1741 & Bap[t] Nov[r] 29th 1741.
Samuel. S. of William & Sara Tates Born Nov 3d 1741 & Bap[t] Dce[r] 12th 1741.
David. S. of Drury & Elizabeth Thwets Born Oct. 27th 1741 & Bap[t] Dec[r] 25th 1741.
Anne. D. of Henry & Elizabeth Toudress Born Aug 15th 1741 & Bap[t] Jan[ry] 3d 1741-2.
David. S. of Samuell & Mary Temples Born Oct. 23d 1741 & Bap[t] Jan[ry] 24th 1741-2.
Miles. S. of Abram & Helenour Tuckers Born Feb[y] 16th 1741-2 & Bap[t] Mar. 14th 1741-2.
Alick. S. of Miles & Sara Thwets Born Jan[ry] 29th 1741-2 & Bap[t] May 9th 1742.
Catharine. D. of Richard & Mary Thomas's Born May 3d 1742 & Bap[t] July 4th 1742.
Anderson. S. of Allan & Mary Tyes Born Mar 11th 1741-2 & Bap[t] July 25th 1742.
Martha D. of William & Sara Traylors Born Oct. 18th 1741 & Bap[t] Aug 14th 1742.
Elizabeth D. of Drury & Elizabeth Thwets born Feb. 10th 1742-3 & bapt[d] March 27th 1743.
Peter S. of Peter & Mary Tatums Born Jan[ry] 27th 1742-3 & bapt[d] May 29th 1743.
Judith D. of John & Judith Thweats born June 19th 1743 & bapt[d] July 23d 1743.
Elizabeth D. of Samuel & Francis Temples born Ap[r] 1st & bapt[d] May 13th 1744.
Jacob S. of Samuel & Mary Temples born Sept[r] 24th & bapt[d] Nov[r] 11th 1744.
Lucretia D. of William & Elizabeth Temples born Sept[r] 16th & bapt[d] Nov[r] 11th 1744.
Mary D. of Joseph & Lucretia Tuckers born Aprile 3d & bapt[d] May 26th 1745.

Nathaniel S. of Rob[t] & Keziah Tatums born March 30th & bapt[d] May 12th 1745.

Edith D. of Drury & Elizabeth Thweats born Aprile 25th & bapt[d] June 30th 1745.

Mary D. of Samuel & Frances Temples was born March 26th 1745.

John S. of James & Sarah Thweats was born June 12th & bapt[d] July 28th 1745.

Mary D. of Edward & Mary Thweats was born Sep[tr] 17th 1745 & bap[td] Nov[r] 3d 1745.

Elizabeth D. of William & Anne Turners was born Sep[tr] 3d & bap[td] Nov[r] 10th 1745.

Elizabeth D of Richard and Sarah Taylors born 29th June 1736.

George S of Ditto born 23d June 1738.

Richard Son of Ditto born 26th Decem[r] 1739.

Nanney D of Ditto born 1st May 1742.

Alice Taylor departed this life 17th August 1750.

Jack Male Slave of Richard & Sarah Taylors born 14th June 1750.

Frankee Daughter of Drury & Eliz[a] Thweat born ——— bap[t] Feb 17th 1750.

Tabitha, Daughter of James & Sarah Thweats born 27th May 1749.

James Son of Ditto born April 3d 1752.

Frank Male Slave of Ditto June 15th 1748.

Feby Female Slave of ditto born Septem[r] 14th 1750.

Nan Female Slave of Ditto born March 11th 1752.

Ned Male Slave of Rich[d] & Sarah Taylors born May 12th 1753.

Thom, Son of Betty, a Slave belonging to John Thweatt, born November 25th 1791, & baptized April 9th 1792.

Charlotte, Dau[r] of Cate, a Slave belonging to the same, born April 9th 1791, & baptized April 9th 1792.

Aleck, Son of Cressy, a Slave belonging to Richard Taylor, born March 1st, & baptized April 29th 1792.

Mary-Henry, D[r] of Henry Tench & Nancy his Wife, born March 12th & bap: June 21st 1792.

Notise, Dau[r] of Abby, a Negro Slave belonging to John Thweatt, was born January 25th & baptized Nov[r] 18th 1792.

William Taylor, of the Town of Petersburg, died December 30th 1792 and was buried January 1st 1793.

Candace, Dau[r] of Peter Temple & Nanny his Wife, born July 18th 1792 & baptized January 4th 1793.

William Eppes, Son of Eppes Temple & Elizabeth his Wife, born Dec[r] 16th 1792 & baptized March 24th 1793.

Edward, S, of Dorcas, a Mulatto slave belonging to John Thweatt, was born December 17th & baptized April 1st 1793.

U–V

Abigaell dau: of John & Elinor Vaughan departed this life feb: 23th 1720–1 in the 6th year of her Age.

James son of Rich & Alice Vaughan born Jan: 23th last bap[t] March 4th 1721–2.

Eliz dau of Wm & Ann Vaughan born 14th Sep[r] last bap[t] Nov[r] 8th 1721.

Anne dau: of Hen: & Martha Vauden born 19th Jan[r] last bap[t] 21th March 1722.

Pearc son of Wm & Prissilla Vaughan born 15th March last bap[t] 16th Sep[t] 1722.

Luis son of Nico: & Ann Vaughn born 20th feb 1719 bap[t] June 7th 1722.

Abra son of ditto born 16th March 1721 bap[t] June 7th 1722.

Joss son of Dan: & Eliz: Vaughan born 14th decem last bap[t] feb: 3d 1722–3.

Martha D of Rich & Alice Vaughan born 18th Nov: last bap[t] Sep[tr] 12th 1724.

Wm son of Wm & Priss Vaughan born 5th August last bap[t] Jan 10th 1724–5.

Jane a negro belonging to Wm Vaughan Sen[r] born 25th Nov[r] 1724.

Williams s of Dan: & Eliz: Vaughan born 14th August last bap[t] Jan[r] 17th 1724–5.

Hen: s: of Hen: & Martha Vaden born 6th feb[r] last bap[t] March 28th 1725.

Isham Son of Daniel and Eliz Vaughan born feb[r] y[e] 4th 1725.

James Son of Wm and Prissillah Vaughan born 6th March bap[t] 18th sep[t] 1725.

Eliz^a D of Jno and Catherine lee born ———.
James Thompson Son of Sarah Vaughan born 24th Sep^t 1726.
Henry Son of Henry and Eliz^a Vodin born 12 Sep^t 1694.
Sipio M Slave of Wm and Julia Vaughan born 31 Decemberr 1726.
Richard Son of Richard and Alce Vaughan born 16th Oce^m 1726.
Eliz^a D of Nicolas and Ann Vaughan born 18th Aprill 1727.
Ann D of Daniel and Eliz^a Vaughan Born 15th Dec^m 1727.
Susannah D of Wm and prissilla Vaughan Born 25th Decm^r 1727.
Frances D of William and frances Vodin Born 18th Sep^t 1728.
Nicolas Son of Nicolas and ann Vaughan Born 20th febr 1728.
Susannah D of Henry and Martha Vodin Born 19th Novmber Bap^t 26th Decm^r 1728.
abigal D of Wm and Mable Vaughan Born 15th 1729 Jan^r.
Peter Son of Daniel & Eliz^a Vaughan Born 28th Sepr 1730.
Caleb son of Wm & Mable Vaughan born 25th January 1731 bap^t Ap^l 30th 1732.
Mary dat^r of Hen^y & Mary Voden born 14th Jany 1731 bap^t May 7th 1732.
Phebœ dat^r of Robt & Martha Vaughan born 18th May 1732 Bap^t June 1st 1732.
Ann dat^r of Danl & Ann Vaughan born 10th of Octr 1732 bap^t Novr 12th 1732.
Wilmot D^r of Isham & Temperanc Vaughan Born 3d March 1732 Bap^t 3d June 1733.
Mary D^r of William & pricilla Vaughan Born 12th November 1732 Bap^t 27th May 1733.
Burrell Son of Henry & Martha Voden Born 2d Sepr 1733 Bap^t 21th octb^r.
abner Son of William & Mable Vaughan Born 25th feb^r 1733 Bap^t 28th ap^r 1734.
Mary daughter of Daniel & Ann Vaughan born ye 1 January 1734–5 Bap^t 9 Febrary.
Henry Son of Morris and Rebecca Vaughan born 14 Decr 1734 Bap^t 9th February.
Peter male Slave of Wm & Julia Vaughan Born 14 Feb^ry 1734.

Sarah D of John and Sarah York Born 17th of Feb[ry] 1734 Bapt 4 May 1735.[*] Carry'd to Y.

James S. of Elizabeth Valentine Born August 27th 1733.

Nicholas S. of Robert. and Martha Vaughan Born the 21st Novr 1734.

Sarah D. of Samuel & Margrett Vaughan Born 29 July 1735.

Anne D of William and Mary Vaughan Born 7th Jan[ry] 1735.

Mabel D of William & Mabel Vaughan Born January ye 12 1740.

Ruth. D. of Nathanael & Amith Vaughans Born Decr 28th 1741 & Bap[t] Mar. 7th 1741-2.

Abram S. of Peter & Annê Vaughans Born Mar. 11th 1741-2 & Bap[t] Apr 18th 1742.

Anne D. of William & Mary Vaughans Born Jan[ry] 20th 1741-2 & Bap[t] June 13th 1742.

Thomas S. of Thomas & Elizabeth Vaughans Born July 12th 1742 & bap[t] Septr 12th 1742.

David S. of Morris & Rebecca Vaughans born Jan[ry] 1st 1741-2.

Sylvana D. of Samuel & Margret Vaughans born Aug. 1st & bapt[d] Nov[r] 7th 1742.

Phebe D. of Daniel & Anne Vaughans born Nov[r] 12th 1743 & bapt[d] Jan[ry] 1st 1743-4.

Phebe D. of Salathiel & Anne Vaughans born Nov[r] 23d 1743 & bapt[d] Jan[ry] 8th 1743-4.

Martha D. of Maurice & Rebecca Vaughans born March 10th 1743-4 bapt[d] May 13th 1744.

William S. of Salathiel & Anne Vaughans born Feb. 16th 1744-5 bapt[d] Aprile 14th 1745.

Silvester S. of Samuell & Margaret Vaughans born March 14th 1744-5 & bapt[d] May 19th 1745.

James S. of Joshua & Sarah Vaughans was born Jan[ry] 22d, bapt[d] Feb 23d 1745-6.

David Son of Salathiel & Anne Vaughans born ——— bap[t] 4th March 1749-50.

Ezekiel Son of Henry and Eliz[a] Vaughans born 29th Decem[r] 1750.

Jessee Son of Joshua & Sarah Vaughans born ——— Bapt[d] 28th Ap[r] 1751.

---

* Erased in original.—C. G. C.

Jemina Daughter of Morris & Rebecka Vaughans born ——— bap[t] 21 June 1752.

Mary D of Williams & Ellinor Vaughans born July 26th 1752.

John, Son of Howel Underhill (of Sussex County) & Nancy his Wife, born March the 3d, & baptized April 6th 1792.

Anne Unckle, Dau[r] of Lewis Unckle, was buried September 22nd 1792.

Sally Newsum Dau[r] of John Verell jun[r] and Martha his Wife, born April 15th, and bap: September 23rd 1792.

Lucetta, Dau[r] of Sarah a Negroe Slave, belonging to John Verell jun[r] was born February 24th and baptized September 23rd 1792.

Peg, Dau[r] of Peg, D[o], D[o], was born March 4th and baptized September 23rd 1792.

Mary-Ann-Elizabeth, Dau[r] of Drury Vaughan & Susannah his Wife born April 21st & baptized July 14th 1793.

Robert Winn, Son of Enoch Vaughan & Mary his Wife, born April 3rd & baptized October 13th 1793.

W

Martha dau: of Cha: & Eliz: Williams born 18th octob[r] last bap[t] 20th Nov: 1720.

Martha dau: of Joss: & Mary Wynn born 1st May last bap[t] 8th Jan[r] 1720–1.

Tho: son of Tho: & Mary Webster born 20th June last bap[t] March 5th 1720–1.

Gardner son of Geo: & Eliz: Wilson born 15th feb: last bap[t] March 26th 1721.

Daniel son of Wm & Rosamund Worsham born last Nov: bap[t] March 26th 1721.

Martha dau of Wm & Dorcas Worsham born 18th Nov last bap[t] Aprill 21th 1721.

David son of Geo: & Sibbil Williams born 22th of Aprill last bap[t] May 28th 1721.

Tho: son of Tho: & Amy Wilson born June 21th 1721 bap[t] June 21th 1721.

Jeremiah son of Hen: & Mary Walthall born 28th Aprill lest bap[t] June 4th 1721.

Martha dau: of Wm & Dorcas Worsham born 26th march last bap[t] June 4th 1721.

Abraham son of Wm & Sarah Whitamore born 14th feb: last bap[t] Octob[r] 8th 1721.

Sarah dau: of David & Sarah Williams born 15th March last bap[t] July 18th 1721.

Stevens son of y[e] decd: Hen: Wilson & Mary his relict born 15th sep[tr] last bap[t] octob[r] 8th 1721.

Dan: son of John & Cath: Walker born feb[r] 14th 1712–3 bap[t] Nov[r] 2d 1721.

Wm son of John & Mary West born 12th Sep[tr] last bap[t] Nov 8th 1721.

Ann dau of Rich & Mary Walthall born 25th octob[r] last bap[t] 5th March 1721–2.

Sarah dau of Rich: & Judith Wilson born 23d decem last bap[t] March 11th 1721–2.

Eliz: dau of Rob[t] & Mary West born 21th March last bap[t] May 13th 1722.

Eliz: dau of Cha: & Eliz: Williams born 24th Aprill last bap[t] May 27th 1722.

Wm son of Wm & Rose: Worsham born 27th sep[t] last bap: Nov 25th 1722.

Rich: son of Rich: & Rebecca White born 13th Nov: 1721 bap[t] March 27th 1722.

Cha: son of Ja: & Olive Williams born 23d feb: 1721 bap[t] March 29th 1722.

Mary dau of Rob[t] & Mary Wynn born 26 Nov: 1722.

Joss son of ditto born 3d August 1722.

Joss son of Joss & Mary Wynn born 24th Jan last bap[t] Aug: 13th 1722.

Cha son of Cha & Ann Williams born 26th May last bap[t] 13th Aug: 1722.

Eliz dau of Hen: & Phebe Walthall born 10th Jan last bap: March 10th 1722–3.

Burgess son of John & Ann Wall born 22th May 1722 bap[t] June 20th 1723.

Joss: son of Joss & Martha Wall born 21th feb[r] last bap[t] June 20th 1723.

Sibilla dau of Geo & Sibilla Williams born 18th this Inst bap August 22th 1723.

Jude a negro girl belonging unto Hen: Walthall born 31th August 1723

Eliz: D: of Wm & Anne Wall born 6th last sep^{tr} bap^{t} August 6th 1723.

John son of Hen & Mary Walthall born 5th Nov: 1723.

Marg^{a} dau of Cha & Eliz: Williams born 19th of Nov: last bap^{t} 22th decem 1723.

Wm son of Wm & Martha Womack born 10th of sep^{tr} last bap^{t} Jan^{r} 19th 1723-4.

John son of Tho & Eliz: Wilkinson born 25th Nov last bap^{t} Aprill 10th 1724.

Mary d of David & Sarah Williams born 29th August last bap^{t} 10th Aprill 1724.

Wm son of Wm & Martha Womack born 10th sep^{t} last bap^{t} Jan^{r} 19th 1723-4.

Rich s of Dan & Anne Wall born 19th Aprill last bap^{t} June 21th 1724.

Anne d of Wm & Sarah Wells born 8th March last bap^{t} May 20th 1724.

Ephraim son of Fran: & Eliz: West born 2d feb^{r} last bap^{t} sep^{tr} 12th 1724.

Abra son of John & Mary West born 2d feb^{r} last bap^{t} 16th sep^{tr} 1724.

Rich son of Rich & Judith Wilson born 18th May last bap^{t} Nov 1st 1724.

Obedience D of James & Olive Williams born 10th May last bap^{t} Nov 6th 1724.

Rich son of John & Eliz: Williams born 14th Sep^{t} last bap^{t} 6th Nov 1724.

———— of Ja & Kath Wood born ye last of October bap^{t} Aprill 19th 1724.

Maball D: of Hen: & phebe Walthall born 10th of May last bap^{t} June 27th 1725.

Christopher s: of Rich: & Mary Walthall born 28th Jan: last bap^{t} feb^{r} 6th 1724-5.

Marg^{a} D. of Joss: & Mary Wynn born 25th Nov: last bap^{t} feb^{r} 8th 1724-5.

Marg^a D of Ditto born 31th decemb^r 1723.

Drury s of Wm & Ann Wall born ye last July bap^t Jan^r 12th 1724-5.

Isham s: of Joss & Martha Wall born 25th Nov last bap^t May 30th 1725.

Cha: s of Cha & Eliz: Williams born 11th June 1725.

susanah and francis daughters of Robt and Mary west born 2d March bap^t 6th March 1725.

David Son of Jno and Ann Wall born 12: June bap^t 21: aug 1725.

John Williams Departed this life Jan^ry ye 16th 1725.

Sarah Da^t of Charles W^ms And Ann born 20th Sep^t 1725.

henry Son George and Sybellah williams born 4th november 1725.

Daniell Son of Daniell and Amy Wall born 25th march 1726.

Ann Da^t of Th^o and mary Westmoreland born 12 ap^r bap^t June 6th 1726.

John Son of David and Sarah Williams born Jan^r 23d Bap^t June 6th 1726.

Dick Slave of henry Waltal born 15th August Last 1726.

Joseph Son of Jno and Eliz^a William born 15th July 1726.

Margarit D of Joseph and Margaret Wilson born 27th octm 1726.

Thomas Son of Joseph and Mary Wyn born 6th Aprill 1726.

Sarah D of henry and Martha Wilson born 9th Dece^m 1726.

Agnis Waller D of Charity Smithis born 30th May 1726.

francis Son of francis and Eliz^a West born 9th feb^r 1726.

Ann Daughter of Richard and Aann Westmoreland born 2d aprill 1722.

——— of Wm and Ann Wall born born 15th Dce^mr 1726.

henry Son of Joshua and Martha Wall born 3d Jana^r 1726.

Mary Daughter of John and Ann Wall born 13th Dec^m 1726.

Mary D of Charles and Eliz^a Williams born 19th aprill 1727.

Lucy D of Charles and Ann Williams born 6th May 1727.

Jane D. of John and Mary Willingham born 2d May 1727.

John Son of Jno Eliz^a Watts born 10th oct^m 1726.

Joel Son of John and Catherine Willson born 6th November 1727.

Joseph Son of Edward and Martha Willson born 1th feb^r 1727.

Peter Son of Jame and ann Williams born 7th Dce^r 1728.

Henry Son of Essex and ann Worsham Worsham Born 5th august 1727.

Marthew Son of Th° and Margrat Westmoreland Born 18th March 1727.

Martha and th° of Rob[t] and Mary West Born 17th May 1728 Bap[t] June 2d.

Micael Son of John and ann Willson Born 18th aprill 1728 Bap[t] 2d June.

Henry Son of Henry and Phebe Wallton Born 25th June 1728 Bap[t] 19th July.

Helen Son of Charles and Eliz[a] W[ms] Born 3d June 1728 Bap[t] July 28.

Frances D of Wm and Roson Worsham Born 8th feb[r] 1727 Bap[t] 28th July.

Mary D of George and Sibylla Williams Born 15th ocb[r] 1727.

Susan D of Charles and Prissilla Williamson Born 1d march 1727.

Joel Son of Thomas and Frances Walker Born 14th June 1727.

Eliz[a] D of Aron and Mary Wood Born 5th June 1727 Bap[t] July 23d.

Th° Son of Wm and Eliz[a] Walter Born 16th Jan[r] 1727.

Mary D of henry and Martha Willson Born 24th No[m] 1728 Bap[t] 27th Dce[m].

Winiford D of Joshua and Martha Wall Born Jan[r] 20th 1728.

Wm Son of Wm and frances Wells Born 20th oct[r] Bap[t] 25th Dce[r] 1728.

ann D of John and Eliz[a] Williams Born 25th oct[r] Bap[t] 1 Decem[r] 1728.

Laurana D of Eliz[a] Womack Born 20th March 1728.

——— of George and Sibellah W[ms] Born 12th oc[tr] 1728 Bap[t] 6th aprill 1729.

Robert Son of David and Mary Walker Born 10th oct[r] 1729 Bap[t] 26th octr.

Alexander Son of Ditto Born 3d octob[r] 1727.

Linder female Slave of Ditt° Born 2d august 1728.

Simon Male Slave of Ditto Born 20th June 1727.

Phebe female Slave of Ditto Born 12 Sep[t] 1729.

Martha D. of Dan[l] & Amy Wall. Born 23d June 1729 Bap[t] 26th Oct[r].

John Son of Charles & Ann Williams Born 17th March. Bap[t] Sep[r] 2d 1729.

Edward Son of Tho[s] & Eliz[a] Winingham. Born 3d May 1729.

Susannah & Abigall D[rs] of Joseph & Isabella Westmoland born 30th Aprill 1729.

John Son of Rob[t] & Temporance West Born 10th May 1729.

John Son of frances and Eliz[a] West Born 2d March 1729.

ann D of Wm and Margret Whood Born 24th March Bap[t] oct[r] 2d 1729.

Jn[o] Son of Charles and Eliz[a] Williams Born 11th March 1729 Bap[t] 10th May 1730.

Amy D of Th[os] and francis Walthal Born 19th feb[r] 1729 Bap[t] 10th May 1730.

Jack Slave of Garrat Waltal born 14th March 1725.

Lusie Dater of Rob[t] and and Mary West Born feb[r] 4th 1729 Bap[t] 31th May 1730.

Gerrat Son of Gerrat and Eliz[a] Walthal Born 25th feb[r] 1729 Bap[t] 10th May 1730.

John Son of Charles and Prissilla Williamson Born 24th 1730 Bap[t] 10th May 1730.

Miles Son of James and Olive Williams Born 15th Jan[r] 1729 Bap[t] 31th May 1730.

Richard Son of aron &: mary Wood Born 15th Sep[r] 1729.

John Son of francis and Eliz[a] West Born 2d March 1729 Bap[t] 2d May 1730.

Phebe and Mary D[s] of Jn[o] and Mary Willson Born 16th June 1730.

Sarah D of John & Susannah Write Born 2d august 1730 Bap[t] 30th octb[r].

Precillah D of Thomas & Eliz[a] Winingham Born 30th June 1730.

Mary D of Richard & Mary Walthal Born 15th Sep[r] 1730 Bap[t] 9th Dce[r].

Mary D of Robert & Temporance West Born 7th Sep[r] 1730.

Eliz[a] D of Henry & Martha Willson Born 28th Sep[r] 1730.

Francis son of Henry & Mary Wyatt Born 29th March 1731.

Zachariah Son of John and ann Wall Born 25th July 1731 Bap[t] aug[s] 29th.

David son of Wm & francis Wells Born 23d November 1730 Bap[t] Jan[r] 10th.

Anne D: of Edward Whit Born 11th Dce^r 1730 Bap^t 17 Jan^r Eliz^a his Wife.

Benjamine son of francis & martha Walthal Born 9th feb^r 1730 Bap^t 3d march 1730.

Richard Son of Henry & Phebe Walthal Born 15th June 1731 Bap^t July 27th.

Ruben Son of abraham & Sarah Wells Born 28th July 1731 Bap^t 30th august.

Henry Son of Isack & Sarah Winingham Born 16th June 1731 Bap^t 12th Sep^r.

Jones of David & Sarah Williams Born 23d ap^r 1731 Bap^t 12th august.

Martha D: of Henry & Martha Willson Born 7th sep^r 1731 Bap^t 7th octb^r.

Tabitha D: of Joshua & Mary Wynn Born 23d May 1731 Bap^t 10th octb^r.

Mary D: of Charles & anne Williams Born 5th august 1731 Bap^t 10th octbe^r.

Samuel Son of Jno & anne Willson Born 31th octb^r 1730 Bap^t 23d ap^r 1732.

David & Mary twinns of David & Mary Walker Born 6th March 1731 Bap^t 23d ap^r 1732.

Joell Son of Edward & Mary Winfield born 30th Decem^r 1731.

Christian dat^r of Robt & Mary West born Ap^l 8th 1732 bap^t May 7th 1732.

Edward son of Jerrott & Eliz^a Walthall born Mar. 17. 1731 bap^t June 4th 1732.

Wm Son of of Wm & Sarah Winingham born 16th Decr 1731 bap^t July 2d 1732.

Christian dat^r of Jno & Mary Winingham born 20th March 1731 bap^t July. 7. 1732.

Robert son of Robt & Eliz^a Williams born 17th June 1732 bap^t 13th Augt 1732.

Essex son of Essex & Ann Worsham born 11th June 1732 bap^t 20th Augt 1732.

Edward Son Cha & Eliz^a Williams born 11th June 1732 bap^t 10th Sepr 1732.

John Son of John & Mary Willson born 11th Sepr 1732 bap^t 12 Novr 1732.

Mary d of Daniel & amy Wall Born 23d august 1731 Bap^{t} 2 Jan^{r}.
James Son of Joseph & Sybilla Westmoreland Born 28th Sepr 1731 Bap^{t} 2d Jan^{r}.
Susanah D: of John & Susanah Write Born 26th Dce^{r} 1732 Bap^{t} feb^{r} 4th.
Phebe D: of Wm & frances Wells Born 31th Dceb^{r} 1732 Bap^{t} feb^{r} 4th.
Judith D^{r} of Henry & Martha Willson Born 24th feb^{r} 1732 Bap^{t} 28th march 1733.
Elisabeth D: of Francis & Eliz^{a} Wyat Born 22d Dce^{r} 1732 Bap^{t} feb^{r} 25th.
Christian D^{r} of Joseph & Sibylla Westmoreland Born 26th feb^{r} 1732 Bap^{t} 20th may 1733.
Frances of John & Eliz^{a} Williams Born 21th feb^{r} 1732 Bap^{t} 8th ap^{r} 1733.
Mark Son of John & ann Willson Born 20th Novm^{r} 1732 Bap^{t} 20th may 1733.
amy D^{r} of Robert & Temperanc West Born 24th Sepr 1732 Bap^{t} 17th June 1733.
Amy D^{r} of Francis & Eliz^{a} West Born 2d June 1733 Bap^{t} 5th August.
Peter Son of Thomas & Frances Walker Born 19th July 1733 Bap^{t} 28th Sep^{r}.
amy D: of Thomas & Mary Winingham Born 11th august 1733 Bap^{t} Novr 4th.
abram Son of abram & Sarah Wells Born 7th Sepr 1733 Bap^{t} 11 Nov^{r}.
John Son of Daniel & amy Wall Born 10th Dce^{r} 1733 Bap^{t} Jan^{r} 27th.
Elisabeth D of Thomas & Margaret Westmoreland Born 31th octb^{r} 1733.
Elisabeth D of Charles & pricilla Williamson Born Jan^{r} 1733 Bap^{t} 2d feb^{r}.
Josep^{t} Son of Charles & Elisabeth Williams Born 2d Jan^{r} 1733 Bap^{t} 2d feb^{r}.
Ann D: of Henry & phebe Walthall Born 10th March 1733 Bap^{t} 14th ap^{r} 1734.
frances D: of Joshua & Martha Wall Born 11th octb^{r} 1733 Bap^{t} 24th March 1734.

Hannah D: of John & ann Winfield Born 12th feb^r 1733 Bap^t 20th May 1734.

John Son of Charles & ann Williams Born 14th May 1734 Bap^t 4th august.

Mary D: of Adam & Elener Wells Born 18th June 1734 Bap^t 11th August.

John Son of Edward & Mary Whitt Born 10th July 1734 Bap^t 11th august.

John Son of William & Sarah Westbrook Born 4th May 1733 Bap^t July 15th.

Henry Son of Richard & Mary Walthall Born 16th May 1733 Bap^t July 13th.

Daniel Son of francis & Martha Walthall Born 8th march 1732 Bap^t July 13.

Freeman Son of David & Mary Walker Born 3d September 1734 Baptizd ye 9th.

Betty female Slave of Ditto Born ye 15th October 1734.

John Son of Robert & Eliz: Williams Born July 27th 1734.

Martha D. of David and Sarah Williams Born 22d March 1734 Bap^t 4 May 1735.

James S of Henry & Martha Willson Born 19. Decemb^r 1734 Bap^t 9 January.

Mary D. of William and Sarah Westbrook Born 3d January. 1734-5.

Ephraim S. of Robert & Temperance West Born 4th Sep^t 1734.

David S. of Thomas & Francis Walker Born Sep^t 23d 1734.

Gerrald S. of John and Mary Winingham Born ye 1st August. 1734 Baptizd 13th Octo.

Thomas S. of John & Elizabeth Whitmore Born 4th Aprill 1734.

Edward S. of Langsdown & Elizabeth. Washington Born the 18th Octob^r 1734.

Margerett D. of Barnabas and Joyce Wells Born ye 1 Decr 1734.

Jane D. of Abraham & Amy Wells Born 23d Sep^t 1735.

Anne D. of Adam and Eleanor Wells Born 6th Octob^r 1735.

Joseph Son of Susanna Wright born 3d Feb^ry 1734.

Jeremiah Son of David & Sarah Wells Born ye 16. Decr 1735.

Jonathan S of Jonathan & Elisabeth Webster Born ye 11 D November 1740.

Anne D of Henry & Martha Wilson Born ye 10 of Febuary 1740.

Francise D of William & Francise Wells Born y[e] 4th of April 1741.
Deury s of Adam & Elener Wells Born y[e] 4 May 1741.
Roland s of Thomas & Jane Williams Born July y[e] 19 1739.
Jane D. of Thomas & Jane Williams Born June y[e] 12 1741.
Tho[s] S. of Robert & Ann Whitehall B December 17th 1738.
Robert S of Robert & Temperance West B Septem[r] 17th 1740.
John S. of Joseph & Martha Worsham B October 3d 1740.
Robert Hicks Son of Joseph & Sib Westmorland B Sep[r] 16th 1740.
Joseph S of Thomas & Margaret Westmorland B Nov[r] 16th 1740.
William S of Miles & Elisabeth Wootten B Feb[ry] y[e] 14th 1740.
Mary D. of Martin & Anne Wilkisons Born Octob 28th 1741 & Bap[t] Nov[r] 22d 1741.
Drusilla D. of Charles & Priscilla Williamsons, Born Nov[r] 12th 1741 & Bap[t] Dec[r] 27th 1741.
Margret D. of Robert & Francis Wines Born Oct. 25th 1741 & Bap[t] Jan[ry] 17th 1741-2.
John S. of Thomas & Francis Wilsons Born Dec[r] 5th 1741 & Bap[t] Dec[r] 19th 1741.
John S. of Robert & Sara Weeds Born Dec[r] 10th 1741 & Bap[t] Feb[y] 28th 1741-2.
Martha D. of Joshua & Martha Walls Born Aug. 23d 1741 & Bap[t] Apr. 11th 1742.
Amy D. of Robert & Anne Whitehalls Born June 7th 1742 & Bap[t] July 4th 1742.
Daniel S. of Joshua & Martha Worshams Born Apr 29th 1742 & Bap[t] July 4th 1742.
Susanna D. of Francis & Elizabeth Wyats Born June 15th 1742 & Bap[t] July 25th 1742.
Elimelech S. of John & Anne Wilsons Born Apr. 18th 1742 & Bap[t] Aug. 10th 1742.
Edward S. of Edward & Mary Winfields Born July 2d 1742 & Bap[t] Sep[tr] 19th 1742.
Edward S. of Thomas & Elizabeth Woodliths born Nov[r] 9th 1742 & bapt[d] Dec[r] 12th 1742.
Anne D. of John & Elizabeth Wests born Nov[r] 5th & bapt[d] Dec[r] 19th 1742.

William S. of Edward & Mary Wheats born Aug 12th 1742 & baptd Decr 25th 1742.

Henry S. of Henry & Mary Wilkasons born Febry 26th 1742–3 & baptd May 22 1743.

William S. of William & Mary Williams born Aug. 30th 1743 & baptd Octobr 9th 1743.

Isham S. of William & Francis Wells born Aug 4th 1743 & baptd Octob 9th 1743.

Sarah D. of Adam & Helenor Wells born Febry 18th 1742–3.

Thomas S. of Thomas & Jane Williams born Octobr 24th 1743 & baptd Decr 18th 1743.

Winnifred a female slave belonging to Willm Wells born Feb 5th 1743–4 baptd May 14th 1744.

Amie a female slave belonging to Ditto born Janr 9th 1743–4 baptd May 14th 1744.

Henry S. of Adam & Eleanor Wells born Feb 5th & baptd March 15th 1744–5.

Hannah D. of Edward & Mary Winfields born Decr 12th 1744 baptd March 3d 1744–5.

Mary D. of James & Elizabeth Wortham born Decr 13th 1744.

Thomas S. of William & Mary Williams born Decr 27th 1744 baptd March 24th 1744–5.

Mason D. of Robert & Frances Wynnes was born May 29th & baptd Septr 1st 1745.

Agnes D. of Henry & Mary Wilkisons was born Septr 8th baptd Oct 1745.

Katharine D. of Henry & Martha Wilsons born Octobr 24th & baptd Novr 1745.

Millison D. of James & Jane Williams was born Decr 3d 1745 & baptd Janry 6th 1745–6.

Mary D. of Joshua & Martha Worshams was born Novr 4th 1745 & baptd March 2d 1745–6.

Lucy D. of Thomas & Jane Williams was born Janry 2d 1745–6 baptd March 16th 1745–6.

Sarah D. of Mr. Anthony & Anne Walke was born Feb. 16th 1744–5.

Ben	Negroes belonging	Septr 1744	baptd Ap.
Peter Mason	to Ditto born	Decr 6th 1745	2. 1746.

Sloman S. of Joshua & Lucretia Wynne was born Octob. 13th 1745 bapt[d] Feb. 16 1745-6.

Mary D. of Arthur & Alice Wyatts was born Jan[ry] 24th & bapt[d] Feb 23d 1745-6.

Pattie D. of Adam & Eleanor Wells was born Ap. 6th bapt[d] May 19th 1746.

Thomas S of Thomas & Francis Wilson was born March 30th & bapt[d] June 1st 1746.

Robert S of Mr. Antony & Anne Walkes was born Aug. 16th & baptized Sep[t] 1747.

Antony S of Ditto departed this Life Sept[r] 1747.

Neptune a negro boy born Dec[r] 24th 1747 } belonging to Mr.
Bristol born May 1748 } Anthony Walke.

Sarah D of Arthur & Alice Watts was born Jan[ry] 24th 1748.

Richard Son of Richard & Hannah Wells born 17th February 1747-8.

Randolph Son of Adam and Elanor Wells born 15th Feb[y] 1749.

Eliz[a] Daughter of James & Jane Williams Born 21st April 1752.

Frederick Son of ditto Born October 24th 1749.

Joshua Son of Ditto Born ——.

Hannah Daughter of Miles & Martha Williams born June 7th 1752.

Edward Son of Arthur & Alice Watts born April 20th 1753.

Jo[s] Walkers Register.

Gollorthun Walker son of Joseph & Penelope Walker was born Sep[r] y[e] 10th 1745.

Reubin Walker their son was Born march the 20th 1751.

Penelope their Daughter was Born Augus[t] the 3d 1753.

Pattey their Daughter was Born Novem[r] the 19th 1755.

Lettisha their Daughter was Born Feb[r] the 9th 1758.

Martin their son was Born Nov[r] the 16th 1759.

Jean Woolfolk, Wife of Fracis Woolfolk, of Sussex County, died March 21st, & was buried April 6th 1792.

John, Son of Ludwell Williams (of Sussex) & Johannah his Wife, born March 25th 1792.

Sally Allen Dau[r] of John Winn (of Sussex) & Katy his Wife, born Jan[y] 8th & bap: May 13th 1792.

Martha, Dau[r] of Edmund Weathers (of Sussex) & Mary his Wife, born Mar: 18th & bap. May 13th 1792.

William Baird, S, of Joseph Westmore and Elizabeth his Wife, born November 10th 1791 and baptized August 21st 1792.

Henry, S, of Wm Worsham & Clarissa his Wife, born August 17tn 1791 & baptized Dec[r] 28th 1792.

Y

Edw: son of Edw: & Mary Yeans born 5th Jan[r] last bap[t] 14th Aprill 1723.

John: son of Edw[d] & Mary Yanes born 2d July last: bap[t] 26 sep[t] 1725.

Eliz[a] D of Edward and Mary Yeans Born 6th May 1727 Bap[t] oct[m] 1th.

Thomas Son of Edward and Mary Yanes Born 7th feb[r] 1728 Bap[t] novm 23d.

Jane D of John and Sarah York Born 7th Sep[r] 1729.

Francis Cadet Son of Micael cadet and Temperance young Born 25th octb[r] 1731 Bap[t] 25th Dcer.

Martha dat[r] of Jn[o] & Sarah York born 3d June 1732 bap' Aug[t] 13th 1732.

Josiah Son of Edward & Mary yanes Born 17th June 1733 Bap[t] 8th Sep[r] 1733.

John Son of Sam[l] & Judith young Born 10th Sep[r] 1733 Bap[t] Jan[r] 27th.

Sarah D. of John and Sarah York born 17th Feb[ry] 1734 Baptizd 4th May 1735.

James Smith The son of William & Dianer Yarbrough was Born Sep[r] y[e] 2d 1745.

Richard son of Ditto was Born March y[e] 18 1747-8.

Eliz[th] Daughter of Ditto was Born October y[e] 23 1750.

William son of Ditto was Born April y[e] 7th 1753.

Ozwell son of Ditto was Born april 24 1756.

Joseph son of Ditto was Born November y[e] 4 1758.

Ruth Their Negro Girl slave was born Jan[r] y[e] 15 1751.

Marsilva their Negro Girl slave was Born March 22d 1753.

Anthoney their Negro Boy was born March the 1st 1763.

Sukey their Negro Girl was Born January the 31 1766.

Dianer, Wife of William Yarbrough departed this life, may the 18th 1767 aged 42 years.

Tom a Male slave Belonging To William Yarbrough was born may the 3d 1768.

Nanny a Negro Girl belonging to William Yarbrough was Born February the 13th 1769.

Henry. S. of Henry Young & Winney his Wife, of Bath Parish, Dinwiddie, born May 3d and baptized September 17th 1792.

INDEX

Abbet, Agnis 3; John 3; William 3
Abernartha, Mary 2; Robt. 2
Abernarthy, Amy 3; Eliz. 2; Mary 2, 3; Robert 2, 3
Abernathy, Mary 1; Robt. 1
Aberneathys, Frederick 4; John 4; Lucy 4
Abernethys, Charles 4; Ellis 4; Robert 4; Sara 4; William 4
Abernothy, Ann 3; David 3; Lucy 3
Abertnartna, John 2
Abertnarthy, David 2; Eliza. 2; Mary 2; Robt. 2
Abernothy, Ann 3; David; Lucy 3
Adaman, Mary 1; Tho. 1; Wm. 1
Adams, Catherine 2; John 2; Mary 4; Samuel 4; Sarah 2; Thomas 4
Addison, Ann 1, 2; Anne 2; Christophar 2; Christopher 3; Mary 2, 3; Tho. 1; Thomas 2; Winifred 3
Adkins, Binns 4; Howell 4; Susannah 4
Aldridg, Elisabeth 3; Mary 3; Peter 3
Aldridge, Mary 4; Mille 4; Peter 4
Aldrige, Elizabeth 4; Ellis 4; Peter 4; William 4
Alexander, John 3; Martha 3; Robert 3
Alle, Abraham 2; Mary 2; Winefritt 2
Allen, Abra 1; Abraham 3; Drury 1; Eleonore 3; Elizabeth 4; Elkana 2; Lucey 3; Martha 4; Mary 1, 3; Miles 3; Sarah 2; Wm. 2
Allens, Abram 4; Mary 4; Mason 4
Alley, Abigail 4; Abra 1; Ann 1; Drury 4; Hen. 1; Mary 1; Shade 4; Sukey 4; Tally 1; Winifreid 4
Allfriend, William 96
Allin, Elcanah 2; Sarah 2
Anderson, Amey 3; Clyborn 3; Eliza. 2; Elisabeth 3; Elizabeth 3; Henry 2, 3; James 3; Jane 3; John 3; Ruth 3
Andersons, David 4; James 4; Jean 4; William 4
Andrews, Amy 1; Ann 2; Avice 2; Avis 1, 2; Eliz. 2; Ephraim 1; Fran 1; Geo. 1; Henry 2; Isham 1; Jane 1, 2; Jean 2; John 2; Luciana 2; Martha 2; Mary 1, 2, 3; Pheboe 3; Rich 1, 2; Richard 2; Richd. 3; Tho. 1, 2; Winifred 1; Wm. 1, 2
Archer, Alce 3; Alice 3; Ann 2, 3; Anne 1; Elisabeth 3; Field 3; Fran. 1; Frances 2; Frederick 3; Geo. 1, 3; George 1, 2, 3; Jean 3; Judith 1; Mary 1, 2, 3; Phebe 3; Richard 3; Sarah 2; Tabitha 3; Thomas 3; William 2; Wm. 1, 2, 3; William 4
Archers, Mary 4; Richard 3; Roger 3; Sara 4; Tabitha 3; William 3, 4
Atkerson, Roger 4
Atkinsons, Elizabeth 3; John 3; Mary 3
Aycock, Elizabeth 4; Mary 4; Richard 4

Backly, Ann 7; Ester 7; Tho. 7
Baird, John 19; John Bate 19; Polly 19
Baldin, Elisabeth 12; Phebe 12; William 12
Baley, Amy 9; Avis 13; George 9; Henry 7, 8, 9, 13; Martha 13
Balie, Avis 8; Henry 7, 8, 13; John 8
Baly, Ann 7; Avice 11; George 7; Henry 7, 11; William 11
Banister, John 11, 13; Martha 11; Willmuth 13; Wilmet 11
Bankes, James 7; Mary 7; Wm. 7
Banks, Cha. 5; Jam. 6; James 5; Mary 5, 6; Prissilla 6; Sarah 5; Vide 5; Wm. 7
Barber, Abigail 6; Agnis 5, 6, 8, 9, 11; Amy 9; Ann 8; John 6; Rich. 5, 6; Richard 9, 11; Ruth 5, 6
Bardin, Patrick 7; Randolph 7; Rose 7
Barker, Mary Chambless 20; Nathaniel 20; Sally 20
Barnes, Elizabeth 19; James 19; Rebeccah 19
Barten, Lettis 11; Robert 11; William 11
Barret, Mary 9; David 9
Bartlet, Catharine 10; Eliza. 10; Sam 10; William 11
Barttlet, Cattorn 11; Samuel 11; William 11
Batt, Mary 5; Tho. 5; Wm. 5
Batte, Ann 9; Frances 20; John 9; Mary 8, 9; Mary Anne Jones 20; Robert 8; Sarah 19; Thomas 20; William 19; Wm. 8, 9
Batts, Agnes 15, 16; Henry 16; Mary 15; William 16; Wm. 5, 8
Baugh, Elisabeth 12; Eliz. 5, 6, 7; Francis 12; Ja. 6; James 13; Jno. 7; John 12; Luis 7; Margrett 13; Martha 13, 21; Mary Johnson 21; Peter 5; Robert 21; William 13; Wm. 6
Baughs, Adam 15; Ann 17; Anne 15; James 15, 17; John 15; Martha 15, 16; Mary 15; Phebe 16; Thomas 15, 16; Wm. 17
Baxter, James 19; John 19; Patsey 19
Baxters, James 14; Mary 14; William 14
Beavil, Ann 9; John 8, 11; Joseph 9; Lucy 8; Mary 8, 11; Robt. 9; Susanna 11
Beck, Amy 8; Andrew 5, 7, 8, 10; Eliz. 5, 7, 10; Eliza. 10; Jno. 10; John 5; Mary 5, 7; Moses 5, 7
Becks, Charles 15, Joseph 14, 15; Mary 14, 15; Phoebe 14
Beckwith, Ann 13; Charles 15; Henry 13, 15; Nehemiah 13
Belcher, Edward 8; Elisabeth 12; Eliza. 11; George 10, 11; George 12; Mary 5, 8, 10; Robert 11; Tho. 5; William 12; Wm. 5, 8, 10
Belchers, George 14; Lucy 14; Mary 14
Belchair, George 13; Lucy 13; Woody 13
Belsher, Mary 5; Wm. 5
Bentley, John 9; Mary 9; Sarah 9
Bently, Jno. 10, 12; Mary 10, 12; Maryellis 12; Sarah 10
Benton, David 8; Lasurous 8; Winfrit 8
Benwood, Amy 20; Joseph 20; Mary-Anne 20
Berrys, Anne 15; Betty 15; Henry 15
Berten, Abram 8; Lazarus 8; Winefred 8
Bevel, John 12; Martha 12; Mary 12
Bevell, Ann 5, 6, 11; Frances 11; James 5, 6; Robt. 5, 6, 11
Bevill, Ann 7; Robert 7; Wm. 7
Bickwiths, Anne 14; Henry 14; Thomas 14
Biggins, Anne 13; Arthur 16; Elizabeth 13, 15, 16; Lucretia 15; Richard 13, 15, 16
Bingham, John 20; Mary 20; William 20
Birchet, Agnis 5; Drury 17, 19; Edw. 5, 7; Edward 19; Frances 17; Jam 7; John 17; Margret 5; Sarah 19; Theoderick 19
Birchets, Edward 14; Frances 15; Jane 14, 15; Robert 14, 15; William 15
Birchett, Agness 18; Clarissa 31; Daniel 19; David 17; Drurey 18; Edward 19; Edward Junr. 17; Elizth. 18, 19; Ephraim 18; Henry 18; Margaret 6; Peter 17; Robert 20; Sara 18; Sarah 17, 19; William 18
Birchetts, Jane 17, 18; John 17; Martha 18; Robt. 17, 18
Bird, Elizabeth 19; Martha 19; Richard 19; Robt. 19
Blackman, Abraham 13; John 12;

Lucy 12; Suffiah 12
Blackmans, John 16; Sophia 16; Wood 16
Blackmun, Abraham 13; John 13; Sephirah 13
Blackston, Jno. 8; Mary 8; Wm. 8
Blackstone, John 1 3; Mary 13
Blackwell, Anne 20; John 20; Martha 20
Blanchet, Eliza. 9, 12; John 9, 12; Tho. 9; William 12
Bland, Ann 17; Anna Buck 20; Elizabeth 14, 17; Frances 17, 18; Jane 17; John 20, 21; Mary 17, 20; Theod. 18; Theodk. 17
Blands, Francis 14; Theoderick 14
Blaton, Mary 8; Sarah 8
Blaxton, Mary 10; Jno. 10; Rice 10
Blick, Benja. 6, 7; Benjamin 13; Eliz. 6; Elisa. 7; Elizabeth 13; John 7; John junr. 20; Martha 13; Patrick 20; Sarah 20
Blicks, Benjamin 18; Jane 18
Bly, Mary 7, 10; Sarah 7, 10
Bobbitt, Eliza. 10; Liewes 10; Miles 10
Boilsys, John 16; Peter 16; Susanna 16
Boiseau, Anner 18; Daniel 18; James 18
Boisseau, Benja. 18; Eliz. 13; James 13, 17; Jams. 13; John 17; Mary 13, 17, 18; Molley Hold 18; Sarah 13
Boisseaus, James 13; Mary 13; Susanna 13
Bolling, Anne 4, 7; Catharine 20, 21; Lucy 21; Mason 7; Rebecca 20; Rebecah 20; Robt. 4, 7, 20; Robert 20; Robert Stith 20; Seigniora 20, 21; Thomas 21; Thos. T. 20; Yelverton de Mallet 21
Bollings, Alexander 17; George 14; Jane 14; Robert 17; Susannah 17
Bonar, Jesse 21
Bonners, Isham 14; Susanna 14; Thomas 14
Booker, Margaret 19; Mary 19; Mary Brooks 20; Richard 19, 20
Booth, Amie 8; Dorcorrs 8; Tho. 8
Bott, Anne 6; Elisabeth 12; Eliz. 5, 6; Miles 12; Tho. 5, 6; Thomas 12
Bowen, Amy 9, 10; Avis 9, 10; David 10; Ephraim 10; Lucie 9; Robert 9; Robt. 10; William 9; Wm. 9, 10
Bowman, Eliza. 8, 10; Elizabeth 12; Peter 12; Robert 8; Wm. 8, 10, 12
Bowyon, Amy 13; Jesse 13; Wm. 13
Bracy, Eliz. 7; Eliza. 7, 11; Francis 7, 11; Thomas 11
Bradshaw, Ann 7, 10; Anne 6, 7; Benja. 10; Gower 7; Jno. 10; John 6, 7; Wm. 6
Bradsho, Ann 8, 9; Eliz. 8; John 8, 9; Phebe 9
Brag, Eliza 7, 9; Hugh 7, 9; Mary 7, 9
Bragg, Hugh 5, 8; Joel 8; Mary 5, 8; Wm. 5
Brandom, Mary 15; Charles 15; John 15
Brandon, Aaron 19; Elizth. 19; Gabril 19; John 19; Judith 19; Mary 19; Peter 19
Brasey, Elisabeth 13; Francis 13; Samel. 13
Brawdiway, Edward 8; Mary 8; Sarah 12; Thos. 12
Bressie, Eliza. 10; Francis 10; Mary 10
Brewer, James 12; Joseph 7; Letisia 12; Margarit 7; Mary 7; Peter 12
Brice, Margarett 19; Molley 19; Nancy 19; Wm. 19
Broadie, — 21
Broadway, Edm. 6; John 6; Letitia 6; Mary 6; Tho. 6; Wm. 6
Brockwell, Betsey 20; Jemimah 20; Thomas 20
Brodnax, Ann 16; William 16
Brooks, Amy 11; Ann 6, 7, 9, 12; Anne 10, 11; Geo. 6; George 7, 9, 12; John 9; Martha 7, 9; Tho. 6; Thomas 10, 11; Thos. 9, 12
Brouder, Eliz. 12; George 12; Joseph 14; Presilia 12; Winnie 14
Browder, Amy 11; Anne 12; Dorothy 8, 11; Edmond 7, 8; Eliz. 6, 12; Eliza. 7, 9, 11; Elizabeth 9; George 7, 9, 11; Handstess 7; James 7; Jeane 9; John 6, 11, 12; Martha 7, 8; Mary 7, 9; Presilia 12; Sarah 8; William 8, 11; Wm. 6, 8
Browders, Elizabeth 14; Frederick 16; George 14; John 14, 16; Joseph 14; Margret 15; Margt. 16; Mary 14, 16; Mason 14; Susanna 16; William 16; Winnie 14
Brown, Anne 5; Betty 16, 17; Boswell 17; Burwell 14, 17; Eliz. 5; Elizabeth 17, 81; Jesse 17; John 5; Mary 81; Rebeckah 17; Rich. 5; Sarah 16; William 17, 81; Wm. 5; Noah 17
Browns, Burwell 14; Elizabeth 14, 16; Francis 14; Noah 16; Thomas 14; William 14
Broyely, Jno. 6; Prud 6; Rebeca 6
Bruce, Hannah 16; James 16; Margaret 16
Bryally, Dorithy 8; John 8; Rebekah 8
Bryan, Mary 8; Tho. 8; Wm. 8
Bryerly, Jo. 5; Rebecca 5; Wm. 5
Buchanan, David 19; Silias Dunlop 19
Bugg, John 10; Mary 10; Wm. 10
Bullock, Bersheba Chiswell 8; Eliza. 8; Frances 8; Ishmail 8
Bundy, Constance 15; Mary 15; Richard 15
Burch, Jane 5, 9; John 5; Martha 9; Rich. 5; Richard 9
Burchet, Abraham 9; Drury 19; Edw. 6, 7; Edward 9; Jam 7; Margret 9; Mary 6; Susanna 19; Wm. 5
Burchett, Drury 24; Edwd. 24; Mary 24
Burchetts, James 18; Jane 18; Robert 18
Burg, Frances 9; John 9
Burge, Alexander 16; Constant 16; Frederick 15; Mary 5, 16; Richard 16; Tho. 5; Thomas 16; William 16
Burges, Francis 14; Frederick 13; John 14; Mary 13, 15; Thomas 13, 15; Woodie 15
Burn, David 11; Frances 11
Burnet, Debora 13; Joyce 13; Richard 13
Burow, Catherine 11; James 11; Mary 11
Burreys, Anne 14; Joseph 14; Mary 14
Burrough, Henry 9; Johannah 9; John 9
Burrow, Elizabeth 13; William 13
Burrows, Anne 14; Catharine 14; James 14; Martha 13; Mary 16; Nathanael 16; Patty 16; Philip 13
Bursby, Anne 7; Eliza. 9; Martha 7, 9; Simon 7, 9
Burton, Abra. 8, 11; Abraham 7, 8, 9; Ann 10; Catherine 7; Charles 12; Eliz. 7; Fras. 10; Henry 12; Jno. 10; John 7, 8, 12; Lovedy 12; Martha 10; Mary 7, 8, 9, 11; Phebe 9; Rachell 12; Robert 11; Robt. 10; Samuel 7; Sarah 8, 10, 12
Busby, Drury 10; Martha 10; Miles 10; Simon 10
Butler, Ann 9, 10, 12, 19; Betsey 21; Dionicia 20; Eliza. 10; Elizabeth 11; Elizth 18; Fanny 19; James 12; Jno. 10; John 9, 10, 12, 13, 18; Joseph 19; Margaret 13; Margrett 13; Martha 10, 13; Mary 18; Peter 11; Sarah 10, 13, 18; Sion 20; Sterling 20; Thomas 13; William 10, 11, 13, 18; Wm. 13
Butlers, Anne 15; Elizabeth 14, 15; Jesse 14; John 15; Joseph 15; Margret 14; William 14, 15
Butterworth, Ann 6; Cha. 6; Nico. 6
Butterworths, Charles 15, 16; Elizabeth 15, 16; Mary 16
Byrg, Eliza. 9; Frances 9; John 9
Byrge, Frances 8; John 8; Richd 8

Call, Hellen 29; Richard Keith 29; William junr. 29
Cameron, Anne Owen 29; John 29
Cannell, Moses 22; Katharine 22; Robt. 22
Cargell, Cornelias 23; Eliza. Daniell 23; William 23
Caries, Judith 26; Mary 26; William 26
Carlile, Eliz. 22; Kasiah 22; Mary 21, 22; Nath. 21; Rich. 21, 22
Carliles, Elizabeth 27; John 27; Richard 27
Carnill, Daniel 24; George 24; Sandilla 24
Caudle, Eliz. 22; Jno. 22; Mary 22, 23; Tho. 22
Cavanist, George 26; Mary 26
Cawdle, David 24; Jno. 24, 25; Mary 24, 25
Chalmers, Francis 27; Henry 27; Silvia 27
Chambles, Frances 27; Francise 26; Henry 26; John 27; Joshua 26; Sarah 27
Chamles, Elizabeth 27; James 27; John 27

Chamlis, Henry 25; Frances 25; Mary 25
Chandler, Abraham 26; Eliza. 25; Elizabeth 26; Isaac 25; William 25, 26
Chaple, Eliza. 24; Robt. 24
Chapman, Cha. 22; Fran. 22; John 22; Sarah 22
Chappell, [A]braham 23; Anne 21; Eliza. 23; Mary 21; Robt. 21, 23
Cheatham, George 28; Nelly 28; Walker 28
Cheaves, Jno. 25; Mary 25; Thos. 25
Cheeves, Elizabeth 27; Jemina 27; Mary 27; Sarah 27; Tabitha 27; Thomas 27; Thos. 27
Cheives, Mary 26; Susannah 26; Thos. 26
Chevers, Anne 27; John 27
Cheves, Elizabeth 27; Jemina 27; Mary 26, 27; Thomas 27; William 26
Childers, Agnis 25; Robert 25; Susana 25
Childres, Agnis 26; John 26; Robert 26
Childs, Peter 23; Walter 23
Chisnall, Alexander 24; Mary 24
Chiswell, Bersheba 8
Christian, Anne 28; Lucy Grice 28; Richard 28
Christians, James 26; Mary 26
Claibornes, Burnell 27; Hannah 27; Martha 27
Clark, Daniel 26; Elisabeth 26; John 26; Margret 26
Clarke, Bolling 27; Phebe 27; William 27
Clarkes, Elizabeth 27; Joseph 27; William 27
Clay, Amy 22; Charles 25; John 25; Mary 25; Tho. 22
Clayton, Isham 25; John 25; Sarah 25
Clemans, Martha 27; Thomas 27
Clements, James 29; John 28; Mary 28; William 28
Clemmonds, Freeman 26; Lockie 27; Martha 25, 26, 27; Rebeckah 25; Robert 27; Thomas 25, 26, 27
Clemonds, John 27, 28; Joshua 28; Martha 28; Mary 27, 28; Prissilla 27; Thos. 28
Clemonds, Elith. 28; John 28; Margret 28; Mary 28
Clensy, Anne 25; Cornelias 25; Sarah 25
Coalman, Anne 24; Daniel 23, 24; Eliza. 23, 24, 25; Francis 26; Jno. 23; John 24; Margaret 24, 25; Margery 25; Martha 23, 24; Mary 23, 24, 26; Maryligon 24; Sarah 23, 24, 25; Warner 25; William 24, 25, 26; Wm. 23, 24
Cobb, Oather 24; Robt. 24
Cock, Abraham 24; Mary 24
Colbreth, Affa 26; Evin 26; Martha 26
Cole, Anne 28; William 28
Coleman, Amy 22; Benja. 23; Dan. 23; Eliz. 23, 26; Faith 21, 22; Fran. 21, 22;; John 21; Joseph 26; Mary 21, 22; Peter 21, 22; Sarah 25; William 26; Wm. 21, 22, 25
Colvill, Anne 21; Edw. 21; Tabitha 21
Cook, Dinah 23; Eliz. 21, 22; Eliza. 23; Frederick 26; Henry 28; Jean 28; Jno. 23; Nickols 24; Peter-Hannor 21; Rich. 21, 22; Richd. 23; [Ric]hard 23; Richard 28; Robert 26; Robt. 23, 24; Ruth 22; Sarah 23; Winiford 23; Winifrid 26; Winnifred 24
Cooke, Benjamin 27; Elizabeth 27; Frances 27
Corbin, Elizabeth 28; Rosey 28; William 28
Cordle, John 23, 25; Lucretia 23; Mary 23, 25; Sarah 25
Cotton, Becky 60; Celah 60; John 60
Couch, Eliza. 23; Matthew 23; Tho. 23
Cousens, Cha. 21; Geo. 21; Margery 21
Cousins, Anne 24; Charles 24; Margry 24
Covington, Catharine 25; Mary 25; Thomas 25
Cox, Elizabeth 28; Ellinor 28; George 26; John 26; Lucretia 26; Saml. 28; Sarah 26
Coxs, Benjamin 27; Francis 27; Mary 27
Coziear, Dunnim 26; Elizabeth 26; John 26
Crecher, Agnis 22; Hannah 22; Millesin 22; Mourning 22; Titus 22
Crew, David 23; Hannah 23; Samuel 23
Crews, Ann 23, 29; Joseph 29; Samuell 23
Cristwell, Barsheba 21; Luis 21; Margaret 21
Crook, Eliza. 24; George 24; James 24; Joseph 24; Martha 24, 26; Mary 24; Solomon 26; Tabitha 24
Crouder, Jno. 25; John 25; Mary 25
Cross, Ann Ford 26; Martha Holy 26
Crowder, Abra. 23, 26; Abraham 23, 24, 26; Amy 23; Barth 22; Bartho. 21; Batho. 23; Batholomiew 23; David 26; Eliz. 21, 22; Eliza. 23; Febe 23; Fran. 23; Frances 23, 24, 26; [G]eorge 23; Hen. 22; Henry 23; [Hen]ry 23; John 24, 26; Joseph 26; Mary 22, 24, 26; Rich 22; Thomas 24; William 26; Wm. 22
Cureton, Charles 28; Fra. 22; Fran. 22; Frances 23; Frans. 28; Jno. 22, 23; John 23, 28; Louisey 28; Winefred 28; Winifred 28; Winneford 28
Curiton, Eliza. 23; Frances 23; Francis 24; Jno. 24; John 23, 24
Curtis, Elliner 23; John 23

Davis, Elizth. 29; Martha 29; Mary 29; Maxey 29; Polly Baugh 29; Samuel 29; Sarah 29; Shepherd 29; Thomas Jones 29; William 29; Wm. 29
Day, James 30; Levina 30; Lucy Ann Kimbow 30
Denton, John 29; John Creach 29; Margaret 29; Rebeccah Hathorn 29
Dodson, Aggy Franklin 29; Mary 29; William 29
Doram, Jane 23; Patrick 23; Wm. 23
Dun, Jean 29; Lewis Burwell 29; Lucy 29; Mary 29; Thomas 29; William 29
Durand, Mary 29

Edgar, Elizabeth 69; Jane 69; William 69
Edwards, Eliz. 22; John 22; Lewis 30; Mary 30; Mary Danforth 30
Eppes, John 30; Lucretia 30; Richard 30; Susanna 30
Ezell, Buckner 30; Elizabeth 30; Richard 30

Featherstone, Edward 31; Lucy 31; Martha Edwards 31; Sarah 31
Feild, James 31
Fenn, Daniel Baugh 31; Joel 31; Mary 31; Richard 31
Feranondo, Benja. 30; Mary 30
Fernando, Ann 30; Benja. 30; Mary 30
Fernendo, Sarah 30
Fin, Fras. 30; Joel 30; Rosey 30; Sarah 30
Finn, David 30; Frans. 30; Fras. Lisenburg 30; Sarah 30; Thoms. Francis 30
Fisher, Daniel 30; Elizabeth 30; John K. 30
Fitz-Gareld, Anne 35; John 35
Fowler, Marke 64; Mary 64; Matthew 64
Fraser, Ann Laughton 30; Ann Loughton 31; Elizabeth 30; Maria Deas 31; Simon 30; Simon 31; Thomas 31

Galbreaths, Angus 36; Barbara 36; Daniel 36; Duncan 36; Isabel 36; Katharine 36; Margret 36; Mary 36; William 36
Gamliin, Mary 33; Wm. 33
Garratt, Abraham 34; John 34; Susan 34; Susannah 34; Thomas 34
Garret, Anne 31; John 31, 32, 35; Stephen 35; Susan 35; Susanna 32
Garrot, Isack 33; Jno. 33; John 33; Susan 33; Susannah 33
Gary, Elizabeth 37; John 36; Nancy Harrison 37; Josiah 37; Mary 37; Richard 36, 37; Sarah 37
Garys, Elizabeth D. 36; Hannah 36; Richard 36
Gates, Edward 33; Mary 35; Susanna 35; Susannah 33; William 35; Wm. 33
Geddy, Elizabeth Kid 37; Euphan 37; James junr. 37
Gee, Charles 37; Susanna 37; Susannah 37; Thomas 37
Gees, Charles 36; John 36; Mary 36; Sarah 36
Gent, Abra 32; Anne 31; Jane 36; James Williams 36; Mary 31, 32; Moses 32; Tho. 32; Wm. 31, 32
Geralds, Anne 36; John 36
Ghents, Mary 36; Thomas 36
Gibbs, Ann 32; Corns. 34; Eliz. 31; John 31, 32, 34, 35, 36, 37;

Lucey 35; Lucie 34; Martha 36, 37; Mary 31, 32, 34, 35; Mathew 34; Pattie 36; Phebe 34; Richd. 34; Susanna 34; Thos. 34; William 36
Gibs, Agnis 33; John 33; Mary 33; Susannah 33
Gill, Amy 33; Ann 32; Eliz. 32; Erasmus 37; Joss 32; Lucy Jones 37; Martha 31, 33; Sarah 37; Stephen 31, 33; Wm. 31
Gillam, Ann 32; Eliz. 32; Frances 31; Harris 31; Jno. 32; Rebecca 31
Gilliam, Amie 33; Ann 33, 35; Charles 34, 35; Christian 37; Eliza 33, 34; Elizabeth 37; Frances 34, 35; Francis 33, 34, 35; Harris 33, 34, 35; James 35; John 33, 35, 37; Josiah 34; Joshua 35; Lucy 33; William 37
Gilliams, Elizabeth 36; John 36; William 36
Gillom, Fran. 32; Harris 32; Wm. 32
Glas, Joshua 34; Sarah 34
Glascock, John 31; Rachel 31; Robt. 31
Glass, Eliza. 33; John 33; Joshua 33, 34; Mary 34; Sarah 33, 34
Glidewell, Eliza. 33, 35; Robt. 33; Susan 33; Tarance lamb 35
Glidwell, Eliz. 31; Nash 31; Robt. 31
Gloydwells, Martha 36; Nash 36; Peter 36
Golightly, Hugh 31, 32; Jane 31, 32; Mary 31; Tho. 32
Golikely, Hugh Lee 32; Jno. 32
Goodcy, Elizabeth Cain 37; John 37; Sarah 37; Susannah 37
Goodwin, David 32; Martha 31, 32; Tabitha 31; Tho. 31, 32
Goodwyn, Ann 35; John 35; Matthew 35; Susannah 35
Gower, Ann 33; Eliza. 33; Wm. 33
Gracie, Archibald 36; Hester 36; Sarah Rogers 36
Grainger, Ann 33, 34, 35; Anne 33; Benja. 33; Benjamin 35; Benjamine 34; Edith 35; John 33; Joseph 33
Grammars, Elizabeth 36; Joseph 36
Grammer, John 36; Mary Wright 36; Prisceilla 36
Grammers, Elizabeth 36; Joseph 36; Peter 36
Granger, Ann 34; Benja. 34; Frances 34
Grantham, Delilah Peterson 37; James 37; Jean 37
Gray, Alexr. 35; Ann 35; Mary 35
Green, Abigaell 32; Abigal 33, 34; Abigall 33; Amey 35; Ann 33, 34, 35; Dorcus 33; Eliz. 32; Eliza. 33, 34, 35; Esther 35; Fran. 31; George 33, 34; Hen. 32; Henry 33, 34; Jemima 34; John 32, 33, 34, 35; Johnathan 35; Luis 31, 32; Margret 33; Martha 33, 35; Mary 32, 33; Peter 31, 33; Richard 35; Rosamond 33, 34; Susanna 32; William 35; Winnifred 34
Greens, Burwell, 36; Lewis Burwell 36; Mary 36; William Randolph 36
Gregory, Elizabeth 37; Harriott 37; Jane 35; Lucey 35; Mary 32; Richard 37; Tho. 32, 35
Griffin, John 33; Mary 33, 35; Richard 33, 35; Wm. 35
Griffon, Mary 32; Ralph 32; Rich 32
Grig, Abner 35; Mary 35; Wm. 35
Grigg, Amey 35; Burrell 35; Eliz. 32; Eliza. 33; Fras. 34; Frances 33; Francis 33; James 33, 34; Jessey 35; Peter 34; Susan 32; Wm. 32
Grigory, Eliz. 31, 32; Elizabeth 36; John 32; Nance 31; Richard 36; Tho. 31, 32; Wilson 36
Gunter, John 32; Martha 32, 33; Tho. 32; Thomas 33; Mary 33

Hackney, Frances 41; John 43; Sarah 39, 41, 43; Tho. 39, 41; Thomas 43; Wm. 39
Haddon, Becky 47; Francis 47; Peterson 47
Haddons, Edward 45; Frances 44, 45; Francis 44, 45; Lucy 44; Mary 45
Hair, Ann 46; Daniel 46; James 46; Mary 46; Thomas 46
Hall, Edw. 38; Edwd. 40; Eliz. 38; Eliza. 40, 47; Elizabeth 30, 46; Fran. 40; Frances 38; George 38; Instance 44, 45, 47; Instant 38; James 38, 40, 41; Joel Stirdevent 46; John 38, 41; Judith 38; Mary 38, 45, 46; Mary Herbert Stith 47; Patrick 40; Rich. 38; Ruth 40, 41; Salley 46; Theodrick 40; Tinah 30; William 46; Wm. 38
Halls, Anne 45; John 44, 45; Martha 44, 45
Hamilton, Andrew 47
Hamleton, Ann 41; David 41; Eliza. 41; John 41
Hamlin, Anne 43; Peter 42; Phebe 42, 43; Thomas 43; Thos. 42
Hammond, Eliza. 41; John 41; Ruth 41
Hammons, Eliza. 43; John 43
Hankings, Agnis 40; Jane 40; John 40; Mical 40
Hansell, James 44; John 44; Katharine 44
Hardaway, Ann 45; Anne 46; Benjamin Stith 46; Drury 46; Fras. 42; Frances 39; Franis 43; James 38; Jane 38, 39; Jno. 42; John 42, 43; Joseph 45; Lucey 45; Tho, 38, 39; Thomas 43; Wm. 39
Hardaways, Ainsworth 44; Francis 44; John 44; Keren-Happuch 44
Hardey, John 44; Rachell 44; Richard 44
Hardiway, Agnis 44; Drury 42; Jane 42; Mason 45; Susannah 44; Thomas 42, 44
Hardway, Drurey 45
Harmers, Anne 45; Thomas 45
Harper, George 42; Joseph 42; Susanah 42
Harris, Ann 40, 41; Anne 38, 39; Edward 40; Elizabeth 44; Fras. 42; Geo. 39; Mary 42; Richard 44; Tim. 38; Timoth 39; Timothy 40; Wm. 41, 42
Harrison, Arthur 38; Edmund 46, 47; Elizabeth 46; Gab. 38; Grace 38; Henry 46; Martha Ann 47; Mary 47; Marry Murray 47; Peyton 46
Harrisons, Benjamin 45; Elizabeth 45; Richard 45
Harvey, Elizabeth 45; William 45; Willm. 45
Harwell, Anne 42; Eliza. 40; James 40; Jno. 40, 41; John 40, 42; Jon. 40; Lucainna 40; Rebeckah 40, 41, 42; Sarah 40; Susan 40; Tho. 40; Wm. 41
Harwells, Barbara 45; Elizabeth 44, 45; John 45; Peter 45; Randolph 45; Thomas 44; William 44, 45
Harwoods, Barbara 44; David 44; Elizabeth 44; Mary 44; Peter 44; William 44
Hatcher, John 43; Margret 43; William 43
Hattaway, David 43; Edmund 43; Mary 43
Hatton, Ann 47; Delilah Ann Southall 47; Thomas 47
Haukins, Agnis 40; Edward 42; Joshua 40; Micael 40
Hauks, Jeffry 38; John 38; Sarah 38
Hawkins, Agness 40; Agnis 41; David 40; Drury 42; Edward 42; Eleanor 42; Eliza 41; Hanna 43; Harbud 43; Isham 43; Jane 43; John 43; Lucy 43, 44; Martha 42, 43; Mary 44; Mical 41; Michael 40; Richard 44; Ruth 43; Solomon 43; Thos. Boon 42; William 42; Willm. 43; Wm. 43
Hawks, Abram 44; Christian 45; Frederick 45; John 44, 45; Lucy 44
Heath, Armistead 47; Drury 47; Elle 47; Selah 47; Thomas 47; William Rives 47
Heathcote, Edward 46; Michael 46; Mary 46
Hemans, Eliz. 39; John 39; Mary 39
Herbert, Ann 40; Bullard 39; Buller 40, 42; Frances 41; John 39; Mary 39, 40, 42; Phebe 41; Richard 41
Herringham, Betty 46; Mary 46; Prudence 46; William 46
Heth, Agnes 46; Dolly Agness 46; Dolly Anne 46; Jesse 46; William 46; Williamson Bonner 46
Heylins, Winnifred 44
Hickman, Thomas 43
High, David 40; Eliza. 41; Jno. 40, 41; John 40; Mary 40, 41; Susanah 40; Thomas 41
Hiland, Lucy 47; Robert 47; William 47
Hill, Amy 34, 40, 41; Ann 42; Edward 40, 43; Eliz. 38; Eliza. 40; Frances 40, 41; Franis 43; James 40; John 40, 42; Jno. 41; Liewes 41; Mary 40; Micaell 38; William 34, 41; Wm. 40
Hills, Amie 45; Elizabeth 44; Micall 38; Michael 44; Michal 45; Susanna 44, 45
Hinton, Chris 39; Christ 38; Christophar 41; Christopher 42, 43; James 41; John 38, 39; Marga. 38, 39; Margret 41; Margrit 42, 43; Robert 43;

Tho. 39
Hitchcocks, John 44; Mary 44; Ussery 44
Hobbes, Edwards 44; Mary 44, 45; Sarah 45; William 44; Willm. 45
Hobbs, Benjamin 46; Jesse 45; Mary 45; Molly 46; Sarah 46; William 45
Hobby, Eliz. 39; Johanna 39; Johannah 40; Mary 38; Tho. 38, 39; Thom. 40
Hodges, Anne 43; Eliza. 43; Thomas 43
Homes, Ann 40, 41; Anne 40; Isack 40; Mary 40; Saml. 40; Samuel 40, 41
Hood, Abraham 43; Anne 38; John 40; Jane 38, 39, 40, 43; Johanna 39; Magery 43; Margery 42; Martha 42; Sarah 43; Tho. 38, 39, 40; Thomas 43; William 43; Wm. 39, 42
Hope, Thomas 46
House, James 39; Wm. 39
Huccaby, Ann 39; James 39; Mary 39; Sam 39
Hudson, Anne 42; Benja. 40; Charity Smithis 42; Charles 40; Eliz. 39, 40; Eliza. 40, 42; Elisabeth 43; Frances 42; Hall 39, 40, 43; Heven 39; Isaac 39, 42; James 38, 39, 41, 42; Joakim 43; Joshua 40; Martha 38, 39, 40; Mary 39, 42; Obedience 38; Phebe 38, 39, 41, 42; Rich. 38; Richard 40, 41; Tabitha 40; Tho. 39, 40; Thos. 42; William 42, 44; Wm. 38
Hudsons, Anne 45; Margret 45; Obedience 44; Robert 44, 45; Sina 44
Hulem, Mary 42; Wm. 42
Hulone, Mary 43; William 43
Humphris, Catherine 41; Jane 41; Robert 41
Hunt, Ann Lamboth Davis 45; Rossey 45; Samuel 45
Hye, John 38; Joseph 38; Mary 38

Irby, Joshua 49, 50; Mary Blyth 49; Mary Green 49; William 49; Wm. 49; Wilmoth 50
Ivy, Ann 49; Elisabeth 51; Eliza. 49; Thomas 49, 51

Jackson, Daniel 50, 51; Elisabeth 50; Eliza. 51; Joseph 51; Judith 49; Neptune 49; Thomas 49
Jacob, Tabitha 50; Thomas 50
Jacobs, John 51; Tabitha 51; Thomas 51
James, Eliz. 48; Mary 49; Rich. 48; Richard 49
Jane, Eliza. 51; Joshua 51; Moses 51
Jeffries, Anne 52
Jent, Jane 48; Mary 48; Wm. 48
Jinkins, John Hall 52; Mary 52; William 52
Johnson, Ann 49; Dianah 50; Eliza. 50; Eliz. 48; Elizabeth 52; Grace 39, 48, 49; Hubbard 52; Joan 39, 48; Jno. 50; Johannah 49; John 48; Martin 49; Sarah 52; Tabitha 52; Wm. 39, 48, 49
Johnston, Eliza. 48; John 48
Johnstone, Eliz. 48; Isaac 48; John 48; Wm. 48
Jones, Abra. 47, 49, 51; Abraham 48; Abram 52; Amey 41; Amie 49; Amy 48, 50, 51; Ann 48, 49, 52; Anne 51; Batte 49; Benja. 48; Benjamine 48; Berriman 51; Betty 52; Cadwaller 49; Dan 48; Daniel 51; David 51; Dorithy 49, 50; Dorothy 51, 52; Easter 51; Edw. 48; Eliz. 47; Eliza. 48, 50; Elizabeth 51, 52; Eleonar 49; Frances 48, 49; Francis 48, 50; Frederick 47, 52; Henry 49; Holmes 46; James 50; Jas. 50; John 48, 49, 51, 52; John Holmes 46; Judith 41, 49, 50, 52; Ledbetter 47, 48, 49; Lucy 48, 52; Lucrece 48; Ludwell 42, 50; Margrat 49; Margrett 50, 51; Martha 47, 48, 49; Mary 42, 47, 48, 49, 50, 51; Mordica 51; Nathaniel 50; Pelletiah 49; Peter 47, 48, 49, 50, 51, 52; Philip 48; Phillip 49, 51; Prissilla 48; Pru. 48; Rachel 50; Rebecca 50; Rebeckah 48; Rich. 47, 48; Richard 49, 50; Richarda 50; Richd. 50; Ridlie 49; Ridly 49; Samuell 47; Sarah 47, 48, 49, 51, 52; Susan 48; Susaner 49; Susannah 46; Tho. 47, 48; Thom. 50; Thomas 50, 51; Thos. 52; Ursula 50; William 41, 42, 50, 52; William Junr. 52; Wm. 48, 49, 50
Jordain, Mary 49; Samuel 49, 50
Jordans, Edward 52; Mary 52; Milson 52; Samuel 52

Kally, Mary 53; Wm. 53
Keeth, Cornelias 53; Eliza. 53; John 53; Sam. 53
Keith, James 54
Kelly, Mary 53; Sarah 53; Wm. 53
Kemp, Ann 53; Jane 53; John 53
Kennell, Cath. 53; John 53; Robt. 53
Kennon, Agnis 52, 53, 54; Ann 53; Anne 53; Eliz. 52; Fran. 53; Hen. Isham 53; John 53; Martha 54; Mary 53; Rich. 52, 53; Richard 54; Richd. 53; Robert 53; Wm. 53
Kennons, Hannah 54; John 54; William 54
Kent, Tho. 52
Keown, Eleanor 54; Elizabeth 55; Milly 54; John Reading 55
Kileress, Jane 53; Nimrod 53; Robt. 53
Kimbal, Jos. 53; Sarah 53
King, Ann 54, 53; Anne 52, 53; Cha 53; Charles 52, 53, 54; Hannah 53; Hen. 52, 53; Henry 53; James 54; Jane 54; Jno. 53; John 53; Judith 54; Martha 54; Mary 52, 53; Olive 52; Rebeckah 53; Sarah 53; William 54; Wm. 54
Kings, Elizabeth 54; Julian 54; Williaw 54
Kinton, Hannah 54; John 54; Molly 54
Kirby, Elizabeth 54; John 54
Knight, Betsy Collins 55; Billy Stephens 55; Josiah 55; Lean 55; Milly 55; Polly Cheatham 55; Stephen 55
Lajohn, Fran. 55; Jane 55
Land, Martha 60; Patsey 60; Robert 60
Landford, Betsy 60; Elizabeth 60; Euclid 60; Henry 60
Lane, Christopher 58; Elizabeth 58; Mary 58
Lang, Elien 59; Elizth. 59; James 59
Lanier, Anne 60; Catherine 60; Isham Randolph 60; John 60; Rebecca Dressony 60
Laniere, Mrs. — 60
Lanthrop, Anne 57; John 57; Thomas 57
Lanthrope, Joseph 57; Mary 57
Lantroop, John 56; Joss 56; Mary 56
Lantrop, Hannah 59; Joseph 57; Mary 57; Shadrach 59; Thos. 59; William 57
Lantrope, Joseph 56; Mary 56
Lantropes, Elizabeth 59; John 59; Peter 59
Lantrops, Elizabeth 59; John 59; Mary 59
Lantroup, Ann 57; John 57; Joseph 57; Margrat 57; Mary 57
Lard, Francis 60; Nancy 60; Peter Singleton 60
Laurence, Francis Littlepage 60; Winny 60
Laws, Elishaba 56, 58; Eliza. 56; Elizth. 55; James 56; John 55, 56; Joss 56; Littleberry 58; Mary 55, 56; William 58; Wm. 55, 56
Lawsons, Benjamin 59
Leadbetter, Ephraim 59; John 59
Leadbetters, Anne 59; Frances 59; Mary 59; Woodie 59
Leath, Abigill 56; Peter 56; Sarah 56
Ledbetter, Ann 58; Drury 58; Fran. 55; Frances 58; Jno. 56; Johannah 58; John 55; Mary 55, 56; Osbun 58; Rebeca 55; Richard 58; Wm. 55
Ledbiter, Ha[ ] 58; Richard 58; William 58
Lee, Amy 56; Ann 57; Anne 56, 59; Burrill 58; Burwell 59; Cath. 55; Catharine 58; Catherine 106; Daniel 58; Elisabeth 58; Eliza. 106; Fran. 55; Frances 56, 57, 58; Hugh 55, 98; Hugh Junr. 56; Jesse 60; Jno. 55, 105; Joshua 58; Martha 57; Mary 55, 56, 58, 59, 98; Matt. 56; Matthew 56, 57; Peter 57; Polly Marcum 60; Roland 58; Sam. 55; Samuel 56, 60; Samuell 58; Sam'l. 57; Sarah 56, 57, 58; Susanna 56, 98; Tabitha 57; Tho. 55; Thomas 56, 57, 58, 59; William 59; Wm. 55
Lees, Daniel 59; Drury 59; Elizabeth 59; Frederick 59; Mary 59; Nathanael 59; Rebecca 59; Thomas 59
Leeth, Abigaell 55, 56; Abigal 57; Ann 55; Eliz. 55; Elisabeth 58; Frances 56; John 58; Mary 57; Peter 55, 56, 57; Rebacah 58; Tho. 55
Leigh, John Taylor 60; Mary 60; Samuel 60; Sarah 60; Susannah 60; Thomas 60
Leith, [illegible]; Charles 56; Tho. 56

Lenard, Frederick 58; John 54, 58, 59; Mary 54, 58, 59; Patrick 58; Thomas 54; Winifred 59
Lenoard, Jno. 57; John 57; Mary 57
Lenoye, Mourning 58; Thomas 58
Leonard, John 57; Mary 57
Leveret, John 58; Sarah 58
Lewelin, Anne 58; Jesse 58; Thomas 58
Lewis, Ann 55; Elisabeth 57; Eliz. 55; Eliza. 57; Elizabeth 58; Fran. 56; Frances 60; George 59; James 58; Joanah 57; John 55, 56, 60; Joseph 58; Katharine 59; Mary 55, 56, 58, 59; Obedience 58; Rebeccah Parham 60; Susan 56; Tho. 55; Thomas 57, 58; Wm. 56. 57
Liewes, Edward 57; Edwd. 57; John 57; Martha 57; Thomas 57
Liffsay, Joseph 59; Mary 59; Willm. 59
Ligon, Elisabit 57; Eliz. 56; Eliza. 57; Matt 56; Matthew 57; Tho. 56
Lile, Anne 56; Eliza. 57; Jno. 57; John 56; Martha 56; William 57
Lister, Ann 58; Thomas 58; William 58
Locket, Benja. 56, 57; Beja. 56; Winefrit 56; Winnifrit 57
Lockett, Eliz. 55; Hannah 55; Tho. 55
Lockley, Frances Margret 58; Henritta 58; Williams 58
Loffsay, Frederick 59; Mary 59; William 59
Loffsets, John 59; Keziah 59; Mille 59
Loftis, Ann 57; Eliz. 57; Wm. 57
Loftus, Eliza. 54; Thomas 54; Wm. 54
Love, Amoss 59; Mary 59; Winifred 59
Loveit, John 58; Sarah 58
Lovesy, Jane 57; William 57
Lovett, Eliza. 57; John 57, 58; Mary 58; Sarah 57, 58
Luis, Eliz. 56; Mary 56; Tho. 56

McCarter, David 69; Susannah 69; William 69
Mccholler, Anne 67; David 67
McDearmon, Eleanor 65; Richd. 65; William 65
McDowell, James 70; Susanna 70; William 70
McFarlane, Elizabeth 70
McKenny, John 69; Rebeccah 69
McLeod, Isabella 70; John 70
McMurdo, Anne 70; Charles 70; Elizabeth 70; Martha 70

Machie, Susana 66; Wm. 66; Vadrey 66
Maccloud, Daniel 67; Susanah 67; William 67
Maccollo, David 65; Elisabeth 65; Ja[ ] 65
Maccullochs, David 67; Elizabeth 67
MacDowals, Benjamin 68; Elizabeth 68; James 68
MacLauds, Daniel 68; Margret 68; Susanna 68
MacNeils, Malcom 67; Catharine 67
Machen, George Wale 69; Henry 69; Mary 69; Mary Wales 70; Sally 70; Thomas 70
Mackdaniell, Ann 61; John 61
Mackey, Eliza. 64; Sarah 64; Michael 64
Mackinney, Morgan 61; Sibilla 61
Maise, Eliz. 61; John 61; Mary 61
Maitland, Alexander Campbell 71; David 28, 70, 71; David Currie 71; Elizabeth 71; Elizabeth Agnes 70; Mary Currie 28, 71; Robert 71; Susan 71; Susanna 70; William 71
Makinny, James 63; John 62; Morgan 62, 63; Sibilla 62; Sybellah 63
Malcolm, John 70
Mallone, Ann 63; Lucrecee 63; Wm. 63
Malone, Margaret 68; Patrick Smith 68
Man, Agnis 63; Ann 64; Eliz. 61; Eliza. 65; Elizabeth 66, 68; Fran 61; Francis 65; Jane 62; John 63, 64, 66, 68; Lucy 61; Mary 63, 64, 66; Prissilla 61, 62; Robert 65; Samuel 66; Tho. 62, 61; Thom 62; Thomas 62; William 68
Manns, Elizabeth 68; John 68
Manson, John 66; Martha 66; Peter 66
Marchbank, Ann 66; George 66; Joseph 66
Marks, Edward 70; Eliza 70; Johanna 70; John 70; Lewis Lanier 70; Martha 70; Polly 70; Sally 70; William 70
Marshal, Ann 65; Elisabeth 65; Wm. 65
Marshall, Ann 64; Robert 64; Wm. 64
Martin, Jno. 64; John 64; Rachail 64; Rachald 64; Elisabeth 66; Elizabeth 67; Joel 67; Richard 66; Sarah 67; William 66, 67; Wm. 67; Zacariah 64; Zachariah 64
Martins, Anne 67; Elizabeth 67; Isabel 67; Lucy 67; Matthew 67; William 67
Mason, John 69; Lucy 69; Lucy Massenburg 69
Massey, Ann 62; Jno. 62; Ricd. 62
Massie, Ann 64; Richard 64; Tabitha 64
Massy, Ann 61, 62; Rich. 61, 62; Sarah 62
Mathes, Amey 62; Eleonore 62; Joseph 62
Matthews, Eleanore 65; Fran. 61; Henry 64; James 61; Joseph 65; Martha 65; Mary 64; Michal 64
Matthy, Hellen 64; Josep 64; Joseph 64
May, Agnes 67, 68; Anna 70; Betty 67; David 68; Dorithy 63; Elisabeth 64; Ephraim 70; George 70; James 63; Jeane 64; John 63, 65, 67, 68; Lucy 64; Mary 63, 64; Richard 67, 70; Thos. 64; William 65
Mayes, Anne 62; Delilah 66; Drury 63; Elisabeth 65; Eliz. 66; Eliza. 62, 63; Frederick 67; Gardiner 63; George 63; James 63; Jno. 62, 65; Johanna 65; John 62, 63, 64, 67; Julia 62, 63, 64, 65; Lucy 64; Martha 62; Mary 62, 63, 64; Matthew 63, 66; Sara 67; Sarah 64; Winiford 62; Wm. 62, 65
Mays, Eliz. 62; Hen. 62; John 61, 62; Julian 61; Marth 61; Mary 62; Rich 62
Meacham, Jamy Cate 69; Jeremiah 69; Milly 69
Meachen, Jeremiah 70; Jemimah Wyat 70; Milly 70
Meadlands, Jane 67, 68; John 67, 68; Susanna 67
Meadows, Daniel 67; Isham 67; Jane 67
Meanlands, Hannah 67; Mary 67; Richard 67
Mellone, Mary 60
Melones, Anne 67; Reuben 67; William 67
Meredith, Anne 70; John 70; Lettice Hickman 70; Pleasant 70; William 70
Merimon, Anne 62; Fran 62; Marga. 62
Mershall, Anne 66; William 66
Meuse, John 66; Matthew 66; Sarah 66
Micabin, John Bass 60; Margaret 60
Mikedermond, Catherine 66; Micail 66
Miles, David 63, 64, 66; Frances 64; Jane 63, 64, 66; John 66
Miller, Hugh 68
Millers, Anne 68; Hugh 68; Jane 68
Milles, Anne 68; Hugh 68; Jane 68; Robert 68
Mils, David 65; Jane 65; Thomas 65
Mitchel, Eliza. 62; Frances 62; Peter 62
Mitchell, Ann 61; Barbary 61; Dan. 61; Eliz. 61; Fran. 61; Hannah 61; Henry 67; Joab 61; John 61; Joshua 61; Mary 61; Nath. 61; Peter 61; Reaps 70; Rebecca 71; Sam 61; Sarah 67; Susanna 70; Tazewell 71; Tho. 61; Thomy Branch 70; Thos. 71
Mitchels, Addie 68; Henry 68; Sarah 68
Mixon, Eliza. 63; Michaell 63; Wm. 63
Mize, Grace 63; Jerimiah 63; Joshua 63; Robert 63
Molone, Daniel 66; Mary 66; Natha. 66
Moodies, Elizabeth 67; Humphry 67; Jane 67
Moody, Ann 66, 67; Anne 61, 65; Daniel 67; Frances 66; John 61; Laurana 65; Robt. 61; Robert 65, 66, 67
Mooney, Ann 67; Jane 67; John 67
Moor, Alexr. 65; Cath. 60, 61; Eliz. 61; James 61; John 60, 61, 62, 67; Mary 60, 61, 62, 67; Priscilla 61; Rich 62; Ruth 65; Sam 60, 61, 62; Seth 62; Willm. 65; Wood 67
Moore, Eliz. 62; Jams. 67; John 69; Joseph 69; Mark 62; Mary 67, 69; Robert 67
Moorland, Dorithea 67; John 67;

Martha 67
Moors, Elizabeth 67; Mary 67; Roger 67
More, Avis 66; Betty Rutherford 64; Catherine 62, 63, 64; Daniel 65; Eleonore 66; Elionar 63; Eliza. 62, 63, 64, 65; Frances 63, 64; Georg Hunt 63; George 64, 65; James 62, 65; Jno. 62, 63; John 63, 64, 65; Leah 65; Lucia 63; Lucy 63; Margret 63; Mark 62; Mary 63, 65; Phebe 63; Roge 65; Roger 63, 64, 65; Samuel 62, 65; Susannah 63; Thomas 64, 66; Thos. 63; Wm. 62
Moreland, Dorithy 63; John 63
Morgan, Eliza. 65; John 65, 66; Mary 62, 64, 65, 66; Philip 62; Phillip 64, 65; Rhuben 62; Saml. 65, 66
Morland, Dorithy 62; Jno. 62; Mary 62
Morrimont, Fran. 60; Margaret 60; Rosamund 60
Morris, Eliza. 63; Elizabeth 67; Henry 62, 63; John 67; Martha 62; Susan 63; Susanah 63; Susannah 63
Mote, David 66; Jonatha. 65; Jonathan 65, 66; Sarah 65, 66
Munford, Ann 66; Edward 63; Eliza. 63, 65; Elisabeth 66; Elizabeth 66; James 63, 65, 66; Martha 63; Robert 63; Robt. 66; Susannah 66
Munfords, Anne 67; Robert 67; Theodorick 67
Murcollo, David 63; Eliza. 63; Mary 63
Murcollow, David 62; Eliz. 62; Jno. 62
Murray, Anne 68; James 68; John 68; Margaret 68; Mary 68; Thomas 69; William 68

Nance, Ann 73; Dan 71; Daniel 72; Elinor 71; Eliz. 71; Eliza. 72; Giles 72; Jane 71, 72; John 71, 72; Jno. 72; Leanard 72; Lucy 72; Martha 72; Mary 71, 72; Nathaniel 72; Phebe 71; Rich 71; Richd. 72; Richard 72, 73; Tho. 71; Thomas 73; William 73; Wm. 72
Nances, Ann 73; Anne 73; Mary 73; Richard 73; Sarah 73; William 73
Nantzs, Priscilla 73; Sarah 73; Thomas 73
Nash, John 73; Johney 73; Mary 73
Neal, Margrat 72; Sarah 72; Tho. 72
Neel, Frances 71; Marga. 71; Margaret 71; Margret 71, 72; Mary 71; Tho. 71; Thom 71; Thomas 72
Nevil, James 72; John 72; Margret 72
Newhouse, Ann 71; Fran. 71; Raise 71; Tho. 71
Newman, Ann 58, 73; Mary 58; Richard 58, 73
Newsum, Lucy 73
Nipper, Ann 72; John 72; Martha 72
Nobles, Eliza. 72; Mark 72; Robt. 72
Norton, Agness 73; Ann 71; Frances 73; James 71; Mary 71; Patty 73; Sarah 73; Thomas 73; William 73; Wm. 71
Nunally, Eliza. 72; John 72; Obedience 72; Richd. 72; Tho. 72; Daniel 72; Mary 72
Nunnally, Eliz. 72; Thom. 72; Thomas 72; Zachariah 72
Nunnely, Eliz. 71, 72; Peter 71; Tho. 71
Nunsry, Judith 7

Ogilbys, Catharine 74; Elizabeth 74; Nicolas 74
Oliphant, John 75
Oliveer, Amy 74; Drury 74; Martha 74; Mary 74
Oliver, Amy 74; Ann 74; Anne 73, 74; Drury 73, 74; Drury 78; Eliz. 73; Elizabeth 74; John 73, 74; Martha 74; Tho. 74; Wm. 73
Olivers, Anne 74; Elizabeth 74, 75; Isaac 74, 75; James 74; Mary 74; Mildred 74; Thomas 74; William 75
Olivier, Amy 74; Drury 74; Eliza 74; Martha 74; Wm. 74
Organ, David 75; Elizabeth 75; Jean 75
Osborne, Jane 75; John 75; John Harrison 75
Overberry, Abraham 74; Ann 74; Dinah 74; James 74; Jaminah 74; Jane 74; Mary 74; Nicholas 74; Peter 74; Richard 74; Richd. 74; Rubin 74
Overbury, Dinah 73, 74; Eliz. 74; James 74; Lucy 74; Martha 73; Rich. 73; Richard 74; Thomas 74
Overby, Adams 73; Ann 73; Dina 73; Dinah 74; Fran. 73; James 73; Jane 73; Marga. 73; Nico. 73; Peter 73; Rich 73; Richard 74; Robt. 73; Thamar 74; Wm. 73
Owan, Edward 74; Elizbth 74; Joyce 74
Owen, Eliza. 74; Elizabeth 74; Howard 74; John 74; Lanceford 74; Margarat 74; Margret 74; Thomas 74; William 74

Parham, Anne 79; Archer 78, 80; Edward 78, 79; Elisabeth 78; Gower 78, 80; Henry 81; Isham 79; John 78; Lewis 81; Mary 78, 79; Phebe 76; Rebeccah 81; Sarah 78, 81; Thomas 79; William 81
Parhams, Archer 80; Gower 80; Mary 80
Parram, Mary 77; Thos. 77; William 77
Parratt, Nath 76; Penellope 76; Tho. 76
Parrish, Charles 79; David 81; James 81; Martha 79; Mary 79
Parrot, Mary 77; Natha. 77; Penilopy 77
Parrott, James 78; Nathaniel 78; Penellope 78
Parry, Ann 81; Phoebe 81; Wm. 81
Parsons, Batty 77, 80; Edith 75, 81; Frances 81; James Markham 80; Jamime 75; Joseph 81; Mary 75, 77, 80, 81; William 81; Wm. 75, 77, 79, 80, 81
Partrick, Liewes 77; Littleberry 77; Sarah 77
Paterson, Eady 76; Fran 76; James 81; Jane 76; John 76; Mary 81; William 81
Patrick, Luis 76; Sarah 76
Patrum, Jeremiah 75; Sara 75
Patterson, John 77; Liewes 77; Mary 77
Pattison, Jane 75; John 75; Smith 75
Paynes, Amy 80; Edward 80; Mary 80
Peachy, Jean 81; Samuel 81· Thos. G. 81
Pearce, Baldwin 82; Hannah 82; Rebeccah 82
Pearcy, Martha 75; Rebecca 75; Wm. 75
Peebles, Abram 81; Betsy 81; Esaia 81; James 81; Peggie 81; Reuben 81
Pegrams, Daniel 80; Edward 80; Francis 80; Mary 80; Sara. 80; William 80
Peirce, Juliana 80; Sarah 80; William 80
Peircy, John 80; Juliana 80; Wm. 80
Pentecost, Anne 81; George 81; Jane 81
Penticost, Eliza. 79; George 79, 80; Jane 79, 80; William 80
Pentycost, George 80; Jane 80; Lucy 80
Perkins, David 81; Margaret 81; William 81
Perkinson, Alice 77; Eliz. 75; Fran. 75; John 75; Lucy 76; Mary 76, 77; Robt. 78; Seth 76, 77; Wm. 78
Perrys, Mary 80; Thomas 80; William 80
Persons, Joseph 76; Mary 76; Wm. 76
Peterson, Elizabeth 80; Fran. 75, 76; Israell 80; John 75, 76, 78; Magdaline 80; Martha 78; Nathaniel 78; Nathaniell 75; Wm. 76
Petersons, Frances 81; John 81; Martha 81
Pettipool, Anne 79; Frances 79; Martha 79; Seth 79; William 79
Pettypool, Eliz. 75; Ffrances 76; John 77; Martha 75, 77; Seth 75, 77; Stephen 76; Wm. 76
Philipps, Betsy 37; Peninah 37
Phillips, Ann 77; Anne 78, 80, 81; Elizabeth 81; George 81; Isabel 78; Isabell 76, 77; Isabella 80; James 80; Jno. 76; John 77, 78, 80, 81; Joseph 77; Mary 78; Mason 77; Tho. 77; Thomas 76, 78, 80
Pickins, Jno. 78; Obedience 78; Pricilla 78
Pirkenson, Eddith 79; Elisabeth 79; Seth 79
Pistol, Charles 79, 80; Sarah 79, 80; Thomas 79; Wm. 80
Pistole, Charles 79; Sarah 79
Pitchford, Amy 78; Frances 78; Saml. 78
Pittillo, Ann 77; Henry 79; James 76, 77, 79; Lucy 79; Mary 76, 77, 79
Pittypool, Marth 77; Peter 77; Seth 77

Plantine, Frances 77; Peter 77; Sarah 77
Plat, Ann 76; James 76; Mary 76
Plentine, Frances 77; Peter 77; William 77
Pool, Frances 77, 78; Martha 76; Phillip 78; Sarah 76; Seth 76; Tabitha 77; Wm. 77, 78; Wm junr. 76
Pools, Francis 80; Henry 80; William Petty 80
Pope, Ralph 82; Sarah 82
Porter, Elisabeth 80; John 80
Porters, Anne 81; Joshua 81; Lucy 81
Pott, Jane 78; John 78, 79; Mary 79; Peter 78; Rebecca 78; Rebeckah 78; Thos. 79
Powel, Ann 77; Batiah 77; Bathua 77; Batiah 77; Hezekiah 77; John 77; Mary 77; William 77; Zedekiah 77
Powell, Anna 77; Bathia 78, 79; Edward 77, 79; Eliza. 77; Elizabeth 79; Hezekiah 78, 79; John 77, 79; Mary 77, 79; Rebeccah 78; Rebeckah 79; Robert 79; Tho. 77
Powels, Edward 81; Elizabeth 81; Luke 81
Poxon, Anne 76; Olive 76
Poythers, Wm. 76
Poythres, Sarah 77; Wm. 77
Poythress, Mary 82; William 81, 82
Poythress's, Elizabeth 80; Sara 80; Willm. 80
Poythris, Anne Isham 76; Eliza. 78; Francis 78; Hannah 78; Sarah 76, 77, 78; William 78; Wm. 76
Prentis, James 82; Mary 82; William 82
Prescot, Philip 79; Rachel 79
Presise, Mary 80; Patty 80; Thomas 80
Price, Eliz. 75; John 75; Mary 75; Richard 78
Pricheat, Ann 80; Aron 80; John 80
Pritchet, Frances 80; Kaleb 80; Susannah 80
Prichett, John 76; Joss. 76; Mary 76; Wm. 75
Pride, John 75, 78; Pucket 78; Susana 78; Susanna 75; Wm. 75
Pritchet, Catherine 78; Josha. 78
Pritchett, Joshua 77, 78; Martha 77
Probey, Servant 81
Pucket, Drury 79; Eliza. 77; Ephraim 75, 77; Frances 77; Jno. 76; Joel 76; John 76, 77, 79; Judith 76, 77, 79; Mable 75; Mary 77; Phebe 77; Sheppyallin 76; Stephen 77; Wm. 77; Womack 75
Puckett, Isham 76; John 75; Judith 75; Lewis 75; Mable 76; Martha 75; Mary 75; Phebe 75; Rich 75; Wm. 75; Womack 76
Purreah, Ann 80; Morgan 80

Raburn, Jno. 83; Rebecca 83; Rich 83
Rackly, John 82; Mary 82
Radgsdale, Alice 82, 83; Benja. 83; Dan. 82, 83; Edward 83; Eliz. 82, 83; Godfrey 83; Godfry 82; Joseph 83; Martha 83; Peter 82, 83; Tab. 82
Raes, Elizabeth 86, 87; Hugh 86, 87; Neil 87
Ragsdail, Alce 84, 85; Ann 84; Baxter 84; Benja. 83, 84; Benjamine 86; Eliz. 82; Eliza. 84; Godfrey 84; Godfry 82; John 84; Martha 83, 84, 86; Rachel 85; Peter 83
Ragsdale, Benja. 85; Martha 85; Winfred 85
Raines, Mary 85; Shanes 85
Ranie, Peter 84; Roger 84; Sarah 84
Rains, Frederick 85; Jane 85; Richd. 85
Ratlif, Anne 85; Isham 85; John 85
Ravenscroft, Thomas 86
Rawthorns, Anne 86; Samuel 86; William 86
Ray, Elisabeth 86; Hugh 86; John 86
Raybon, Jean 85; Richd. 85
Rayborn, John 84; Rebeckah 84; Thomas 84
Rays, Letty 96; Sally 96
Reading, Joel 87; Martha 87; Susannah 87
Reams, Alse 85; Elisabeth 86; Eliza. 85; Thomas 86; Thos. 85
Reaves, Isham 86; Joseph 85, 86; Josept 85; Sarah 85, 86
Reed, Jemiah 84; Mary 84; Wm. 84
Rees, Mary 84; Tho. 84; Thomas 84
Reese, Charles 86; Diancy 87; Eliza. 85, 86; Francis 84; Hugh 85, 86; Isham 85; Jacob 87; John 85; John Featherstone 87; Martha 85; Mary 84, 86; Roger 85, 86; Sarah 85, 86; Thomas 85, 86; Thos. 84
Reess, Hugh 86; James 86; John 86; Mary 86; Mason 86; Sarah 86; Thomas 86
Reeves, Daniel 83; James 88; John 88; Josep 83; Joseph 84; Judith 87; Mary 84, 86; Priscilla 87; Sarah 83, 84; Timothy 86; Usiller 86; William 87
Reiny, Roger 85; Sara 85; William 85
Reves, Frances 87; John 87; Mary 87; Richard 87; Thomas 87; William 87
Rhaynes, Eliza. 83; John 83; Thom. 83
Rigsby, Ann 84; Eliz. 83; Eliza. 84; Ja. 83; James 84; Mary 83
Riss, Hug 84; Prissilla 84; Sarah 84
Rivers, Hannah 86; Robert 86; Thomas 86
Robarson, George 86; Martha 86; Sarah 86
Roberds, John 86; Judith 86; Michael 86
Roberts, Francis 86; Hanah 86; Hannah 83; Judath 86; Mary 83; Thomas 83; Thos. 86
Robertson, Abraham 83; Anne 88; David 84; Deborah 84; Edward 85; Eliza 84; Elizabeth 88; Elizabeth Archer 87; Henry 84; Israil 83, 84; James 87, 88; Jno. 83, 84; John 85; John Alexander 88; Mark 84; Martha F. 87, 88; Mary 83, 84, 85; Sarah 83, 84; William 87, 88
Robertsons, Henry 86; Peter 86: Susanna 86
Robinson, Ann 82, 86; Charles 86; Christ 82, 83; Christopher 83; Eliz. 82, 83; Eliza. 83; Ffrances 84; Hen. 82, 83; Henry 83, 86; Israel 82, 83; Israil 85, 86; John 83, 84, 86; Liewes 83; Martha 83; Mary 82, 83, 84, 86; Matthew 82; Nath 83; Nicholas 85; Peter 83; Robt. 86; Sara 83; Sarah 82, 83, 85, 86
Robtson, Geo. 83; George 83; Mary 83
Roe, Nancy 88; Patrick 88; Robert 88
Rogers, John 87; Mary 87; Philip 87
Roland, Agnis 84; Ann 84; Benja. 84; Christophar 84; Eliza 84; John 84
Rolland, Ann 85; Christo. 85; Sarah 85
Rollings, Ann 84; Nicholas 84; Thomas 84
Roney, Elizabeth 87; John 87; Patrick 87; Sarah 87; Thomas 87
Roshill, Peter 87; Sarah 87
Rottenbery, Hen. 82, 83; Marga. 83; Martha 82; Rich. 83
Roupers, Anne 86; Charles 86; David 86; Lowerel 86
Rowland, Ann 40, 84; Christopher 40, 84; John 40, 84
Rowlet, Fran. 82; Wm. 82; Daniel 82
Rowlett, Mary 83; Peter 83
Royal, Littleberry 87; Sarah 87; William 87
Royall, Eliz. 82, 84; Fran. 82; Hen. 82; Henry 84; Isabellah 84; James 84; John 84; Partrick 84
Russel, Jenny 87; Robert 87
Russell, Eliz. 82; Martha 82; Mary 82; Rachel 87; Richard 87; Wm. 82, 87
Rutlidge, James 85; Sarah 85; William 85
Ryan, Edmund 87

Sandert, Eliz. 88; James 88
Satterwhite, Elizab 90; Mary 90; Tho. 90
Saunders, Anne 93; John 93; Mary 93; Rebecca 94; William 94
Sauntie, Agge 94; Mary 94
Savage, Ann 92; Mary 92; Thomas 92; Thos. 92
Scoggan, Lutia 90; Martha 90; Mary 90, 92; Richd. 90, 92
Scoggin, James 96; John 88; Mary 88, 89; Rebecca 88, 89; Rich 88, 89; Sally 96; Selah 96; William 96; Wm. 88, 89
Scoggins, Anne 93; Elizabeth 95; George 95; John 93; Matthew 93
Scogin, Anne 92; David 89; Francis 90; Mary 90, 92; Rebeckah 89; Richard 92; Richd. 90; Wm. 89
Scot, Amy 37; Hannah 37

Scotts, Jemima 94; John 94; Stephen 94; William 94
Sental, Ann 92; Henry Fitz 92; Jonathan 90; Mayr 90; Samuel 90
Sentall, Jane 92; Mary 92; Samuell 92
Shackleford, Zachariah 96
Sharp, Margaret Lang 96; William 96; Winnifred 96
Shern, Anne 92; John 92; Mary 92
Shipton, Ann 88, 89; Eliz. 89; Phebe 88
Shore, Anne 97; John 96, 97; Sarah 97; Thomas 96
Shorie, Thomas William 91
Short, Mary 93; Thomas 93
Shorts, Martha 94; Mary 94; Thomas 94
Sidner, Anthony 96
Skipwith , William 95
Smart, Elisabeth 93; Frederick 93; Henry 93; James 93; Matthew 93; Sarah 93
Smarts, Elizabeth 94; James 94; Sylvana 94
Smelt, Maxey 29; Robt. 29; Sarah 29
Smith, Agnis 88, 89, 93; Anne 96; Archiball 93; Benjamin 96; Benjamine 93; Catherine 89; David 89; Eliz. 89; Eliza. 90, 91, 92; Geo. 89; George 90, 93; James 89; Jane 90; Jno. 89, 91; John 89; John Benjamin 96; Joss 89; Mary 89, 90, 93; Moses 91; Partrick 92; Phebe 89; Rich 88, 89; Richard 93; Sarah 89; Susannah 93; Thomas 92; William 96; Wm. 89, 90, 93
Smiths, Clement 94; David 94; Drury 94; Elizabeth 94; George 94, 95; Mary 94, 95; Millinton 95; Lucy 94; John 94; Joshua 94; Obedience 94; Patrick 94; Priscilla 94
Snipes, Elizabeth 93; Susannah 93; Thomas 93
Spain, Batt 92; David 93; Eliza. 91; Frances 91; John 88; Joshua 89; Martha 91, 92; Mary 88, 89, 91, 92; Prisilla 91; Tho. 91; Thom. 91; Thomas 92; Wm. 88, 89, 91, 92
Spencer, Ann Grant 95; Elizth. 95; Richd. 95
Spires, Catharine 94; Henry 94; Joseph 94
Spruce, Elizabeth 96; Polly 96
Stainback, Ann 95; Ann Lamboth 95; Elizabeth 95; Rebecca 95; William 95; Wm. 95
Standley, Eliza. 90; Priscilla 90; William 90
Stanfield, Frances 89, 90; Mary 89; Robt. 89, 90
Stanley, Ann 90; Eliza. 90; Elizabeth 93; James 93; Richd. 90; William 93; Wm. 93
Staples, Fran 89; Frances 98; Ruth 88, 89, 98; Thompson 88, 89, 98
Starkes, Bolling 92; Mary 92; Wm. 92
Stell, Angelica 88; Ann 88; Geo. 88; James 88
Stephens, Mary 93; Patie Tadlock 93
Steward, Ann 93; Charles 95; Fanney 93; Mary Toney 95; Matt 95
Stewart, Elizabeth 94; John 93; Martha 94; Susanna 93
Still, Frances 93; James 93; John 93; Mary 93; Richard Cross 93; Wm. 93
Stillmans, George 94; Goodith 94; Mary 94
Stimpson, Charles 96; Ellen 96; Sally Hall 96
Stirdevent, Ann 95; Ann Isham 95; Joel 95; John 95; Mary Epes 95; Salley 95
Stith, Barthurst 90; Drury 88, 89, 90, 91; Eliz. 88; Eliz. 89; Eliza. 90, 01; Griffin 88; John 89, 94; Thomas 91
Stoaker, Ann 91; Eliza. 91; Elizabeth 93; Margaret 93; Robert 93; Robt. 91
Stoker, Eliz. 89; Eliza. 90; Matthew 90; Robert 90; Robt. 89
Stone, Elizabeth 96; Launcelot 96; Sarah Howlet 96
Stonebank, Mary 88; Tho. 88
Stott, Ebenezer 97; Elizabeth 97; Helen 97
Stow, Abrattam 90; Han. 89; Marga. 89; Margt. 90; Wm. 89, 90
Strachan, Alexander Glass 96; Sarah 96; Sarah Feild 96
Stradford, Clemond 93; Hardship 93
Stroud, David 91; Jane 90; Jean 91; Jno. 90, 91; John 90; Joseph 90, 91; Margaret 90; Mary 90, 91; Olive 90; Wm. 90
Stuard, Edw. 83; Eliz. 88; Eliza. 90; Matthew 90
Stuart, Elizabeth 92; John 93; Mary 93
Stunks, Ann 90; Anne 91; Eliza. 90; Mary 90; Prissilla 91; Tho. 90; Thomas 90, 91
Sturdavant, James 93, 94
Sturdavants, John 93
Sturdefant, Daniel 93; Martha 93; Sarah 93
Sturdevant, John 97; Thompson 97
Sturdifant, Eliza. 90; John 90; Mary 90; Tho. 90
Sturdivant, Ann 95; Biggen 91; Catherine 88; Dan. 89; Daniel 93, 97; Eliz. 89; Eliza. 91; Fran. 89; Francis 94; Isaac 92; Ja. 88; James 90, 91, 92, 93, 95, 96; Jmes. 89; Jno. 90, 91; Joel 96; Joell 91; John 88, 89, 95; Lewellen 92; Luellin 92; Mary 88, 89, 90, 91, 92, 93, 95; Mary Anne Thompson 96; Matthew 90; Nathaniel Birchett 96; Patsey 96; Rebeckah 92; Robert 96; Sally Servant 96; Sarah 91, 93; Susanna 94; Thompson 95, 97; Wm. 89
Sturdivants, Daniel 94, 95; Mally 94; Sarah 94, 95
Sturdvant, Eliza. 90; Lewellin 90; Mary 90
Summerell, Mary 91, 92; Jacob 91; William 92
Summerrell, Jacob 92
Suttawhite, Sarah 92; Thomas 92
Talley, Abra. 97; Anne 97
Tally, Anne 99; Henry 102; Heny. 101; Jno. 100; John 97, 99; Judith 100, 101, 102; Kezia 100; Littlepage 101; Martha 102; Martin 99; Mary 99; Richd. 99; Ruth 99
Tatam, Agnis 100; Emelea 99; Mary 100; Nathaniel 99; Littleberry 101; Mary 101; Nathaniel 99; Peter 101; Robert 99
Tate, Lucia 102; Nathan 102; Sarah 102; William 102
Tates, Samuel. 103; Sara 103; William 103
Tatum, Eliz. 98; Fran. 98; Hen. 97; John 98; Mary 97, 98; Phebe 98; Sam. 98; Wm. 98
Tatums, Keziah 104; Mary 103; Nathaniel 104; Peter 103; Robt. 104
Tatun, Frances 98; Hen. 98; Mary 98
Tayler, Eliza. 101; Jno. 101; Roger 101
Taylor, Eliza. 102; Mary 100; Robert 100; Roger 100, 102; William 100, 102, 105
Taylors, Elizabeth 104; George 104; Nanney 104; Richard 104; Sarah 104
Temple, Amy 101; Candace 105; Eliz. 98, 99, 99; Eliza. 101; Elizabeth 105; Eppes 104; Frances 101; Mary 98; Nanny 105; Peter 105; Rebeckah 101; Sam. 98; Tho. 98; Thomas 101; William 101; William Eppes 105; Wm. 99
Temples, David 103; Elizabeth 103; Frances 104; Francis 103; Jacob 103; Lucretia 103; Mary 103, 104; Samuel 103, 104; Samuell 103; William 103
Tench, Henry 104; Mary-Henry 104; Nancy 104
Tenheart, Ja. 98; Lucy 98; Mary 98
Thacker, Jno. 100; Phelis 100; William 100
Thomas, Catharine 103; David 103; Elisabeth 103; Elizabeth 102; Mary 103; Peter 102, 103; Richard 103
Thompson, Ann 100; Anne 99; James 99, 100; Mary 99, 100
Thomson, Charles 103; Frances 103; John 103
Thorn, Eliza. 102; Richard 102; Willmoth 102
Thweat, Ann 99, 100; Burrell 101; Christian 100; Drury 104; Eliz. 98; Eliza. 100; Eliza. 104; Frances 99; Frankee 104; Geo. 97; Hanna 100; Hannah 97, 98, 99; Hen. 97, 98, 99; Henry 100; Ja. 98; James 98, 99, 100, 101, 102; Jno. 98, 99; John 97, 98, 99, 100, 101; Judith 97, 98, 99, 100, 101; Marth 101; Mary 98; Miles 101; Obedience 99; Sarah 101; Wm. 100
Thweats, Drury 104; Edith 104; Edward 104; Elizabeth 104; James 104; John 103, 104; Judith; Mary 104; Sarah 104; Tabitha 104
Thweatt, Ann 102; Anne 101; Elizabeth 102; James 102;

John 104, 105; Martha 101; Miles 102; Sarah 102; William 102
Thwets, Alick. 103; David. 103; Drury 103; Elizabeth 103; Miles 103; Sara 103
Tidmust, Eliz. 98; John 98; Rich 98
Tillman, Eliza. 99; George 101; John 102; Margret 102; Mary 99, 101; Roger 99; Sarah 101
Tillmon, Eliza. 100; Mary 100; Roger 100
Tilman, Geo. 97, 98, 99; Mary 97, 98, 99; Roger 99; Tabitha 97; Wm. 98
Tolbert, Mary 100; Matthew 100
Tolbot, James 102; Mary 102; Matthew 102
Tomlinson, Eliza. 101; Jane 101; Jno. 101
Totty, Eliza. 100; Margret 102; Mary 99, 100, 102; Thomas 100; William 102; Wm. 99, 100
Toudress, Anne. 103; Elizabeth 103; Henry 103
Trayler, Ann 102; Edmond 99; Elisabeth 99; Jno. 101; Mary 101; Phebe 99; Sarah 102; William 102; Wilmut 101
Traylor, Archer 100; Blanch 101; Edmond 101; Edward 102; Eliza. 101, 102; George 102; John 100, 102; Judith 100, 102; Lucretia 102; Martha 100; Mary 100, 102; William 102
Traylors, Martha 103; Sara 103; William 103
Tucker, Abraham 102; Amy 25, 97, 99, 102; Ann 97, 99, 100, 101; Anne 97, 98, 99; Cath. 97; Dan. 99; Daniel 99, 100; David 100; Drury 97; Elisabeth 101; Eliz. 98, 99; Eliza. 99, 100; Elizabeth 100; Fran. 98; Frances 25, 99, 100, 101, 102; Francis 97, 99, 100, 101; Geo. 99; George 101, 102; Hanna 101; Henry 25, 100, 101, 102; Isham 101; James 97, 100, 101; John 97, 99, 100, 101, 102; Jno. 99, 101; Joseph 98, 100, 101; Joss. 97; Katheren 98; Lucretia 100, 101; Martha 97, 98, 99, 100, 101; Mary 97, 99, 100, 101; Micael 97; Nath. 98; Nevil 100; Robert 101, 102; Robt. 97, 98, 99, 100; Sara 97; Susanna 98; Tho. 100; Warner 101; William 99, 102; Wm. 98, 99
Tuckers, Abram 103; Helenour 103; Joseph 103; Lucretia 103; Mary 103; Miles. 103
Tunks, Anne 103; Thomas 103
Turner, Ann 100; Eliza. 99, 100, 102; Elizabeth 102; Holenberry 100; Jno. 99; Jos. 99; Joseph 100, 102
Turners, Anne 104; Elizabeth 104; William 104
Twitty, Mary 103; Rebeckah 103; Thomas 103
Tye, Agnis 102; Allen 99, 100, 102; Frances 99; Mary 99, 100, 102; Solomon 102; William 100
Tyes, Allan 103; Anderson 103; Mary 103

Unckle, Anne 108; Lewis 108
Underhill, Howel 108; John 108 Nancy 108

Vaden, Hen. 105; Martha 105
Valentine, Elizabeth 107; James 107
Vauden, Anne 105; Hen. 105; Martha 105
Vaughan, Abigaell 105; Abigal 106; Abner 106; Alce 106; Alice 105; Ann 105, 106; Anne 107; Caleb 106; Dan. 105; Daniel 105, 106; Danl. 106; Drury 108; Elinor 105; Eliz. 105; Eliza. 106; Enoch 108; Henry 106; Isham 105, 106; James 105; James Thompson 105; John 105; Joss 105; Julia 106; Mabel 107; Mable 106; Margrett 107; Mary 106, 107, 108; Mary-Ann-Elizabth 108; Martha 105, 106, 107; Morris 106; Nico. 105; Nicolas 106, 107; Pearc 105; Peter 106; Pheboe 106; Pricilla 106; Priss 105; Prissilla 105, 106; Prissillah 105; Rebecca 106; Rich 105; Richard 106; Robert 107; Robert Winn 108; Robt. 106; Samuel 107; Sarah 106, 107; Susannah 106, 108; Temperanc 106; William 106, 107; Williams 105; Wilmot 106; Wm. 105, 106
Vaughans, Abram 107; Amith 107; Anne 107; Daniel 107; David 107; Eliza. 107; Elizabeth 107; Ellinor 108; Ezekiel 107; Henry 107; James 107; Jemina 108; Jessee 107; Joshua 107; Margaret 107; Mary 107, 108; Martha 107; Maurice 107; Morris 107, 108; Nathanael 107; Peter 107; Phebe 107; Rebecca 107; Rebecka 108; Ruth. 107; Salathiel 107; Samuel 107; Samuell 107; Sarah 107; Silvester 107; Sylvana 107; Thomas 107; William 107; Williams 108
Vaughn, Abra 105; Ann 105; Luis 105
Verell, John junr. 108; Martha 108; Sally Newsum 108
Voden, Burrell 106; Henry 106; Martha 106; Mary 106
Vodin, Eliza. 106; Frances 106; Henry 106; Martha 106; Susannah 106; William 106

Walke, Anne 118; Anthony 118; Sarah 118
Walker, Alexander 112; Cath. 109; Dan. 109; David 112, 114, 116; Frances 112, 115; Francis 116; Freeman 116; Gollorthun 119; Joel 112; John 109; Joseph 119; Lettisha 119; Martin 119; Mary 112, 114, 116; Pattey 119; Penelope 119; Peter 115; Robert 112; Reubin 119; Thomas 112, 115, 116
Walkers, Jos. 119
Walkes, Anne 119; Antony 119; Robert 119
Wall, Amy 12, 111, 112, 115; Ann 109, 111, 113; Anne 110; Burgess 109; Dan. 110; Daniel 12, 115; Daniell 111; Danl. 112; David 111; Drury 111; Eliz. 110; Frances 115; Henry 111; Isham 111; John 12, 111, 113, 115; Jno. 111; Joshua 111, 112, 115; Joss. 109, 111; Martha 109, 111, 112, 115; Mary 111, 115; Rich 110; Winiford 112; Wm. 110, 111; Zachariah 113
Waller, Agnis 111
Walls, Joshua 117; Martha 117
Wallton, Henry 112
Waltal, Garrat 113
Walter, Eliza. 112; Tho. 112; Wm. 112
Walthal, Amy 113; Benjamine 114; Francis 113, 114; Martha 114; Mary 113; Richard 113; Thos. 113
Walthall, Ann 109, 115; Christopher 110; Daniel 116; Edward 114; Eliz. 109; Eliza. 114; Francis 116; Hen. 108, 109, 110; Henry 115, 116; Jeremiah 108; Jerrott 114; John 110; Maball 110; Martha 116; Mary 108, 109, 110, 116; Phebe 109, 110, 115; Rich. 109, 110; Richard 116
Walton, Phebe 112
Washington, Edward 116; Elizabeth 116; Langsdown 116
Watts, Alice 119; Arthur 119; Edward 119; Eliza. 111; Jno. 111; John 111; Sarah 119
Weathers, Edmund 120; Martha 120; Mary 120
Webster, Elisabeth 116; Jonathan 116; Mary 108; Tho. 108
Weeds, John 117; Robert 117; Sara 117
Wells, Abraham 114, 116; Abram 115; Adam 116, 117, 118, 119; Amy 116; Anne 110, 116; Barnabas 116; David 113, 115; Deury 117; Elanor 119; Eleanor 116, 118, 119; Elener 116, 117; Frances 112, 115; Francis 113, 118; Francise 117; Hannah 119; Helenor 117; Henry 118; Isham 118; Jane 116; Jeremiah 116; Joyce 116; Margerett 116; Mary 116; Pattie 119; Phebe 115; Randolph 119; Richard 119; Ruben 114; Sarah 110, 114, 115, 118; William 117, 118; Willm. 118; Wm. 110, 112, 113, 115
West, Abra 110; Amy 115; Christian 114; Eliz. 109, 110; Eliza. 111, 113, 115; Ephraim 110, 116; Fran. 110; Frances 113; Francis 111, 113, 115; John 109, 110, 113; Lusie 113; Martha 112; Mary 109, 110, 111, 112, 113, 114; Robert 113, 115, 116, 117; Robt. 109, 111, 112, 113, 114; Susanah 111; Temperanc 115; Temperance 116, 117; Temporance 113; Tho. 112; Wm. 109
Westbrook, John 116; Mary 116; Sarah 116; William 116
Westmoland, Abigall 113; Isabella 113; Joseph 113; Susannah 113
Westmore, Elizabeth 120; Joseph 120; William Baird 120
Westmoreland, Aann 111; Ann 111; Christian 115; Elisabeth 115;

James 115; Joseph 115, 117; Margaret 115, 117; Margrat 112; Mary 111; Matthew 112; Richard 111; Robert Hicks 117; Sib 117; Sibylla 115; Sybilla 115; Tho. 111, 112; Thomas 115, 117
Wests, Anne 117; Elizabeth 117; John 117
Wheats, Edward 118; Mary 118; William 118
Whit, Anne 114; Edward 114; Eliza. 114
Whitamore, Abraham 109; Sarah 108; Wm. 108
White, Rebecca 109; Rich. 109
Whitehall, Ann 117; Robert 117; Thos. 117
Whitehalls, Amy 117; Anne 117; Robert 117
Whitmore, Elizabeth 116; John 116; Thomas 116
Whitt, Edward 116; John 116; Mary 116
Whood, Ann 113; Margret 113; Wm. 113
Wilkasons, Henry 118; Mary 118
Wilkinson, Eliz. 110; John 110; Tho. 110
Wilkisons, Agnes 16, 118; Anne 117; Henry 16, 118; Martin 117; Mary 16, 117, 118
William, Eliza. 111; Jno. 111; Joseph 111
Williams, Ann109, 111, 112, 116; Anne 114; Cha. 108, 109, 110, 111, 114; Charles 111, 112, 113, 116; David 108, 109, 110, 111, 114; Edward 114; Elisabeth 115; Eliz. 108, 109, 110, 116; Eliza. 111, 112, 113, 114, 115, 119; Frances 115; Frederick 119; Geo. 108, 110; George 111, 112; Hannah 119; Henry 111; Ja. 109; Jame 111; James 36, 110, 113, 118, 119; Jane 117, 118, 119; Jno. 113; Johannah 119; John 110, 111, 112, 113, 115, 116, 119; Jones 114; Josept. 115; Joshua 119; Lotty 81; Lucy 111, 118; Ludwell 119; Marga. 110; Martha 108, 116, 118; Mary 110, 111, 112, 114, 118; Miles 113, 118; Millison 118; Obedience 110; Olive 109, 110, 113; Page 81; Peter 111; Rich 110; Robert 114, 116; Robt. 114; Roland 117; Sarah 109, 110, 111, 114, 116; Sibbil 108; Sibilla 110; Sibylla 112; Sybellah 111; Thomas 117, 118; William 118
Williamson, Charles 112, 113, 115; Elisabeth 115; John 113; Pricilla 115; Prissilla 113, 114; Susan 112
Williamsons, Charles 117; Drusilla 117; Priscilla 117
Willingham, Jane 111; John 111; Mary 111
Willson, Ann 112, 115; Anne 114; Catherine 111; Edward 111; Eliza. 113; Henry 112, 113, 114, 115, 116; James 116; Joel 111; Jno. 113, 114; John 111, 112, 114, 115; Joseph 111; Judith 115; Mark 115; Martha 111, 112, 113, 114, 115, 116; Mary 112, 113, 114; Micael 112; Phebe 113; Samuel 114
Wilson, Amy 108; Anne 116; Eliz. 108; Francis 119; Gardner 108; Geo. 108; Hen. 109; Henry 111, 112, 116; Joseph 111; Judith 109, 110; Margaret 111; Margarit 111; Martha 111, 116; Mary 109; Rich. 109, 110; Sarah 109, 111; Stevens 109; Tho. 108; Thomas 119
Wilsons, Anne 117; Elimelech 117; Francis 117; Henry 118; John 117; Katharine 118; Martha 118; Thomas 117
Wines, Francis 117; Margret 117; Robert 117
Winfield, Ann 116; Edward 114; Hannah 116; Joell 114; John 116; Mary 114
Winfields, Edward 117; Edward 118; Hannah 118; Mary 117, 118
Winingham, Amy 115; Christian 114; Edward 112; Eliza. 112; Gerrald 116; Henry 114; Isack 114; Jno. 114; John 116; Mary 114, 115, 116; Precillah 113; Sarah 114; Thomas 113, 115; Thos. 112; Wm. 114
Winn, John 119; Katy 119; Salley Allen 119
Womack, Aliza. 112; Laurana 112; Martha 110; Wm. 110
Wood, Aron 112, 113; Eliza. 112; Ja. 110; Kath 110; Mary 112, 113; Richard 113
Woodliths, Edward 117; Elizabeth 117
Woolfolk, Fracis 119; Jean 119
Wootten, Elisabeth 117; Miles 117; William 117
Worsham, Ann 112, 114; Clarissa 120; Daniel 108; Dorcas 108, 109; Essex 112, 114; Frances 112; Henry 112, 120; John 117; Joseph 117; Martha 108, 109, 117; Wm. 120
Worshams, Daniel 117; Joshua 117, 118; Martha 117, 118; Mary 118
Wortham, Elizabeth 118; James 118; Mary 118; Rosamund 108' Rose. 109; Roson 112; Wm. 108, 109, 112
Wright, Joseph 116; Susanna 116
Write, John 113, 115; Sarah 113; Susanah 115; Susannah 113
Wyat, Elizabeth 115; Eliza. 115; Francis 115
Wyats, Elizabeth 117; Francis 117; Susanna 117
Wyatt, Francis 113; Henry 113; Mary 113
Wyatts, Alice 119; Arthur 119; Mary 119
Wyn, Joseph 111; Mary 111; Thomas 111
Wynn, Joshua 114; Joss. 108, 109, 110; Marga. 110; Martha 108; Mary 108, 109, 110, 114; Robt. 109; Tabitha 114
Wynne, Joshua 119; Lucretia 119; Sloman 119
Wynnes, Frances 118; Mason 118; Robert 118

Yanes, Edward 120; Edwd. 120; John 120; Josiah 120; Mary 120; Thomas 120
Yarbrough, Dianer 120, 121; Elizth. 120; James Smith 120; Joseph 120; Ozwell 120; Richard 120; William 120
Yeans, Edw. 120; Edward 120; Eliza. 120; Mary 120
York, Jane 120; Jno. 85, 120; John 107, 120; Martha 85, 120; Sarah 85, 107, 120
Young, Francis 120; Henry 120; John 120; Judith 120; Micael Cadet 120; Saml. 120; Temperance 120; Winney 120